RECASTING WORKERS' POWER

Work and Inequality in the Shadow of the Digital Age

Edward Webster

With Lynford Dor

BRISTOL
UNIVERSITY
PRESS

First published in Great Britain in 2023 by

Bristol University Press
University of Bristol
1–9 Old Park Hill
Bristol
BS2 8BB
UK
t: +44 (0)117 374 6645
e: bup-info@bristol.ac.uk

Details of international sales and distribution partners are available at bristoluniversitypress.co.uk

© Bristol University Press 2023

British Library Cataloguing in Publication Data
A catalogue record for this book is available from the British Library

ISBN 978-1-5292-1878-7 hardcover
ISBN 978-1-5292-1879-4 paperback
ISBN 978-1-5292-1880-0 ePub
ISBN 978-1-5292-1881-7 ePdf

Cover design: Lyn Davies Design
Front cover image: Alamy/Jesús Martinez
Bristol University Press uses environmentally responsible print partners.
Printed and bound in Great Britain by CPI Group (UK) Ltd, Croydon, CR0 4YY

FSC
www.fsc.org
MIX
Paper | Supporting
responsible forestry
FSC® C013604

Contents

List of Figures and Tables

Figures

Tables

List of Abbreviations

4IR	Fourth Industrial Revolution
ADP	advanced digital production
AFADWU	Agricultural Food and Allied Democratic Workers Union
ANC	African National Congress
ANCEFA	African Network Campaign on Education For All
APF	Anti-Privatisation Forum
ATGWU	Amalgamated Transport and General Workers' Union
BCEA	Basic Conditions of Employment Act
BEE	Black Economic Empowerment
BIA	Bridge International Academies
BOM	Brothers of Melville
BRT	Bus Rapid Transit
BSU	Business Support Unit
BUSA	Business Unity South Africa
C4C	Casuals for Company
CCMA	Commission for Conciliation, Mediation and Arbitration
CEO	chief executive officer
CEPPWAWU	Chemical, Energy, Paper, Printing, Wood and Allied Workers Union
COSATU	Congress of South African Trade Unions
CPI	Consumer Price Index
CWAO	Casual Workers Advice Office
DEMAWUSA	Democratic Municipal and Allied Workers Union of South Africa
DITSBO	Department of Informal Trade and Small Business Opportunities
DoL	Department of Labour
DRC	Democratic Republic of Congo
EACHRights	East African Centre for Human Rights
EFF	Economic Freedom Fighters
EI	Education International

EMIEF	eThekwini Municipality Informal Economy Forum
EPWP	Expanded Public Works Programme
ERP	Enterprise Resource Planning
FAWU	Food and Allied Workers Union
FES	Friedrich Ebert Stiftung
FMCG	Fast-Moving Consumer Goods
GCE	Global Campaign for Education
GEAR	Growth, Employment and Redistribution policy
GIWUSA	General Industries Workers Union of South Africa
GLU	Global Labour University
GPE	Global Partnership for Education
GPS	global positioning system
GUF	global union federation
HMI	human–machine interface
ICLS	International Conference of Labour Statisticians
ICT	information and communication technology
IDP	Integrated Development Plan
IFAT	International Federation of App-based Transport Workers of India
IFC	International Financial Corporation
ILO	International Labour Organization
IMF	International Monetary Fund
IPO	initial public offering
IT	information technology
ITF	International Transport Workers' Federation
ITUC	International Trade Union Confederation
JMC	Johannesburg Metropolitan Council
JMPD	Johannesburg Metro Police Division
KAMBE	Kampala Metropolitan Boda Boda Entrepreneurs
KNUT	Kenya National Union of Teachers
KZN	KwaZulu-Natal (province)
LPT	labour process theory
LRA	Labour Relations Act
MNC	multinational corporation
MTC	Metro Trading Company
MWA	Migrant Workers Association
NBCCI	National Bargaining Council for the Chemical Industry
NEDLAC	National Economic Development and Labour Council
NGO	non-governmental organisation
NIHSS	National Institute for the Humanities and Social Sciences
NMWA	National Minimum Wage Act

NPO	non-profit organisation
NTM	National Transport Movement
NUM	National Union of Mineworkers
NUMSA	National Union of Metalworkers of South Africa
NUT	Nigeria Union of Tailors
NUTGTWN	National Union of Textile, Garment and Tailoring Workers of Nigeria
PAC	Pan Africanist Congress
PB	personal best
PFG	PFG Building Glass
PPP	public–private partnership
PRA	power resources approach
R204	Recommendation 204 (ILO)
SACCAWU	South African Commercial, Catering and Allied Workers Union
SACCO	Savings and Credit Cooperative
SACP	South African Communist Party
SACTWU	South African Clothing and Textile Workers Union
SADSAWU	South African Domestic Service and Allied Workers Union
SAITA	South African Informal Traders Alliance
SAMWU	South African Municipal Workers Union
SANCO	South African National Civic Organisation
SAP	Structural Adjustment Programme
SATAWU	South African Transport and Allied Workers Union
SAWPA	South African Waste Pickers Association
SBO	shared business ownership
SCIS	Southern Centre for Inequality Studies
SDA	Skills Development Act
SER	standard employment relationship
SERI	Socio-Economic Rights Institute of South Africa
SETA	Sectoral Education and Training Authority
SEWA	Self-Employed Women's Association [of India]
SI Cobas	Intercategory Syndicate [Italy]
SMME	small, medium and micro enterprises
SVA	Street Vendors Alliance
TAWU-K	Transport and Allied Workers Union of Kenya
TES	temporary employment service
TLA	Textile Labour Association
TUiT	Trade Unions in Transformation [project]
UBS	Uganda Bureau of Statistics
UIF	Unemployment Insurance Fund
UNATU	Uganda National Teachers' Union

UNIDAPP	Unión de Trabajadores de Plataformas
UNIDO	United Nations Industrial Development Organization
UU	United Ugandans
WDR	World Development Report
WEF	World Economic Forum
WIEGO	Women in Employment: Globalizing and Organizing
WISA	Waste Integration in South Africa

Preface

There is a widespread view that labour as a counter-hegemonic force has come to an end. We saw this in the work of Manuel Castells (1996) and his notion of the network society, then Guy Standing's (2011) notion of the global precariat, and now Klaus Schwab's (2016) idea of a 'Fourth Industrial Revolution' (4IR). There is a lot going for these arguments; there is no question that there has been a decline of union membership and density in the Global North, although in some countries more than others. For example, in liberal market economies such as Australia union membership has declined from 50 per cent to 15 per cent, and in the United States from 20 per cent to 11 per cent. In coordinated market economies such as Germany it has declined from 35 per cent to 18 per cent. Even a social democratic country such as Sweden has lost union members, from 78 per cent to 68 per cent (Visser, 2019: 15).

But the problem with the pessimistic 'end of labour thesis' is that it reifies globalisation and the digital age, giving them a logic and coherence that they do not have. It adopts a form of linear analysis that takes little account of historic structural shifts and cycles, or what Karl Polanyi (1944) called the double movement, and what Marx saw as the relentless drive of capital to accumulate by exploiting labour and thereby generating ongoing struggles against it (Marx, 1990).

Most importantly, the pessimists present workers as victims. The result is that labour can only act defensively – fight militantly to defend a demand, even when it is unrealistic. The result is that labour is seen as an actor without agency that cannot think of alternatives or imagine a future towards which labour can work. We need to rethink the way we view digitalisation, and reject a preconceived notion about the development of globalisation.

An important event in this rethinking was a global project on innovation in trade unions, Trade Unions in Transformation (TUiT), initiated by the Friedrich Ebert Stiftung (FES), with a focus on power resources (Herberg, 2018). The studies that form part of the TUiT project restore a focus on worker agency and demonstrate how workers are responding innovatively to globalisation. We draw on the power resources approach (PRA) to examine the new forms of worker organisation emerging among large swathes of precarious and informal labour in Africa and South Africa. We identify examples where workers on the margins are beginning to cross the divide between the protected and the unprotected, the established workers and those marginalised by liberalisation.

In developing a Southern approach to work and labour, a research agenda evolved where we have begun to identify the new forms of organisation and sources of power that are emerging in the Global South. The focus of these studies has, we argue, not been the institutional setting of labour relations or the overall impact of major trends like globalisation on labour, but rather the strategic choice of workers in responding to new challenges and changing contexts.

We demonstrate in these studies that workers' structural power has been constrained by increased competition between workers globally, by intensified managerial control at workplace level deepened by digitalisation and by unfriendly strike regulations. However, in addition to structural power we identify how workers are able to mobilise other sources of power. 'Self-employed workers' with low structural power tend to create new forms of associational power, which diverge from traditional trade unions. We identify modest but significant examples of the new forms of organisation and sources of power that workers are experimenting with in the Global South. To what extent they can form a counter-movement to liberalisation in the Global South remains to be seen. What is clear is that Southern workers are developing innovative responses to the challenge of an increasingly insecure world.

Instead of the bright new world painted by Schwab and others, like the global tech companies, what is emerging is a return to the working conditions of the nineteenth century. In many ways digitalisation, and what we call algorithmic management, is a return to Frederick Taylor's ideas of scientific management. Management could strengthen its hand in the struggle to speed up production, Taylor wrote at the beginning of the last century, if 'managers assume ... the burden of gathering all of the traditional knowledge which had been possessed by the workmen and then classifying, tabulating and reducing this knowledge to rules, laws and formulae' (Braverman, 1974: 12). A second principle was that 'the work of every workman is fully planned out by the management ... and each man received in most cases complete written instructions, describing in detail the task which he is to accomplish' (Braverman, 1974: 118). In other words, management must use its monopoly over knowledge to control each step of the labour process and its mode of execution. Indeed, the current world of work could be described as a form of 'digital Taylorism'.

As Kamath and Sarkar (2020) argue in their problematisation of algorithm-based decision making embedded in Enterprise Resource Planning (ERP), 'standardisation and modularisation of tasks have made wide inroads in workers' lives, resulting in a replication of Taylorist mass-production techniques'. They point out that the algorithmic nature of ERP technology has made work processes far more standardised and routinised, 'making the modern skilled worker as replaceable as Braverman's factory worker' (Kamath and Sarkar, 2020: 116). However, a clear difference from the Fordist assembly line is that workers in the digital age are often atomised into micro or individual workplaces and are not easily able to combine in large numbers to build worker power and confront employers. This points to the need to target state and other national institutions which have the power to deliver services such as pensions, unemployment benefits and other forms of social protection.

Furthermore, the entry of China and former Soviet countries into the global labour force and the economic liberalisation associated with globalisation has resulted in labour and hence capital goods being cheap to produce in emerging Asian economies (Milanovic, 2016: 106). Consequently, although globalisation leads to income gains for the global top income earners and the middle class in emerging Asian economies, this comes at the expense of the working class of the Global North and the poor globally, with those in the lower percentiles of global income distributions experiencing minimal changes in their real income (Milanovic, 2016: 5). The implications of Milanovic's research is that large parts of the Global South are excluded from the gains of globalisation and the new technologies; and, although the members of the working class of the Global North are poor, they are still wealthier than the poor in the Global South.

While the gap 'between rich and poor nations, powerful and powerless nations ... caused by colonization and imperialism is now slightly less substantial, a large citizen premium still exists with a lot of our income [depending] on the accident of birth' (Milanovic, 2016: 139.) Not only is the number of hours worked by labourers greater in the poorer countries, but the real wage rates for the same occupations that involve the same amount of effort are also lower in the Global South (Milanovic, 2016: 140). This ongoing exploitation of Southern labour, colonialism's legacy of global inequality, is what we mean by 'working in the shadow of the digital age'.

The innovation in the volume lies in the way in which it links emerging forms of worker organisation – both formal and informal – that respond to the changing nature of capital and the world of work. In recent times we have seen the emergence of a new business model among the global IT giants, such as Apple and Amazon, that successfully evade nation state corporate governance codes, laws and policies (like anti-trust and competition policy). Control is exercised by a small, mathematically proficient elite dominating decision making and policy by owning and controlling the 'algorithm'. In the process, even greater (income and wealth) inequalities are created and entrenched. This unprecedented concentration of wealth and power is generating resistance to the precarious employment conditions in these giant tech companies, leading to increasing attempts to regulate the sector; this resistance is coming chiefly from global unions and international non-governmental organisations (NGOs) in combination with local worker organisations. As Tony Atkinson (2015: 303) argues in his last book, 'The direction of technological change should be an explicit concern of policy-makers, encouraging innovation in a form that increases the employability of workers'.

This points to the importance of bolstering global institutions such as the International Labour Organization (ILO) and Global Unions which are supporting the organisation of precarious workers. The ILO is the only tripartite United Nations (UN) agency that incorporates worker, trade union, and employer representatives. This is crucial, since it allows nation states to adopt empowering legislation such as Recommendation 204 (R204), which permits informal economy workers to transition into the formal economy. It also points to the importance of pressurising particularly weak nation states to adopt worker rights in a variety of areas including in laws governing migrants, social protection, labour, local government, small business and other arenas impacting on workers' lives. If labour is to revitalise its role in relation to global capital, it needs to organise at different levels: global, nation state and local. This will involve new and experimental ways of organising and implementing worker rights. Crucially, nation states need to strengthen inspectorates to monitor state institutions in their delivery of worker benefits and services. Laws and regulations are useless without successful delivery, an area which worker organisations must oversee.

We take this debate further in four ways. First, we contribute to discussions on the future of work by filling a gap in knowledge on how new technology is shaping the world of work in the Global South. Second, we shift the debate from the dominant narrative of technological determinism to the power dynamics among precarious workers and what these dynamics mean for the future of labour. Third, we stress the importance of organisation at the local level to ensure that global and national rights and regulations are implemented and that bargaining with local state institutions can take place. This importantly includes the role of trade unions, as well as other players in cooperatives and associations. This level takes on a new importance as work becomes more precarious and the informal economy at a local level grows. Finally, we contribute to the debate on the forces driving the production and reproduction of inequality in the Global South (Kanbur, 2019). Today the South faces unprecedented levels of poverty and inequality without the safety net of the welfare state. As argued elsewhere, the study of inequality 'must be rooted in the lives of those who experience inequality ... and be informed by the experiences of those most affected' (Francis et al, 2020: 17).

The central theme of this volume is the impact of new technology on the future of work(ers) and labour organising in the Global South. Our theoretical approach is quite eclectic and draws on global labour studies, inequality studies and African political economy. More specifically, it puts labour process theory in conversation with the PRA.

The methodology followed is predominantly ethnographic, drawing on the experiences of precarious workers through in-depth interviews and observation. We believe this is the most authentic way of uncovering the invisible world of the informal economy and precarious workers. It is their experiences that inform the search for new organisational forms and ways to respond to the challenges of new technologies.

What began as a journey of occasional collaboration has become a collective project drawing together joint research over the past six years. When I began researching the world of work and workers 50 years ago, the employment relationship was seen as a simple binary between an employer and employees. The growth of informal work and the increasing recognition that the majority of the world's workforce are not organised into traditional trade unions set me off on a new journey into the study of precarious work and the future of labour.

I believe that all knowledge is collectively produced, and this book is no exception. The book grew in an ad hoc way. Six years ago I met Dr Carmen Ludwig, a German PhD student at the time, researching the increasingly precarious municipal workforce in Johannesburg. We began to collaborate on a number of research projects, defining and applying the PRA to trade unions. She contributes to Chapters 6 and 7 in this volume. In 2019, I undertook a joint study with Dr Kally Forrest on the response of traditional unions to vulnerable workers. A version of that research appears in Chapter 2. We have continued to collaborate on a number of research projects, and I have benefitted enormously from her extensive knowledge and deep insight into the labour movement. It has also been a great privilege working with Fikile Masikane on a pioneering study of the platform economy. Fikile is a PhD student and one of the bright emerging Black scholars being produced by the National Institute for the Humanities and Social Sciences (NIHSS). Our joint research appears in Chapter 5. Finally, I must acknowledge the contribution of PhD student Lynford Dor. I drew Lynford into this project after reading his Masters research report on organising casual workers east of Johannesburg. He had worked for five years as an organiser, and Chapter 4 was written by him. He also helped conceptualise and write Chapter 1, and on that basis I have included him as co-author of this book.

Of course, at the centre of the 'hidden abode' of the publishing labour process is our editor, Karin Pampallis. She played, and has played many times before, the crucial role of bringing it all together and advising on the publishing process. I also need to thank my colleagues at the Southern Centre for Inequality Studies (SCIS) – the Director Professor Imraan Valodia, and his Deputy Director David Francis, as well as my wonderful colleagues in the Future of Work(ers) project led by Dr Ruth Castel-Branco.

References

Atkinson, A. (2015) *Inequality: What Can be Done?*, Cambridge, MA: Harvard University Press.

Braverman, H. (1974) *Labor and Monopoly Capital: The Degradation of Work in the Twentieth Century*, New York: Monthly Review Press.

Castells, M. (1996) *The Rise of the Network Society, The Information Age: Economy, Society and Culture*, Volume 1, Malden, MA, and Oxford, UK: Blackwell.

Francis, D., Valodia, I. and Webster, E. (eds) (2020) *Inequality Studies from the Global South*, London: Routledge.

Herberg, M. (ed.) (2018) *Trade Unions in Transformation: Success Stories from All Over the World*, Berlin: Friedrich Ebert Stiftung.

Kamath, R. and Sarkar, E. (2020) 'The engineer ... no longer a person but a number on an Excel sheet: Enterprise Resource Planning and commoditisation of labour', *Global Labour Journal*, 11(2): 103–17.

Kanbur, R. (2019) 'Inequality in a global perspective', *Oxford Review of Economic Policy*, 35(3): 431–44.

Marx, K. (1990 [1867]) *Capital: A Critique of Political Economy*, Volume 1, London: Penguin Books.

Milanovic, B. (2016) *Global Inequality: A New Approach for the Age of Globalisation*, Cambridge, MA: Harvard University Press.

Polanyi, K. (1944) *The Great Transformation*, New York: Farrar & Rinehart.

Schwab, K. (2016) *The Fourth Industrial Revolution*, Geneva: World Economic Forum.

Standing, G. (2011) *The Precariat: The New Dangerous Class*, London: Bloomsbury Academic.

Visser, J. (2019) 'Can unions revitalise themselves?', *International Journal of Labour Research*, 9(1–2): 17–48.

The End of Labour? Rethinking the Labour Question in the Digital Age

Nearly three decades ago, Manuel Castells (1996) triumphantly declared that the atomising effects of the new technologies of the 'information age' and the dislocating effects of globalisation presaged the 'end of labour'. By labour, Castells was referring to the organisations that represent the collective interests of workers – that is, the labour movement[1] – which he suggested had been historically superseded.

There is little doubt that the labour movement worldwide is no longer the social force it was in the twentieth century. But much of the debate on the future of work and the consequences for worker organising has focused on responses to technological trends in the Global North. More evidence is required to understand how these trends are impacting on work and workers in the Global South. In this introductory chapter, we discuss the need to rethink the labour question in the digital age. We focus on two major drivers of ongoing structural change – globalisation and digitalisation – and their implications for labour. The innovation in our approach lies in the way in which we contest Castell's provocative claim by linking emerging forms of worker organisation – both formal and informal – to the changing nature of capital and the ways in which the working class is constantly being restructured.

We have divided the chapter into four parts. In Part I we attempt to 'rethink the labour question' within an African context. We suggest that labour scholarship in South Africa would benefit from looking towards Africa to learn from comparative processes of precarisation of work and the struggles emerging against it. We compare economic and labour market indicators from South Africa, Kenya and Uganda – the three countries from which the case studies contained in this book originate.

Part II begins with an analysis of the impact that globalisation and the new global production regime has had on labour. We examine those who have wrestled with Polanyi's (1944) notion of capitalisms' pendulum-like swings between periods of market domination and state regulation. This literature draws on Polanyi to explain the rise of the neo-liberal world order and to search for what he saw as 'counter-movements' to 'protect society' from neo-liberalism's rampant commodification of land, money and labour (Polanyi, 1944). We introduce Burawoy's (2010) critique of the 'false optimism' of contemporary Polanyian labour studies. We contrast Burawoy's 'uncompromising pessimism' with Silver and Zhang's (2009: 174) somewhat more optimistic argument that 'where capital goes, capital-labour conflict follows'. This returns sociology to Marx's theory of the inherent logics of capital accumulation and the fundamental contradictions of wage labour.

In Part III we return to the labour process and Marx's formulation of the labour question as it relates to exploitation. This is especially pertinent for scholars in the Global South, as we argue that the form that precarity and exploitation takes in some parts of the Global South represents a return to nineteenth-century working conditions. In revisiting Marx and the origins of industrial capitalism we can better understand this 'movement forward towards the past' (Ravenelle, 2019: 111) and how it is generating forms of counter-mobilisation, not into traditional trade unions but into new hybrid forms of worker organisation. While these embryonic forms of organisation remain on the margin, they point towards the possibilities of a new trajectory of worker struggles emerging in the Global South.

Throughout our analysis we foreground the role of power in rebuilding the labour movement and advancing struggles of the exploited and the dispossessed. Some of labour's proponents and sympathisers have called for such struggles to be cast as a Marx–Polanyi dialectic (Silver, 2003; Burawoy, 2010; Munck, 2013). We consider the usefulness of the proposed dialectic to explain how the cyclical nature of capital accumulation compels workers to continuously mobilise and build their power.

In Part IV we set out our analytical framework for the chapters that follow. Our framework centres on the relationship between capital's restructuring of labour processes, how this effectively restructures the working class as a result, and the dynamics of struggle that emerge from different sections of the working class in response.

Part I: Labour markets and precarious work in South Africa, Kenya and Uganda

Labour played a central role in the 1980s and early 1990s in the transition to democracy in South Africa, winning significant worker rights in the process (Adler and Webster, 1995). In 1995, the post-apartheid Labour Relations

Act (LRA) was introduced to cement workers' 'organisational rights' to form or join trade unions and to promote collective bargaining through industry-level bargaining councils. The LRA also established the Commission for Conciliation, Mediation and Arbitration (CCMA) to resolve disputes between workers and employers in order to prevent 'avoidable' industrial action and enforce the minimum protections established in the Basic Conditions of Employment Act (BCEA) and other new labour legislation.

But the transition to democracy in 1994 has been described as a triple transition – a political transition to democracy, an economic transition towards global competitiveness and a societal transition to a post-colonial society (Webster and Adler, 1999; Von Holdt, 2003; Webster and Omar, 2003). The interlinked processes of democratisation, economic liberalisation and decolonisation meant that South Africa would have to come to terms with its colonial past as well as with its present location in the division of the world that leaves it vulnerable to patterns of value extraction and domination under global capitalism. 'This perspective, which seems to be common sense in the rest of Africa', wrote Kenyan Africanist Frank Njubi Nesbitt (2002: 5), 'went against the grain in South Africa where a myth of exceptionalism had taken root in both scholarship and the popular imagination'. Indeed, Mahmood Mamdani (1996) challenged the idea of South African exceptionalism, arguing that apartheid was the 'generic form of colonialism'.

Of course, South Africa does have certain distinctive historical, political and economic features in relation to the rest of the continent, and this has contributed to the belief that it could chart a unique path in the post-apartheid period. Debates in the 1980s and 1990s considered the potential for South Africa to embark on a 'high road' development path of high skills, high wages, high productivity and lower costs of living that would be rooted in a compromise between a powerful union movement and capital, as outlined in the Industrial Strategy Project developed by the Congress of South African Trade Unions (COSATU) (Joffe et al, 1995).

However, instead of this high-road development path, the post-apartheid era has seen the decline of trade unionism, the shrinking coverage of collective bargaining, increasing abuse of workers' basic rights and a rise in precarious forms of work. But despite its shrinking industrial base, the relative size, allure and economic dominance of the formal sector continues to distinguish South Africa from much of the rest of the continent, where social reproduction rests to a far greater extent on informal and subsistence work (Francis and Valodia, 2022). Table 1.1 uses data from the ILO to show how rates of informality and informal employment still differ significantly in Southern Africa from the rest of the continent. This data can be read to demonstrate the continued hegemony of the formal sector in South Africa despite the rise of informal sector activity in the post-apartheid era.

Table 1.1: Informality in different parts of Africa

	Africa	Northern Africa	Sub-Saharan Africa	Central Africa	Eastern Africa	Southern Africa	Western Africa
Informal employment as a % share of total employment*	85.8	67.3	89.2	91.0	91.6	40.2	92.4
Informal employment in the informal sector as a % share of total employment**	76.0	58.1	79.2	83.5	82.9	27.6	79.6

*Informal employment in households, the informal sector and the formal sector.

**Figures represent only informal employment and not formal employment in the informal sector.

Source: ILO (2018: 27), using ILO data for 2016.

South Africa now has the highest unemployment rates in the continent, with a labour market that is characterised primarily by extreme competition for low-wage and low-skill formal sector jobs (ILO, 2018). Indeed, it is hard to find a better example of an internal industrial reserve army in almost any other country in the world today. The abundance of idle labour plays a defining role in the contemporary South African political economy by buttressing capital's primary economic demand for low wages on the one hand, yet posing an ever-present threat to the political stability of the system on the other.

Figure 1.1 reveals the large discrepancy in unemployment rates between South Africa and its continental neighbours, Kenya and Uganda. A similarly useful indicator to demonstrate the gap is the employment-to-population ratio shown in Figure 1.2.

Using Gross Domestic Product (GDP) as a proxy to establish the performance of national economies, we can see from Figure 1.3 that the South African economy remains much stronger than its counterparts, despite the volatility it has experienced in the wake of the 2008 financial crisis.

Ultimately, however, these exceptions do little to prove that South Africa is an exceptional developmental case. Castells, writing during the first decade of democracy in South Africa, repeated the metaphor of the divergent developmental roads (or paths) that lay ahead for the country. He noted

Figure 1.1: Total unemployment as a percentage of the labour force

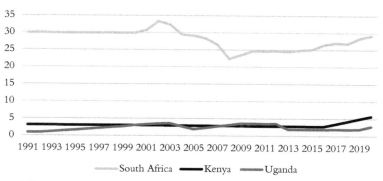

Note: Modelled ILO estimate.

Source: Created by Lynford Dor using open-access World Bank data from https://data.worldbank.org

Figure 1.2: Total employment to population ratio, 15 years and older

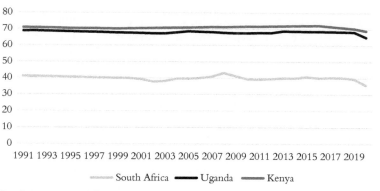

Note: Total per cent; modelled ILO estimate.

Source: Created by Lynford Dor using open-access World Bank data from https://data.worldbank.org

South Africa's distinctive developmental potential but also warned about the dangers of descending down the low road:

> If the political fate of South Africa is indeed linked to its African identity, its developmental path continues to diverge from its ravaged neighbours – unless the end of the gold rush, a lagging technological capability, and increasing social and economic tensions push South Africa towards the abyss of social exclusion from which the African National Congress fought so bravely to escape. (Castells, 2000: 126)

The high road never materialised, and South Africa finds itself increasingly confronted with the reality of its location in the Global South – that is,

Figure 1.3: Current GDP (USD): South Africa, Kenya and Uganda

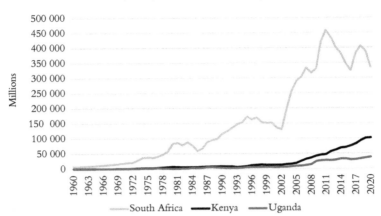

Source: Created by Lynford Dor using open-access World Bank data from https://data.worldbank.org

with a future tied far more closely to its continental neighbours than many had anticipated, or even hoped. In our contribution to the debate on the future of labour, and writing this book from South Africa, we therefore find it useful to put local case studies into conversation with cases from Kenya and Uganda despite the contextual differences that workers are faced with. It is workers' experimental responses to the rise of precarious work in each country that is the common thread and that justify putting these cases into conversation with each other.

We will return in the concluding chapter to an analysis of the future of labour in Africa where we address the labour question in its broader political economic context. For now, however, we go beyond Africa to paint a picture of the new global work order under neo-liberalism. To do so, we explore in Part II the sociological debates that have grappled with the changes to the global economy under this phase of capitalism. In large part, these debates centre on the tension between explaining the specific character of the neo-liberal phase in relation to two of capitalism's distinct yet interlinked modes of accumulation – that is, dispossession (or commodification) and exploitation. Central to our focus, of course, is the desire to understand what the changes under neo-liberalism mean for the labour movement and workers' struggles going forward.

Part II: Labour and neo-liberal globalisation

Globalisation has enabled large parts of the globe that were previously insulated from global capitalism to be penetrated by multinational corporations (MNCs), including central Europe, the former Soviet Union,

India and China. At the same time capital has become more mobile via financialisation, trade liberalisation, the deskilling of manufacturing production processes and the growth of global logistics networks.[2] This has left the rest of the Global South ripe for harvest. And with the expansion of the capitalist mode of production on such a grand scale over the last 50 years, there has been the growth of what increasingly presents as a single global labour market (Munck, 2002; Ness, 2016). Crucially, these 'new' elements of the working class are generally constituted in the Global South and enter the global labour market 'unprotected', without the rights and social benefits that workers won in North America and Western Europe during the period of welfare capitalism.

Debates on globalisation and the search for a counter-movement

It is this creation of a new global production regime, based upon heightened competition between workers, governed by de-regulated and highly financialised markets and accompanied by rampant commodification of previously non-capitalist sectors that has characterised the shift towards capitalism's neo-liberal phase. For many, these far-reaching changes represented a 'second great transformation' in global capitalism as it returned to a project of wholesale market domination (Munck, 2002, 2004; Burawoy, 2003; Silver, 2003; Webster et al, 2008; Block and Somers, 2016). Karl Polanyi's forgotten classic, *The Great Transformation*, was retrieved by the social sciences to put up a defence against the rapidly hegemonising discourse of neo-liberal economic orthodoxy. His concept of 'embeddedness' – the idea that the economy is not autonomous but subordinated to social relations – was a direct challenge to economic liberalism and its assumption that the free market tends towards equilibrium, making it the most effective way to produce and distribute resources for society.

The opening page of *The Great Transformation* seemed like a call to action to build a counter-movement: 'Our thesis is that the idea of a self-adjusting market implied a stark utopia. Such an institution could not exist for any length of time without annihilating the human and natural substance of society' (Polanyi, 1944: 3–4).

In search of evidence for an emerging counter-movement and to understand the effects of growing competition from neo-liberal globalisation and increasing insecurity in the workplace and workers' households, Webster et al (2008) began a study over 20 years ago on workers in three countries producing white goods – fridges, washing machines, micro-ovens. The dominant response they found was one of defeat. In Electrolux Australia the response was one of resignation in the face of the relocation of the plant to China. Most workers interviewed felt fatalistic about the future of the plant and intended to fall back on the modest social protection provided by the Australian welfare system (Webster et al, 2008: 141–6). In South Korea workers responded to intensified international competition by working harder. Overtime increased and workers responded to the threat of downsizing by investing in individual insurance and pension schemes (Webster et al, 2008: 127–40). In South Africa, on the other hand, workers retreated into the household to engage in various survivalist-type strategies in the informal economy (Webster et al, 2008: 108–26).

Despite the immediate signs of defeat, the authors identified the emergence of new sources of power that workers were testing out, in the recognition that they were engaging in a radically new terrain of struggle. Their 'structural power' to stop production had been weakened by increased labour competition, and so they began to look elsewhere to harness forms of 'societal power' to respond to the new global order. In this way, the authors framed the study in terms of Polanyi's notion of a 'double movement' whereby ever wider extensions of free market principles generated broad-based and potentially transnational counter-movements to 'protect society' (Webster et al, 2008: 4–5).

In a review of Webster et al's (2008) book – and a range of similar books dealing with labour and globalisation – Michael Burawoy (2010) critiqued what he described as 'the false optimism of global labour studies'. He argued that the adaptation of the Polanyian double-movement hypothesis leads inevitably to an unfounded optimism around the prospects for labour successfully responding to neo-liberal globalisation. We first need to decide, he suggested, 'where one sits in relation to … exploitation (Marx) or commodification (Polanyi) – [as this will] dictate the strategy one deploys in moving forward' (Burawoy, 2010: 307). We can either promote transnational labour alliances, he said, or one could build local alliances embracing all those impacted by market-driven commodification. But by posing the local and the global as alternatives – either you go global or you organise locally – Burawoy was presenting the reader with a false dichotomy. The global is often in the local and it is no longer possible to see trade union organisation as a purely local activity, as we demonstrate in this book's Chapter 7 on transnational union activism.

But for Burawoy (2010: 308) the reason for the 'false optimism' of Polanyian labour studies lies in a deeper weakness – 'in [Polanyi's] failure to take the logic of capitalism seriously'. In rejecting the idea of laws of history associated with orthodox Marxism, Burawoy argued, 'Polanyi also jettisons the logic of capital, in particular its recurrent deployment of market fundamentalism as a strategy for overcoming its internal contradictions'. Burawoy went on to reconstruct Polanyi in terms of three waves of marketisation: the first wave, from 1795–1914, involved the marketisation of labour; in the second wave, 1914–1973, the marketisation of labour continued but now money was commoditised; and then in the third wave, 1973–?, the marketisation of nature, money and labour took place (Burawoy, 2010: 309). He concluded: 'Optimism today has to be countered by an uncompromising pessimism, not an alarmist but a careful and detached analysis of the way capitalism combines the commodification of nature, money and labour and thereby destroys the very ground upon which a counter-movement could be built' (Burawoy, 2010: 312).

Burawoy continues along similar lines a decade later: 'Today, the working class has lost its leverage with capital. The shoe is now on the other foot, labour has become more dependent on capital, making concessions to capital, fearing redundancy' (Burawoy, 2021: 15). He describes this process as a shift from de-commodification of labour (under welfare capitalism), to re-commodification (in the turn to neo-liberalism), and finally to ex-commodification (as reserves of labour power increasingly sit idle).

The importance of Burawoy's critique is his suggestion that Polanyi 'had lost sight of the imperatives of capital accumulation that lie behind the resurgence of market fundamentalism' (Burawoy, 2010: 308). This requires that we examine more closely the accumulation 'fixes' under neo-liberalism and, for our purposes, the location of South Africa and Africa in the new global production regime.

For Harvey (2003: 87), capitalism's ability to survive through crisis and reinvent itself despite its inner contradictions is a 'mystery worth illuminating'. He borrows from Marx's theoretical insights into the tendency for the rate of profit to fall to argue that it is the 'lack of profitable opportunities that lies at the heart of' the major crises that are generated episodically under capitalism (Harvey, 2003: 88). The solution for capital is found in a series of 'spatial-temporal fixes' that 'stave off, if not resolve, the tendency towards crisis formation under capitalism' (Harvey, 2003: 88). Ultimately, Harvey argues (2003: 180), the resurgence of market fundamentalism on a global scale under neo-liberalism is driven by the imperative to overcome (or fix) obstacles to accumulation through an intensified form of 'accumulation by dispossession'. By this he means capital's appropriation or commodification of non-capitalist spheres of the globe – that is, through privatisations of welfare and socialist states and through the domination of previously non-capitalist modes of production.

However, in an online debate with Harvey (2018) on the nature of 'the new imperialism' of the twenty-first century, Smith (2017) argues that it is in fact the outsourcing and relocation of production to low-wage countries that is the single most important transformation of the neo-liberal era. He describes this as a fundamental transformation in the dominant mode of 'surplus value extraction' that now takes place through the 'global labour arbitrage-driven globalization of production' (Smith, 2017: 1). In other words, under the phase of neo-liberal-financialised capitalism, surplus value is increasingly created through low-paid, labour-intensive work in the Global South and appropriated by MNCs (and their financial backers) that are headquartered in the Global North. Again, we see this tension between exploitation (Marx) and commodification (Polanyi) as two intricately connected but theoretically distinct processes of accumulation that each operate as explanatory factors in the reconstruction of the new world order under neo-liberalism.

If sociology and political economy have understandably drifted towards the latter to explain the overwhelming power of the market under neo-liberalism, the rise of literature on precarity has forced us to think more clearly about how capital has overcome obstacles to accumulation through the creation of new patterns of exploitation and surplus value extraction on a world scale. We pause here to emphasise the central role played in this process by a rapidly globalising reserve army of labour.

Precariousness and the global reserve army

Standing's (2011) book, *The Precariat: The New Dangerous Class*, is possibly the most well-known contribution to the concept of precariousness. For Standing, workers under 'new', vulnerable forms of employment in formal industries, workers in the informal economy and the unemployed are beginning to develop into a new globalised 'class of their own' – a class that he describes as being unpredictably volatile. The precariat, in Standing's schema, is treated separately from the traditional concept of the working class or the proletariat and is ultimately viewed as a phenomenon that is unique to neo-liberalism.

In a critical reconstruction of Standing's work, Munck (2013) warns that anyone who introduces a new concept into the social sciences ought to have clear theoretical and empirical reasons for doing so. Ultimately, Munck suggests that Standing jumped into the deep end of class theory without grasping the foundational insight of class as a social relation within a given mode of production – in other words, class as a relation towards the ownership or lack thereof of the means of production.

For many Southern-based scholars, Standing's portrayal of global precariat expansion misses an important variation, particularly between the Global North and the Global South. Both Braga (2016) and Scully (2016) argue that Standing's analysis does not appreciate the extent to which precarity has been a long-standing feature of labour in the South. The different trajectory of labour in the South is asserted most forcefully by Scully (2016: 161), who associates Standing's analysis with a 'Eurocentric historical narrative' and a 'simplistic assumption of global convergence'. He contends that current features of the precariat, such as a 'detachment from labour' and lack of citizenship rights, have been present in the South for quite a long time – well before the late twentieth-century shift that Standing associates with the rise of the precariat. Scully suggests the need for greater attention to the particularities of contemporary precarity in the South. Indeed, the concept of the informal sector to describe the unregulated and invisible economic activities of the urban poor of the developing world was first identified by researchers in Global South in the early 1970s (ILO, 1972; Hart, 1973). The urban poor were not unemployed, these studies argue; they were working, although often for low and irregular returns.

A second important critique of Standing comes from Bellamy Foster and Jonna (2016) who note that the concept of precariousness has a longer history than is generally acknowledged in the new literature on precarity. 'Precariousness', they suggest, was first notably employed in relation to the development of the reserve army of labour in Engels' (1845) *The Conditions of the Working Class in England* as well as in Marx and Engels' (1848) *The Communist Manifesto*. By returning to the theory of the reserve army, they argue, we can better explain the phenomenon of growing precariousness under neo-liberalism and its North–South dimensions. For example, it can be argued that the neo-liberal restructuring of the global production regime constitutes an effort to exploit what Marx (1867) would refer to as the 'latent surplus populations' in the Global South. This section of the working class was initially proletarianised through centuries of colonialism as people were moved off their land and forced into rural and urban townships. As the proletarianisation of latent surplus population continues under neo-liberalism, through processes of 'accumulation by dispossession' (Harvey, 2018), it drags down the bargaining power of the active army of labour. This is, of course, because the precarious existence of the latent population means that there are numerous would-be workers willing to accept very low wages (Marx, 1867). And as capital developed the means with which to exploit this group across the globe, it pits workers against each other and begins to render more precarious sections of the working class in the Global North.

Similarly, neo-liberal restructuring at a company or industry level, which is characterised by the turn to lean production methods, resulted in the explosion of precarious forms of employment all over the world. It can be argued that this has increased, in relative terms, the size of the 'floating populations' which move in and out of formal sector employment more regularly. But, as with the previously mentioned case, this simultaneously renders more precarious the jobs of even those workers who have more permanent employment – the active army of labour. By treating the concept of precariousness in relation to the role that the reserve army of labour plays in the accumulation of capital, we can see how the increasingly precarious existence of a certain section of the working class under neo-liberalism does not result, as Standing argues, in its separation into a new class. Rather, the fragmentation of the working class under neo-liberalism and the growing weight of the different sections of the reserve army only serves to drag down the entire class into greater levels of precariousness. This approach does not preclude us from acknowledging the particularities of precarity and exploitation in different parts of the world.

Instead, it allows us to view the uneven global developments in class formation and exploitation in their totality.

The 'Fourth Industrial Revolution' and the degradation of work

Today the new digital technology has accelerated the transformation of the labour market landscape. In 2016 Klaus Schwab, Founder and Executive Chairman of the World Economic Forum (WEF), announced that a 'Fourth Industrial Revolution' (4IR) had arrived (Schwab, 2016).[3] The 4IR is characterised by the convergence and complementarity of emerging technology domains, including nanotechnology, biotechnology, new materials and advanced digital production (ADP) technologies. The latter includes 3D printing, human–machine interfaces (HMIs) and artificial intelligence, and is already transforming the global industrial landscape.

There is no doubt that the new information technology (IT) that we are now using has the capacity to increase productivity and human connectivity across the globe in unprecedented ways. The history of industrial capitalism is the history of growing technological innovation starting with the steam engine, electricity, the telephone, the computer through to digitalisation and machine learning (Frey, 2019).

The World Bank (2019) in their annual World Development Report (WDR) optimistically rejected the widespread view that we had entered a world without workers. Instead, the authors argue, work is constantly being reshaped by technology, bringing new opportunities and new ways of producing goods and services. The rise of digital platforms means, they write, that technological effects reach more people faster than ever before. The Mastercard Foundation estimates that within the next ten years between 30 and 80 million people in sub-Saharan Africa will be employed in digital labour, helping to meet a spectacular shortfall in jobs for African workers by absorbing a 'substantial segment of the total 2030 labour force of 600 million' (BFA/Mastercard Foundation, 2019: 33, cited in Mallet, 2020: 272).

From this viewpoint, the 'gig economy' will bring jobs to the unemployed through flexible and autonomous work arrangements, helping people to 'become their own boss' while simultaneously improving both the quality and competitiveness of the modern-day service industry (BFA/Mastercard Foundation, 2019: 33, cited in Mallet, 2020: 272). These arguments are echoed by big business and various high-level international organisations such as the World Bank.

But there is a growing body of literature that believes that this new technology can best be seen through a 'precarity lens' that goes beyond the workplace 'to explore the broader social and political implications of insecure work' (Mallett, 2020: 274). So when the WDR 2019 points to the limited role of trade unions and collective bargaining in conditions of economic austerity, its authors obscure the fact 'that not all responses to uncertainty and insecurity within the labour market take a standardised form' (Mallett, 2020: 281). Mallet (2020) cites studies that show that labour agency is often 'multi-scaled', widely divergent in its visibility and amplitude, channelled in ways that may be far from organised or connected to the wider workforce and it may also take 'unruly' forms of spontaneous and direct action. He concludes that 'in contrast to popular claims that gig workers are anomic and essentially unorganisable, the brief cases considered here illustrate that possibilities for the expression of collective agency and contentious politics are to be found in multiple and diverse forms' (Mallet, 2020: 282).

Whether an identified 4IR exists or whether it is a continuation of the Third Industrial Revolution is a matter of debate (Cooper, 2021; Moll, 2021: 4). What is clear is that 'for all its app-enabled modernity, the gig economy resembles the early industrial age, where workers worked long hours in a piecemeal system, workplace safety was non-existent, and there were few options for redress. Despite payment systems and review systems, the sharing economy is truly a movement forward to the past' (Ravenelle, 2019: 111). To understand this 'movement forward to the past' and the working conditions that resemble the early industrial age, we need to revisit the origins of industrial capitalism and Marx's formulation of the labour question (Chachhi, 2014).

Part III: A movement forward to the past – revisiting the labour process and labour's power

In the context of the rise in the prevalence of precarious work throughout the world, the question of exploitation, as analysed by Karl Marx, has been put back on the agenda – and with it a renewed interest in labour process studies, as detected by Kenny and Webster (2021). And so, in our interest in understanding what future there may be for labour, we return to the foundational logic of Marx, and primarily the idea that 'where capital goes, capital–labour conflict follows' (Silver and Zhang, 2009: 174).

Marx and the labour process

There are two parts to Marx's approach to the labour question. The first component, spelled out in *Capital Volume One* (Marx, 1990 [1867]), is a demonstration of how work is progressively transformed as capital overcomes the impediments to capital accumulation and extends its control over the labour process. Three phases of the transformation of the labour process are identified: cooperation, when the craft worker still had control over the content and performance of work; manufacture, when the process of job fragmentation and deskilling began; and machinofacture, when work became mechanised and 'emancipated from human subjectivity'. In what was to become in the 1970s labour process theory (LPT), a new generation of scholars engaged in a lively debate as to whether automation had led to a fourth phase where all manual interventions would be eliminated (Thompson and Vincent, 2010). The Brighton Labour Process Group challenged this idea of a fourth phase, drawing on Chapter 16 of Marx's *Capital*, which makes a distinction between formal and real subordination of labour to capital. Under real subordination, they argued, capital has power in the very heart of production itself – they call this 'valorisation in command' (Brighton Labour Process Group, 1977: 20). This involved the conscious application of science and technology to the labour process.[4]

While Marx was concerned with demonstrating how capital, through its relentless drive for profit, progressively increases its control over the labour process, real subordination is never complete. By calling labour power variable capital, Marx made it clear that surplus value was not determined in a mechanical way. If powerful enough, employers can vary the surplus created. If they are strong enough, workers can also vary this. The term 'variable' draws attention to the fact that the surplus created varies according to the relative strengths of the combatants and their relative control over the labour process.

Thus, the second component of Marx's approach to the labour question was his belief that the evolution of industrial capitalism provided the pre-conditions for collective organisation by drawing workers together in large numbers and creating deprivations which spurred them to combination. However, the limited economic achievements of these trade unions led workers to adopt more political forms of action and ultimately to directly challenge the whole structure of class domination.

This privileging by Marx and Engels of production and workers as the agents of emancipatory potential, not only of themselves, but of all components of society, proved to be hopelessly optimistic in their lifetime. Much to their disgust, trade unions initially became exclusive preserves of the aristocratic minority of privileged craft workers (Lane, 1974: 63–90).

Since the death of Marx and Engels in the late nineteenth century, the development of both trade unions and capitalist society has further undermined the credibility of the simple thesis propounded in their early writings. The most influential accounts of twentieth-century socialist theory (such as those by Lenin, Michel and Trotsky) and social analysis (such as those by Wright-Mills, Dahrendorff and Lipset), writes Hyman (1972: 11–37), have focused on aspects of trade unions which inhibit any overt challenge to capitalism. With organisation, he suggests, comes oligarchy, a decline in militancy, and integration and incorporation of trade unions into capitalist society.

Harry Braverman, who contributed so much to the renewal of interest in the labour process through his book *Labour and Monopoly Capital*, shared this pessimistic interpretation of the role of trade unions in capitalist society. He wrote:

> The unionized working class weakened in its original revolutionary impetus by the gains afforded by the rapid increase in productivity, increasingly lost the will and ambition to wrest control of production from capitalist hands and turned ever more to bargaining over labour's share of the product. ... The critique of the mode of production gave way to the critique of capitalism as a mode of distribution. Trade unions were prepared to accept increased [capitalist] control over production in return for better wages. (Braverman, 1974: 150)

The re-emergence of industrial conflict in advanced capitalist society in the 1960s led to a critical reappraisal of the pessimistic one-sidedness of industrial relations orthodoxy. Foremost among these critics was Richard Hyman, who emphasised the ambivalence inherent in the trade union function. Influenced by the militant rank-and-file movements challenging union officials in the United Kingdom in the late 1960s and early 1970s, he drew attention to the potential of trade unions:

> Pure and simple trade union activity does pose a substantial threat to the stability of the capitalist economy in certain circumstances. ... The iron law of oligarchy is subject to important constraints. Attempts to extend the process of incorporation do meet significant obstacles to success. To this extent, the 'optimistic' interpretation of trade unionism cannot be rejected outright. (Hyman, 1972: 37)

Rediscovering labour's power

In earlier research in the 1980s on the transformation of work and worker resistance in the metal industry in South Africa, Webster (1985: 11–12) argued that Marx's 'optimism' was not an article of faith; his analysis of the role of the working class rested on a materialist account of the contradictory nature of capitalist development. The precise impact of the changing labour process on forms of workplace organisation is not explored by Marx, it was argued, although his theory postulated such a link. There is also, Webster went on to argue, an absence in Braverman's study of an account of the way in which the development of machine-based production generates important sources of leverage for effective workplace organisation. Webster (1985: 231–60) identified the new bargaining power conferred on unskilled and semi-skilled workers when mechanisation replaced craft skill, and demonstrated how an increasingly confident semi-skilled Black labour force emerged creating a powerful shop steward movement in South Africa's industrial heartland.[5]

Contrary to the projections in the 1980s to 1990s that 'the labour movement seemed to be historically superseded' (Castells, 1997: 360), or even earlier that the working class was no longer a force for social transformation (Gorz, 1983), the recent upsurge in labour struggles in the platform economy globally has once again brought labour to the forefront (Ness, 2016).[6] If by the labour movement we mean not just the traditional trade union movement (which is indeed under threat internally and externally, especially in the North), but this wider movement where self-defined workers organise, protest and struggle as workers as well as citizens, there is no doubt that the labour movement retains the potential to drive processes of social change.

Making, unmaking and remaking the labour movement

In *Forces of Labour*, an influential account of the global trajectory of the labour movement through the twentieth century, Beverley Silver (2003) begins by identifying how capital overcomes impediments to accumulation through various fixes (spatial, production, financial and technological). And accompanying such fixes, especially where new iterations of capital formation are concerned, are processes of new class formations. Or as Munck (2013) argues, these fixes result in cyclical processes of capital formation that 'make, unmake and remake' the working class.

Ultimately, Silver advances the argument that two distinct 'types' of struggles are generated in response to capital's efforts to overcome impediments to accumulation. Struggles of the old sections of the working class that resist the 're-commodification' or 'ex-commodification' of their labour power through the attack on both wages and the social wage (or even attacks on its employment altogether) are framed as 'Polanyi-type'. This is generally seen as the section of the working class that had made material gains during the heyday of social democracy – essentially to de-commodify their labour power by regulating its sale and ultimately taking it out of the free market. Often the attack on this section of the class results in the 'unmaking' of its traditional location within the relations of production. 'Marx-type' struggles, on the other hand, are presented as emerging from new sections of the working class that are made or re-made through various capital fixes and new capital formations. Silver traces how this process unfolds on a global scale as impediments to accumulation in the auto industry forced it to relocate production to cheaper parts of the world, thus generating new workers and new struggles against it.[7]

As Silver and Zhang (2009: 174) succinctly put it some years later, 'Where capital goes, labour–capital conflict follows'. But this is obviously not a seamless process purely determined by the logic of capital. In some cases class-based action is harder to achieve due to the specificities of local economic, cultural and political dynamics (Harriss-White and Gooptu, 2001). The initial response of the traditional labour movement to the rise of neo-liberalism was to rely on the dominant 'social dialogue' and social partnership strategy of engagement expressed through tripartite 'political exchange'. But, as Sweeney (2018) argues, the social dialogue approach was simply out of step with the realities facing workers in most of the world.

In the 1990s there was a global shift to a 'social power' approach, willing to challenge, in one form or another, 'existing arrangements of ownership and power, mainly by asserting, or reasserting, calls for public or social ownership and democratic control over key sectors' (Sweeney, 2018: 31). With the growing rediscovery of the power of labour by militants in the labour movement, we see the emergence of a group of scholars beginning to theorise the power of labour through the PRA.

The power resources approach

The intellectual foundations of the PRA were laid over two decades ago by two American Marxist sociologists, Erik Olin Wright (2000) and Beverly Silver (2003). The two key concepts – structural power (the power stemming from labour's position in the economic system and production process), and associational power (the power arising from collective political or trade union associations) – provided the basis for this approach. In the decade that followed, labour scholars went on to identify two other sources of workers' power – first societal power (Chun, 2009), and then institutional power (Dörre et al, 2009; see also Schmalz et al, 2018 and 2019).

The concept of symbolic power – or societal power – was added into the PRA by researchers arguing that workers with limited structural power were able to compensate for the lack of associational power 'by drawing upon the contested arena of culture and public debates about values' (Chun, 2009: 7). Societal power can be expressed in two ways – by building coalitions with other social groups such as social movements and by influencing the public discourse. The concept of institutional power was introduced by researchers from Germany, who saw institutionalised labour rights and dialogue procedures as sources of power that labour could rely on even when structural and associational power was weakened (Dörre et al, 2009; Schmalz and Dörre, 2013; Urban, 2013). Figure 1.4 summarises these four aspects of the PRA. In addition to these debates on the nature of labour power, scholars from Canada argued that specific capabilities are needed to mobilise the individual power resources. Lévesque and Murray (2010, 2013) identify four such capabilities: the ability to learn from the past (learning capability); the ability to resolve conflict and build consensus (intermediation capability); the ability to develop

Figure 1.4: Trade union power resources

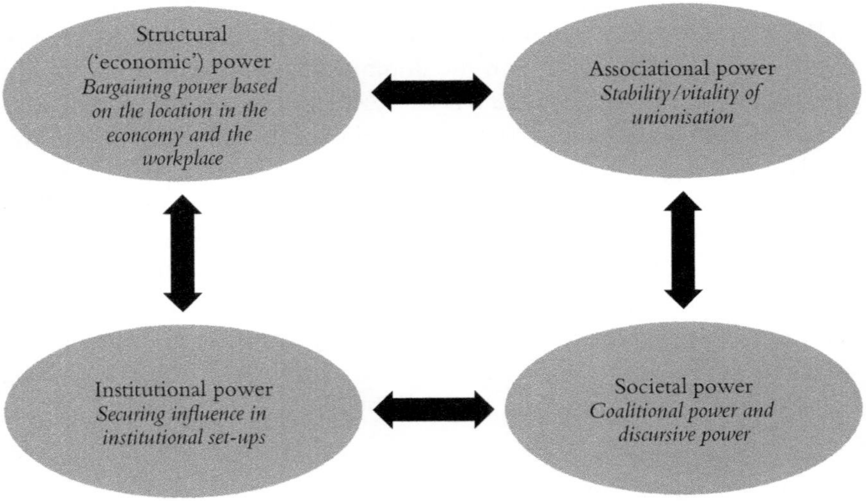

Source: Schmalz et al (2018: 116). Expanded chart based on Gerst et al (2011).

new strategies and establish an autonomous agenda (framing capability); and the ability to adapt organisational traditions to changing policy needs (organisational flexibility).

Silver (2003) argues that weaknesses in structural power might encourage experiments with new forms and ways to strengthen workers' associational power. Webster et al (2008) took this analysis further by introducing logistical power as particularly relevant in the light of rising labour protests in the Global South. Logistical power can be regarded as a form of structural power which rests primarily on workers' ability to disrupt flows of capital and people in public spaces. It is therefore based on the ability of workers to extend disputes from the workplace into the public domain.

However, PRA has been subject to critique. First, it is argued that it is not a universal formula and has to be situated in an analysis of the relationship between capital and labour (Gallas, 2018). It is a tool that can be utilised to understand and build worker organisation. But context matters (Schmalz et al, 2019). For example, while institutional power can guarantee trade union rights such as freedom of association and participation in labour-market and conflict-resolution institutions on the one hand, it also restricts unions' capacity, creating a frame that constrains trade union strategies and actions. Therefore, institutional power is dependent on context and labours' political traditions.

Others have criticised the PRA for allegedly supporting a social democratic and corporatist model of trade unions developed in post-war Western Europe (Nowak, 2018). In their response to this argument Schmalz et al

(2019) suggest that the PRA tends rather to highlight the primary sources of workers' power (structural power), based on the ability to wage conflicts and the vitality of labour organisations (associational power) and the possibility of cooperation with social movements (societal power), while taking into account institutional configurations (institutional power). The PRA challenges the assumption that there is no alternative: it highlights the possibility of worker agency in the face of globalisation processes and the 'strategic choice' of trade unions to revitalise and establish new forms of action beyond established routines. Schmalz et al (2019) go on to suggest that new movements and forms of organisation are emerging. These organisations of informal or precarious workers often differ from traditional unionism in their structures and strategies. Where trade unions have taken up the issues of these workers, as we will show later, unions have been forced to undergo fundamental transformations. Where they have resisted such changes, unions have often been severely weakened.

Part IV: Analytical framework and outline of the book

With the aim of contributing to the debates concerning the future of the labour movement in the twenty-first century, this book begins by exploring how workers and worker organisations have responded to the changing nature of work, to marketisation, to technological change and to the rise of new industries over the last few decades in South Africa, Kenya and Uganda. Figures 1.5, 1.6 and 1.7 demonstrate changes in the share of total employment in three overarching economic sectors (agriculture, services and industry) for South Africa, Uganda and Kenya.[8] Agriculture still registers over 70 per cent

Figure 1.5: Employment in agriculture in South Africa, Uganda and Kenya

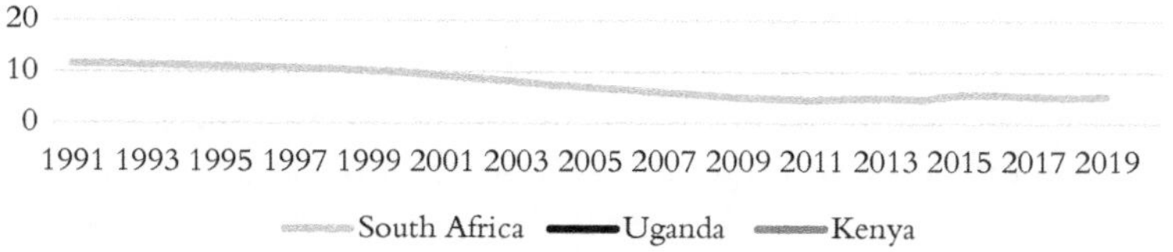

Note: Percentage of total employment; modelled ILO estimate.

Source: Created by Lynford Dor using open-access World Bank data from https://data.worldbank.org/indicator

Figure 1.6: Employment in services in South Africa, Uganda and Kenya

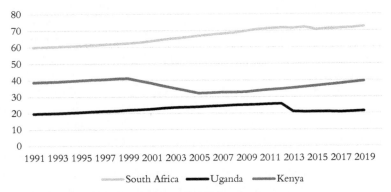

Note: Percentage of total employment; modelled ILO estimate.

Source: Created by Lynford Dor using open-access World Bank data from
https://data.worldbank.org/indicator

Figure 1.7: Employment in industry in South Africa, Uganda and Kenya

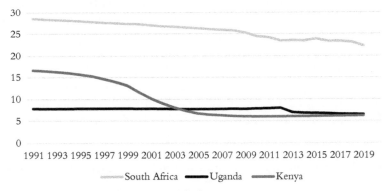

Note: Percentage of total employment; modelled ILO estimate.

Source: Created by Lynford Dor using open-access World Bank data from
https://data.worldbank.org/indicator

of total employment in Uganda. In Kenya services contribute a significant
share of employment, while in South Africa services are by far the dominant
sector. The share of employment in industry has tailed off in South Africa,
along with the general economic decline of many of its subsectors.

We have concentrated much of our research on the growth of 'atypical'
workers in casual and insecure work in the formal sector, as well as informal
workers attempting to make a living in various informal sector activities.
It is these workers who often experiment most with alternative means of
building their power.

After decades of neo-liberal reforms that have radically altered class relations in all corners of the globe, struggles around work in the 'digital age' are quite simply no longer taking place in linear or predetermined ways and are certainly not occurring purely in the previously hegemonic union forms. So, when we refer to 'labour' or 'the labour movement' in this book, we are not referring only to what is sometimes narrowly understood as 'organised labour'. Instead, we are referring to all possible forms of collective worker action, organisation and representation, no matter how big or small, or how permanent or temporary.

It is widely recognised that unions need to revitalise themselves and broaden their constituency if they are to stay relevant. Jelle Visser (2019: 19) has identified four trends in unions globally. First is their ongoing marginalisation, where unions face a further loss of members, resources and relevance. Second is dualisation, where unions defend existing strongholds and focus on those workers in stable jobs, reproducing the dualities in labour markets. Third, substitution describes a scenario where unions are no longer the only actors and other organisations such as social movements, cooperatives and NGOs fill the vacuum by providing specific services and alternative organisational strategies. Finally, unions can successfully revitalise. But to revitalise, Visser (2019: 19) argues, unions need 'the courage to innovate and experiment with new forms of association, use digital tools, and broaden unions' reach through coalition-building with other groups'.

In each of the chapters in this book we see signs of these competing trends. This characterises the nature of the broader labour movement in the current period, as it responds in diverging ways to the defeats suffered over recent decades. It is starkly different to those moments of upsurge, in which a single organisational form or tactical approach establishes itself as hegemonic, as we saw with industrial unionism and the shop steward movement in South Africa in the 1970s and 1980s.

In our concluding chapter we reconstruct Visser's schema based on our case studies to introduce a fifth category: 'experimentation'. Visser's categories all assume the traditional union form to be hegemonic, whereas this is not the case in much of the Global South, and is even changing in industries in South Africa where industrial unions once were the hegemonic form. The chapters in this book each detail how workers are experimenting with different approaches to organising and building power – approaches that differ significantly from the categorisation of 'union revitalisation', as Visser describes it.

To understand the variegated trajectories of worker struggles that emerge in the accounts of this book, we follow Silver (2003) and Munck's (2021) approaches by locating changes in the labour movement within broader processes of class formation and restructuring. Silver's *Forces of Labour* studies the unmaking of old and the making of new elements of the working class in relation to capital's spatial fixes – or, more simply, through the relocation of production to low-wage spheres of the world – what Harvey (2003) described earlier as capital's spatial fixes. Silver tracks the ebbs and flows of worker resistance in different geographical locations, and how these correspond with phases of industrialisation and deindustrialisation. Fine (2019) and Ashman et al (2011), on the other hand, have made important contributions on how the working class within a given country (South Africa) is restructured through another of capital's measures to overcome its accumulation problems, namely through financial fixes – or through financialisation (Fine, 2019). This book complements that literature by returning to the labour process to examine how changes in production within a given geographical location have the effect of unmaking and remaking the older sections of the working class and making new sections in the process, as capital searches for ways to extract higher rates of surplus value. We focus our attention on the restructuring that takes place at workplace, firm or industry level, which we describe as 'labour process fixes'.

Crucially, we explore how such fixes, which include capital's introduction of new technologies and new forms of labour control in production, generate struggles from both older and newer sections of the workforce. In general, labour process fixes have the effect of attacking the conditions of the permanent and unionised section of the workforce, often with the intent of expelling them from production altogether. Through these fixes, capital ultimately seeks to buy labour power from workers on a more 'flexible' (that is, exploitable) basis, which either entails turning the old permanent workforce into a casualised one or bringing a whole new section of the working class into production for the first time. Importantly for capital, this new layer of workers generally comes into the workplace without experience of organised politics and is more likely (at least initially) to accept more precarious employment standards.

We chose our case studies from three countries to explore how labour process fixes across different industries have the effect of restructuring different sections of the working class. In South Africa, our case studies reveal how these processes are unfolding in the informal sector, the public sector, in industry and in the service sector. In Uganda we look at transport and in Kenya at education.

In Chapter 2 we consider the making of an informal sector workforce in post-apartheid South Africa which, although not as large as in its continental neighbours, now makes up a significant section of the country's labouring class. Table 1.1 (near the beginning of this chapter) shows how rates of informality and informal employment still differ significantly between Southern Africa and the rest of the continent. This chapter explores how South Africa's largest labour federation, COSATU, has acknowledged the growing threat of informalisation in the South African labour market at different moments in the last 30 years, but has largely been unable to reorient itself towards various types of vulnerable workers, especially in the informal sector.

In Chapter 3 we turn our attention to the public sector. Our study focuses on privatisation of the Johannesburg municipality, which abruptly unmade a permanent workforce and remade it into an outsourced one on far more precarious conditions.

In Chapter 4 we focus on labour process fixes in manufacturing. Looking at four manufacturing workplaces in Ekurhuleni (east of Johannesburg), we highlight how changes in production have the potential to significantly restructure the character of the industrial workforce. In these case studies we see how the permanent unionised workforce has been expelled from the factory over time, and replaced by workers in more precarious forms of employment. We consider how this process generates struggles from both the 'old' and 'new' layers of industrial workers, who use different approaches to mobilise their power.

In Chapter 5 we examine the emergence of a new worker in the digital economy – the online platform-driven food courier rider. Instead of clocking in with a timecard as at a traditional workplace, 'gig' workers log into an 'app'. In so doing they become subject to a new business model based on a form of algorithmic management. The chapter concludes by suggesting that the new digital technology is a double-edged sword. On the one hand, it leads to an extension of authoritarian managerial control over workers, increasing their insecurity and deepening levels of inequality. On the other hand, this technological linkage has increased workers' workplace bargaining power, providing them with the ability to develop collective solidarity and even strike action.

In Chapter 6 we go beyond South Africa to focus on the Amalgamated Transport and General Workers' Union (ATGWU), a Ugandan transport union which successfully revitalised by crossing the divide between formal and informal workers, and organising the new workers emerging in the informal economy. The union has been substantially transformed from 5,000 paid-up members 15 years ago to become a hybrid organisation – something between a 'traditional' trade union and an informal association of micro-businesses. It is now one of the largest transport unions in Africa with nearly 100,000 members.

In Chapter 7 we show how the introduction of digital technology is a contested process, and how the global union federations (GUFs) are playing an intermediary coordinating role in supporting the exercise of power by trade unions at the supranational level. Through transnational activism in Kenya and Uganda, the GUF Education International (EI) has effectively resisted the de-professionalisation of teachers through a global campaign against the privatisation of education by for-profit operator Bridge

International Academies (BIA). At the centre of BIA's business model is the standardisation of education through digital technology. We argue that global unions played an important role in facilitating local unions' resistance to global corporations. Although the power of global capital makes it a deeply unequal contest, global union federations are facilitating the development of unions' counter power at both local and global levels.

We return in our concluding chapter to Silver's notion of the Marx/Polanyi dialectic introduced earlier in this chapter. Drawing on insights from six different case studies of precarious work, we assess the ways in which the African working class is being unmade and remade, and explore initiatives, both union and non-union, to organise on this shifting terrain.

We conclude by suggesting that the future of labour is above all a question of power. The defeats suffered by the traditional labour movement globally under neo-liberalism means that it is more accurately a question about the potential that workers have to build power once again. In order to pursue these questions, we argue that it is crucial to locate them in an analysis that appreciates the dramatic changes that have taken place to the labour process across industries and geographies under neo-liberalism, which are, most notably, the advances in information and productive technologies, the rise of precarious forms of employment, and capital's dependence on low-wage work in the Global South. It is essential to return to the labour process and its changes, because the workplace remains an important terrain in which struggles against exploitation and domination take place.

Notes

[1] In this book we also use the term labour to mean the labour movement. In other words, we do not use the term labour as a synonym for work.

[2] Capital mobility is felt throughout the circuit of capital. Money capital (financialisation), productive capital (deskilling of production processes), and commodity capital (trade liberalisation with global logistics networks) have all been rendered more mobile under neo-liberalism.

[3] Not everyone has accepted the idea of a Fourth Industrial Revolution. Dave Cooper (2021) suggests that the current period is a continuation (albeit a deeper second phase) of the technological innovations still rooted in the initial information and communication technology (ICT) software and biotechnological innovations of the Third Industrial Revolution. Ian Moll (2021: 4) argues something similar when he concludes a careful analysis of the First, Second and Third Industrial Revolutions by concluding that the 'changes in the twenty-first century are generally the continued evolution of the Third Industrial Revolution'.

[4] In Chapter 5 of this book we suggest that the application of the algorithm in the digital economy is possibly the most advanced technological example of what Marx meant by real subordination of labour to capital.

[5] As Tony Elger (1979: 84) argued:

> The weakness of Braverman's account is that the working-class struggle is accorded the status of a merely transient or frictional reaction to capital,

rather than being located as the articulation of contradictions within the forms of valorization dominating a specific period of capital accumulation. For Braverman it was only the existence of craft skills that presented an obstacle to capitalist development; consequently, the transformation of the labour process is conceptualized in terms of a switch from thorough-going craft control to pervasive capitalist direction of the labour process.

[6] See, for example, the Leeds Index of Platform Labour Protest, a database of platform worker protest events around the world, which identifies 1,271 instances of worker protest between January 2017 and July 2020 (Bessa et al, 2022). Furthermore, platform worker protests showed a strong tendency to be driven from below by worker self-organisation, although trade unions also had an important presence in some parts of the world (Bessa et al, 2022).

[7] Burawoy (2010) provided a different view, suggesting that 'Marx-type' struggles are specifically about exploitation in production, while 'Polanyi-type' struggles are about marketisation or commodification. This framing allows Burawoy to suggest that Polanyi's emphasis on commodification allows for greater scope to link struggles of social movements over privatisation and market domination (which he calls the dominant mode of struggle under neo-liberalism) with worker struggles that he casts as struggles against the exploitation of labour power.

[8] World Bank data allows us to make these comparisons. Industry covers the subsectors of mining, construction and manufacturing. Services groups wholesale and retail in with financial services, as well as various state or government services. Agriculture also includes forestry and fishing.

References

Adler, G. and Webster, E. (1995) 'Challenging transition theory: the labor movement, radical reform, and transition to democracy in South Africa', *Politics & Society*, 23(1): 75–106.

Ashman, S., Fine, B. and Newman, S. (2011) 'The crisis in South Africa: neoliberalism, financialization and uneven and combined development', *Socialist Register*, 47: 174–96.

Bellamy Foster, J. and Jonna, R.J. (2016) 'Marx's theory of working-class precariousness', *Monthly Review*, 69(11): 1–19.

Bessa, L., Joyce, S., Neumann, D., Stuart, M., Trappmann, V. and Umney, C. (2022) *A Global Analysis of Worker Protest in Digital Labour Platforms*, ILO Working Paper 70, Geneva: ILO.

BFA/Mastercard Foundation (2019) *Digital Commerce and Youth Employment in Africa*, Available from: https://mastercardfdn.org/research/digitalcommerce/ [Accessed 7 March 2023].

Block, F. and Somers, N. (2016) *The Power of Market Fundamentalism: Karl Polanyi's Critique*, Cambridge, MA: Harvard University Press.

Braga, R. (2016) 'On Standing's *A Precariat Charter*: confronting the precaritisation of labour in Brazil and Portugal', *Global Labour Journal*, 7(2): 148–59.

Braverman, H. (1974) *Labor and Monopoly Capital: The Degradation of Work in the Twentieth Century*, New York: Monthly Review Press.

Brighton Labour Process Group (1977) 'The capitalist labour process', *Capital and Class*, 1: 3–26.

Burawoy, M. (2003) 'For a sociological Marxism: the complementary convergence of Antonio Gramsci and Karl Polanyi', *Politics and Society*, 31(2): 193–261.

Burawoy, M. (2010) 'From Polanyi to Pollyanna: the false optimism of global labor studies', *Global Labour Journal*, 1(2): 301–13.

Burawoy, M. (2021) 'Going public with Polanyi in the era of Trump', in L. Hossfeld, E.B. Kelly and C. Hossfeld (eds) *The Routledge International Handbook of Public Sociology*, New York: Routledge, pp 11–21.

Castells, M. (1996) *The Rise of the Network Society, The Information Age: Economy, Society and Culture*, Volume 1, Malden, MA, and Oxford, UK: Blackwell.

Castells, M. (1997) *The Power of Identity, The Information Age: Economy, Society and Culture*, Volume 2, Malden, MA, and Oxford, UK: Blackwell.

Castells, M. (2000) *End of Millennium, The Information Age: Economy, Society and Culture*, Volume 3, Malden, MA, and Oxford, UK: Blackwell.

Chachhi, A. (2014) 'Introduction; the "labour question" in contemporary capitalism', *Development and Change*, 45(5): 895–919.

Chun, J. (2009) *Organizing at the Margins: The Symbolic Politics of Labor in South Korea and the United States*, Ithaca, NY: Cornell University Press.

Cooper, D. (2021) 'Why does the Davos World Economic Forum proclaim the second phase of a post-1970s industrial revolution as the "4IR"?', in T. Ngwane and M. Tshoaedi (eds) *Fourth Industrial Revolution: Myth or Reality?*, Johannesburg: Jacana Media, pp 33–58.

Dörre, K., Holst, H. and Nachtwey, O. (2009) 'Organising – a strategic option for trade union renewal?', *International Journal of Action Research*, 5(1): 33–67.

Elger, T. (1979) 'Valorization and "deskilling": a critique of Braverman', *Capital and Class*, 3(1): 58–99.

Engels, F. (1993 [1845]) *The Conditions of the Working Class in England*, Oxford: Oxford University Press.

Fine, B. (2019) 'Post-apartheid South Africa: it's neoliberalism, stupid!', in J. Reynolds, B. Fine and R. van Niekerk (eds) *Race, Class and the Democratic State*, Pietermaritzburg: University of KwaZulu-Natal Press, pp 75–96.

Francis, D. and Valodia, I. (2022) 'The informal economy and informal employment in South Africa', in G. Mills, M. Jonas, H. Bhorat and R. Hartley (eds) *Better Choices: Ensuring South Africa's Future*, Johannesburg: Picador Africa, pp 120–33.

Frey, K. (2019) *The Technology Trap: Capital, Labor, and Power in the Age of Automation*, Princeton, NJ: Princeton University Press.

Gallas, A. (2018) 'Class power and union capacities: a research note on the power resources approach', *Global Labour Journal*, 9(3): 348–52.

Gerst, D., Pickshaus, K. and Wagner, H. (2011) 'Revitalisierung der gewerkschaften durch arbeitspolitik? Die initiativen der ig metall – szenario für arbeitspolitik in und nach der krise', in T. Haipeter and K. Dörre (eds) *Gewerkschaftliche Modernisierung*, Wiesbaden: Springer.

Gorz, A. (1983) *Farewell the Working Class: An Essay on Post Industrial Society*, London: Pluto Press.

Harriss-White, B. and Gooptu, N. (2001) *Mapping India's world of Unorganised Labour*, Socialist Register, London: Merlin Press.

Hart, K. (1973) 'Informal income opportunities and urban employment in Ghana', *Journal of Modern African Studies*, 11(1): 30–49.

Harvey, D. (2003) *The New Imperialism*, New York: Oxford University Press.

Harvey, D. (2018) 'Realities on the ground: David Harvey replies to John Smith', *Review of African Political Economy*, [online] 5 February, Available from: https://roape.net/2018/02/05/realities-ground-david-harvey-replies-john-smith [Accessed 9 May 2019].

Hyman, R. (1972) *Marxism and the Sociology of Trade Unionism*, London: Pluto Press.

International Labour Organization (ILO) (1972) *Employment, Incomes and Equality: A Strategy for Increasing Productive Employment in Kenya*, Geneva: ILO.

International Labour Organization (ILO) (2018) *Women and Men in the Informal Economy: A Statistical Picture*, 3rd edn, Geneva: ILO.

Joffe, A., Kaplan, D., Kaplinsky, R. and Lewis, D. (1995) *Improving Manufacturing Performance: The Report of the Industrial Strategy Project*, Cape Town: International Research Development Centre and UCT Press.

Kenny, B. and Webster, E. (2021) 'The return of the labour process; race, skill and technology in South African labour studies', *Work in the Global Economy*, 1(1–2): 13–32.

Lane, T. (1974) *The Union Makes Us Strong*, London: Arrow Books.

Lévesque, C. and Murray, G. (2010) 'Understanding union power: resources and capabilities for renewing union capacity', *Transfer: European Review of Labour and Research*, 16: 333–50.

Lévesque, C. and Murray, G. (2013) 'Renewing union narrative resources: how union capabilities make a difference', *British Journal of Industrial Relations*, 51(4): 777–96.

Mallett, R. (2020) 'Seeing the changing nature of work through a precarious lens', *Global Labour Journal*, 11(3): 271–88.

Mamdani, M. (1996) *Citizen and Subject: Contemporary Africa and the Legacy of Late Colonialism*, Princeton, NJ: Princeton University Press.

Marx, K. (1976 [1867]) *Capital: A Critique of Political Economy*, Volume 1, London: Penguin Books.

Marx, K. (1990 [1867]) *Capital*, Volume 1, London: Penguin Books.

Marx, K. and Engels, F (1964 [1848]) *The Communist Manifesto*, London: Penguin Books.

Moll, I. (2021) 'The myth of the fourth industrial revolution', *Theoria*, 68(167): 1–32.

Munck, R. (2002) *Globalisation and Labour: The New 'Great Transformation'*, London: Zed Books.

Munck, R. (2004) 'Globalization, labor and the "Polanyi" problem', *Labor History*, 45(3): 251–69.

Munck, R. (2013) 'The precariat: a view from the South', *Third World Quarterly*, 34(5): 747–62.

Munck, R. (2021) 'Labor and globalisation: complexities and transformations', *Tempo Social, Revista de Sociologia da USP*, 33(2): 253–66.

Nesbitt, F.N. (2002) 'African intellectuals in the belly of the beast: migration, identity and the politics of exile', *African Issues*, 30(1): 70–5.

Ness, I. (2016) *Southern Insurgency: The Coming of the Global Working Class*, London: Pluto Press.

Nowak, J. (2018) 'The spectre of social democracy: a symptomatic reading of the power resources approach', *Global Labour Journal*, 9(3): 353–60.

Polanyi, K. (1944) *The Great Transformation*, New York: Farrar & Rinehart.

Ravenelle, A. (2019) *Hustle and Gig: Struggling and Surviving in the Sharing Economy*, Berkeley, CA: University of California Press.

Schmalz, S. and Dörre, K. (eds) (2013) *Comeback der Gewerkschaften? Machtressourcen, innovative Praktiken, internationale Perspektiven*, Frankfurt and New York: Campus.

Schmalz, S., Ludwig, C. and Webster, E. (2018) 'The power resources approach: developments and challenges', *Global Labour Journal*, 9(2): 113–34.

Schmalz, S., Ludwig, C. and Webster, E. (2019) 'Power resources and global capitalism', *Global Labour Journal*, 10(1): 84–90.

Schwab, K. (2016) *The Fourth Industrial Revolution*, Geneva: World Economic Forum.

Scully, B. (2016) 'Precarity north and south: a southern critique of Guy Standing', *Global Labour Journal*, 7(2): 160–73.

Silver, B. (2003) *Forces of Labor: Workers' Movements and Globalisation since 1870*, Cambridge: Cambridge University Press.

Silver, B. and Zhang, L. (2009) 'China as emerging epicenter of world labour unrest', in H. Hung (ed.), *China and the Transformation of Global Capitalism*, Baltimore, MD: Johns Hopkins University Press, pp 174–87.

Smith, J. (2017) 'David Harvey denies imperialism', *African Review of Political Economy*, [online] 10 January, Available from: http://roape.net/2018/01/10/david-harvey-denies-imperialism [Accessed 8 September 2019].

Standing, G. (2011) *The Precariat; The New Dangerous Class*, London: Bloomsbury Academic.

Sweeney, S. (2018) *Trade Unions and Just Transition: The Search For a Transformative Politics*, Trade Unions for Energy Democracy Working Paper 11, New York: Murphy Institute, City University of New York.

Thompson, P. and Vincent, S. (2010) 'Labour process theory and critical realism', in P. Thompson and C. Smith (eds) *Renewing Labour Process Analysis*, Houndmills: Palgrave Press, pp 47–69.

Urban, H.-J. (2013) *Der Tiger und seine Dompteure: Wohlfahrtsstaat und Gewerkschaften im Gegenwartskapitalismus*, Hamburg: VSA.

Visser, J. (2019) 'Can unions revitalise themselves?', *International Journal of Labour Research*, 9(1–2): 17–48.

Von Holdt, K. (2003) *Transition from Below: Forging Trade Unionism and Workplace Change in South Africa*, Pietermaritzburg: University of Natal Press.

Webster, E. (1985) *Cast in a Racial Mould*, Johannesburg: Ravan Press.

Webster, E. and Adler, G. (1999) 'Towards a class compromise in South Africa's "double transition": bargained liberalization and the consolidation of democracy, *Politics and Society*, 27(3): 347–85.

Webster, E., Lambert, R. and Bezuidenhout, A. (2008) *Grounding Globalisation: Labour in the Age of Insecurity*, Malden, MD, Oxford, UK, and Carlton, Australia: Blackwell Publishers.

Webster, E. and Omar, R. (2003) 'Work restructuring in post-apartheid South Africa', *Work and Occupations*, 30(2): 194–213.

Wright, E.O. (2000) 'Working-class power, capitalist-class interests, and class compromise', *American Journal of Sociology*, 105(4): 957–1002.

World Bank (2019) *World Development Report, 2019: The Changing Nature of Work*, Washington, DC: World Bank, [online] Available from: https://openknowledge.worldbank.org/handle/10986/30435#:~:text=The%202019%20World%20Development%20Report%20will%20study%20how,smooth%20the%20transition%20and%20guard%20against%20rising%20inequality [Accessed 25 June 2022].

World Bank (2022) *Indicators*, [online] Available from: https://data.worldbank.org/indicator [Accessed 25 June 2022].

2

Precarious Work after Apartheid: Experimenting with Alternative Forms of Representation in the Informal Sector

With Kally Forrest

The Congress of South African Trade Unions (COSATU) had been at the centre of the internal struggle for democracy since its formation. Therefore, expectations were high in 1994 among its members that South Africa's first democratic government would usher in a worker-friendly labour regime. But from the beginning, the new labour regime proved complex and contested. For employers, labour market flexibility became a mantra as they grappled with intensified global competition. For labour, however, democracy was not delivering on the expectations of more and better jobs, as employers were bypassing the new labour laws.

The world of work was changing and COSATU's membership was not diversifying significantly to include the growing numbers of outsourced, casual, migrant or informal sector workers. This became a concern to the federation as it felt the pressure of large-scale retrenchments and informalisation of employment practices. The labour relations system based on the traditional employer/employee binary was being eroded by labour broker intermediaries (Kenny and Webster, 1998). COSATU responded to these and other challenges in 1997 by setting up a Commission on the Future of Trade Unions, known as the September Commission (after Connie September, Deputy President of COSATU at the time).

Chapter 7 of the September Commission report focused on the rise of vulnerable work and made recommendations on how COSATU should respond.[1] The report categorised vulnerable work into four areas: vulnerable sectors, vulnerable layers of workers (in all sectors), the informal sector, and migrant workers. The report recommended that COSATU commit to the 'strategic objective' of organising against vulnerable work on all levels and warned against the consequences of not doing so. For example, it argued that should COSATU not organise in vulnerable sectors its 'position in the labour market would be weakened, and this would be likely to affect its influence at a political level, and at NEDLAC [National Economic Development and Labour Council]'. Furthermore, if it did not organise 'vulnerable layers' of workers in the formal sector, the report warned that 'COSATU could end up being based in a shrinking section of the working class, as has happened to trade unions in a number of countries' (COSATU, 1997: Chapter 7).

Despite the report's warnings, over the decades that followed COSATU, and the trade union movement more generally, failed to respond adequately to the rise of precarious and vulnerable work in all its forms. This has been well documented (Theron, 2005; Von Holdt and Webster, 2005; Bischoff, 2015). A COSATU survey revealed that 90 per cent of its members were in permanent employment in 2014 despite the proliferation of informal and temporary work practices (Bischoff and Tame, 2017: 66). Bischoff and Tame (2017) note that COSATU's post-apartheid orientation towards organising workers in white-collar and public-sector work (and effectively away from vulnerable work) eventually generated a debate over whether the federation came to represent a 'labour aristocracy' (Buhlungu, 2006).

It was in this context that COSATU set up the Vulnerable Workers Task Team (VWTT) in 2012 to examine ways of representing precarious workers more effectively. In this chapter we focus on the activities of this Task Team and of the Organisation of Informal Traders in the South African Informal Traders Alliance (SAITA). By examining these two case studies we suggest that experimentation in representation on the periphery of the labour movement is crucial for our exploration of the future of labour.

In Part I of this chapter we focus on the VWTT. COSATU's 2012 Congress mandated the federation to explore the organisation of non-standard workers, and the VWTT was subsequently launched. Between 2013 and 2014, it brought together representatives from its affiliates, as well as two informal worker associations (SAITA and the South African Domestic Service and Allied Workers Union [SADSAWU]), two international organisations of informal workers (Women in Employment: Globalizing and Organizing [WIEGO] and the global union StreetNet International), and a number of research organisations. The aim of the Task Team was to encourage and assist the recruitment of precarious workers through a campaign. Because the VWTT debates occurred outside of established unions, this was a moment of significant experimentation in the representation of precarious workers. Sadly, however, events overtook this imaginative initiative. After meeting regularly in 2013 and 2014, the VWTT ceased to function at the end of 2014, due to ruptures within its parent organisation. In November 2014, COSATU's largest affiliate, the National Union of Metalworkers of South Africa (NUMSA) was expelled, followed by the expulsion of the federation's general-secretary, Zwelinzima Vavi in March 2015. While the issues that led to the split had no direct bearing on the VWTT (Craven, 2016), the split did mark the death knell of the Task Team.

In Part II of the chapter, we contrast the VWTT with an initiative that preceded it and which took place outside of traditional unions: the Organisation of Street/Informal Traders.

These two cases are worth comparing because of their shared focus on organising street traders – a new class of workers that formed in the post-apartheid period. Street or informal traders were not allowed to operate under apartheid and had to fight for their right to work under the new dispensation. On the one hand, there is the largest trade union federation in the country, with its base in formal industry and the public sector, which (to a limited extent) recognises the need to reposition itself towards new layers of workers in a changing labour market. On the other hand, there are the workers themselves, organising from below and making alliances with organisations such as StreetNet International and various NGOs to advance their interests. StreetNet's efforts to support street traders sought to advance their interest through strong tripartite institutions (such as the National Economic Development and Labour Council, NEDLAC). But these institutions ultimately play a contradictory role. They offer precarious workers the opportunity to have their policy interests pursued via representatives or organisations sympathetic with their cause, but also act as a barrier to established unions crossing the divide between formal and informal as it signals a vested interest in the labour relations status quo.

Clearly established unions benefit from strong institutional power, making it less urgent for them to transform themselves (Paret, 2015). As Gallas (2016) highlights, institutional power is a double-edged sword that can also constrain unions into positions contrary to workers' interests. Over time the unions have become increasingly dependent on sectoral bargaining (Theron, 2014) and on the alliance with the ruling party to secure their power (Paret, 2015). They became prisoners, as it were, of the institutional framework they negotiated, losing their ability to question the wider social organisation of society, the increasing numbers of precarious workers, and the rapidly deepening inequalities of the neo-liberal period.

Ultimately this chapter argues that an examination of experimentation in organising and representation on the periphery of the labour movement is crucial for our exploration of the future of labour. The primary focus on the informal sector allows us to see how older and newer sections of the working class, as well as the organisations that they belong to, respond to a changing labour market terrain. As they look to mobilise their power and advance their interests, this new class of workers (the street traders) and their organisations find themselves caught between strategies that attempt to harness the institutional power amassed by the traditional labour movement in the past and the recognition of the limits of this double-edged form of power.

Part I: The Vulnerable Workers Task Team

Central to the activities of the VWTT was the need to overcome the 'representation gap' between established unions and growing numbers of workers outside of standard employment (Webster and Bischoff, 2011). The term refers to 'the percentage of workers who desire union representation but who currently do not have access, primarily because they are located in workplaces without trade union recognition' (Heery, 2009: 352). The core unions in the Task Team were SADSAWU, the Food and Allied Workers Union (FAWU), the South African Transport and Allied Workers Union (SATAWU), and the Street Vendors Alliance (SVA). It met monthly and soon realised that a diversity of sectors and forms of employment existed. Early on the VWTT established that employment status – self-employed or wage worker, employer or own account worker – was central to understanding changing structures of employment and the possibilities for organising.

Henry Bernstein (2007) suggests that Africa's labour market is best understood as divided into 'classes of labor'. There are people who sell their labour power in some kind of market – either directly as wage labour or indirectly through a product market. Categories like worker, peasant, employed and self-employed are fluid. Working people alternate between 'earning a living' through wage labour and 'making a living' through various livelihood strategies (Webster, 2005). Bernstein writes:

> In practise what you have in African cities is a large group who simultaneously and ambiguously combine employment and self-employment. ... In the shantytowns are large numbers of individuals who are sometimes unemployed and work intermittently in wage labour in small workshops or performing services. In short, there is no 'homogeneous proletarian condition' within the 'South', other than that essential condition ... the need to secure reproduction needs (survival) through the (direct and indirect) sale of labour power. (Bernstein, 2007: 5)

This ambiguity over class location raises difficult questions for union organisers. Who is a worker? Is a person who owns one minibus and drives it a worker? What about someone who owns two minibuses and hires a person to drive the second one? If the person owns 200 minibuses, are they a worker or an entrepreneur? (Barrett, 2018).

Work in standard employment usually occurs at certain fixed times in defined built spaces such as factories, offices or shops. The regulated workplace is crucial for organising workers into unions. In contrast, precarious work – whether formal or informal – takes place in a variety of spaces (some invisible), such as streets, workers' homes or cyberspace.

Although the central focus of the VWTT became a campaign, the meetings mirrored a range of activities involving the organisation of precarious workers. These included discussions on a national minimum wage,[2] a workshop on migrant labour, and a workshop on precarious work and the future of labour. Taking place in 2013, this workshop was subsequently turned into an edited volume (Webster et al, 2017). In discussion it emerged that legal advice offices were re-emerging to service precarious workers not represented by traditional unions, and two research organisations were commissioned to conduct a survey of these services. Six site visits and nearly 130 telephone interviews with advice offices were conducted (Webster and Englert, 2020).

The core Task Team targeted three sectors: farm and domestic workers in casual employment and street traders (own account workers). It was agreed to campaign from July to October 2014 around five decent work demands: the right to make or earn a decent living, work security, comprehensive social protection, safe and healthy workplaces, and full organisational rights for all workers (VWTT, 2013a: 4).

The aim of the campaign, according to the Task Team was that it:

> must first and foremost build organisation. We must find a balance between collecting demands from below and providing leadership and direction as a Task Team. A set of demands can draw workers together to stand 'shoulder to shoulder' in preparation for moving forward to deepen organisation. (VWTT, 2013b: 2)

For the Task Team, the campaign was about recruitment and 'listening and learning'. The demands 'must unite and be linked to an agreed strategy to make the links between workers who are fragmented through sub-contracting, labour broking, part time work, etc'. The campaign, it was agreed, should also engage public perceptions of waste pickers as 'scavengers'. The demand for a safe and healthy workplace was added to the four core demands. The Task Team concluded by emphasising, 'Worker knowledge of rights and state enforcement is critical to achieving rights – if they are there on paper but not implemented they are worth nothing' (VWTT, 2013b).

The wording of the first demand – for a living wage – was challenged as some informal workers did not earn wages. It was changed to 'decent work and livelihoods for all' and extended to include, 'Respect for own account workers (the self-employed), including rights and access to materials, markets and space' (VWTT, 2013b).

The second demand was expanded to include, 'direct access to work opportunities for both employed workers and own account workers – away with middlemen!' – a reference to labour brokers (VWTT, 2013b). Under social protection, a demand was made for the introduction of a Basic Income Grant and the extension of the Unemployment Insurance Fund (UIF) 'to include all those without employment' (VWTT, 2013b: 3).[3] It was proposed that the UIF be brought under the control of the unions rather than the Department of Labour (DoL). The fourth demand for union rights was amended to:

> Full representational and organisational rights for all workers: the right of all workers to meet and gather in every work place regardless of who the employer is, including shopping malls, farms, homes, airports, stations and other multiple employer work spaces and in the case of own account workers, public spaces; the statutory right to representation and collective bargaining for both employed workers and own account workers; the right of access of organisational representatives to all work places to recruit and represent workers. (VWTT, 2013b: 3)

We turn now to a discussion of the three targeted sectors. It is worth noting the difference between the VWTT's targets to address the representation gap for vulnerable workers and the categorisation of vulnerable work that was used in the September Commission report. The VWTT chose to narrow its focus of vulnerable work to domestic work, farm work and street traders. It did not confront vulnerability that exists at the heart of the formal sector and the public sector in which COSATU's established union affiliates organise. Those forms of vulnerability are addressed in the chapters that follow.

Domestic workers

Of the vulnerable work targeted by the VWTT, domestic work was identified as the most difficult to organise. Shireen Ally (2010: 3) cited Hondagneu-Sotelo as saying, 'Paid domestic work is distinctive not in being the worst job of all but in being regarded as something other than employment'. Ally argues that it is rarely recognised as employment because it is often seen as an extension of women's apparently 'natural' roles. It is seen as a continuation of kinship rather than contractual obligations. Importantly, Ally (2010: 3) observes, the arrival of the South African democratic state began from the premise 'that domestic work was a form of work like any other, and should be formalised, modernised, and professionalised as a form of employment'. In spite of domestic workers acquiring rights to organise, they have been 'politically incorporated as "vulnerable"' and the state has substituted itself 'for the union and demobilised domestics' (Ally, 2010: 162). She argues convincingly that the state can manipulate their victimhood but acknowledges that domestic workers are in a weak bargaining position, especially because 'domestic work is an intimate form of labour'(Ally, 2010: 10). Under these circumstances, the democratic state can become a crucial ally in the same way it has intervened to set a minimum wage for vulnerable workers.

This 'vulnerability' emerged in the VWTT discussions when the South African Domestic Service and Allied Workers Union representative, Eunice Dhladhla, urged VWTT participants to encourage their domestic workers to join SADSAWU. She spoke in terms of the need to get assistance with union education, recruitment pamphlets and recruitment generally (VWTT, 2013c: 6). Dhladhla emphasised the need for state Sectoral Determination and urged participants 'to participate in hearings, as part of an organising strategy' (VWTT, 2013c: 6). The meeting encouraged her to make use of Department of Labour provincial offices.

The dependence of domestic workers on the goodwill of employers and the issue of sexual harassment emerged as key to their vulnerability. Dhladhla spoke of 'persistent and repeated sexual harassment, including rape silenced through bribery, which sometimes even results in pregnancy'. She argued that 'silence and acquiescence of the workers is a major problem, compounded by the dependence of workers on the employer for accommodation in "back rooms". The notion of domestic workers being part of the family is not as it is – workers are workers and nothing else' (VWTT, 2013c).

The campaign made little impact on domestic recruitment, and no advice office for these workers has been established. The strongest support the VWTT offered was to recommend that the COSATU Central Executive Committee encourage their domestic workers to join a union (VWTT, 2013c). Subsequently a new registered domestic worker association driven by younger women has emerged in Pretoria to challenge SADSAWU; it is the United Domestic Workers Union of South Africa. "They got sick of SADSAWU saying they couldn't represent workers", commented Jane Barrett, Director of WIEGO's Organisation and Representation Programme (Barrett, 2019a).

Farmworkers

Union density in the agriculture sector is low, about 3 per cent, and the impact of informalisation on union organising is profound (Webster and Nkosi, 2013: 73–5). In the VWTT, the Food and Agricultural Workers

Union targeted recruitment of 250,000 members by 2015 (VWTT, 2013b: 4). Importantly, at the same meeting FAWU proposed a new recruitment strategy that 'follows the value chain'. It involved connecting with shop stewards in supermarkets and city markets 'where the prices of products are also determined' (VWTT, 2013b: 5). This meant tackling retailers who determine prices, and exploring with COSATU the possibility of a merger between FAWU and the South African Commercial, Catering and Allied Workers Union (SACCAWU).

These were innovative ideas. Regular reports were given at Task Team meetings, and capacity-building workshops were proposed in KwaZulu-Natal, Limpopo and Mpumalanga provinces. Some progress was made including cane growers being recruited at Illovo Sugar, with the next target being Tongaat Hulett, another major sugar producer. However, a major hitch occurred when the Department of Labour stopped its roving safety project (mobile health and safety teams moving from farm to farm). Provinces had succumbed to pressure from employers, who saw the project as 'having the intention to organise workers' (VWTT, 2013d: 9).

FAWU has not reached its targets. In 2019 it had 124,000 members; few cane growers have been recruited; unity with SACCAWU has not been pursued and inter-union competition in the formal sector is high with FAWU capturing SACCAWU's Choppies supermarket membership. Innovative ways of organising have not been explored, although in the approach to its 2020 congress such discussions did occur. FAWU exited COSATU in 2016 and joined the new South African Federation of Trade Unions (SAFTU), which has "few resources to engage with organising vulnerable workers", according to Katishi Masemola (2019), FAWU's general secretary at the time.

Street traders

Street traders were initially represented in the VWTT by the South African Informal Traders Alliance. Earlier in 2005 'COSATU agreed to establish a project to organise street traders to campaign for the right to trade, for access to financial and government services such as ID papers, social insurance and cooperatives' (COSATU, 2013). The federation intended street traders to work with the South African Municipal Workers Union (SAMWU) to implement demands; however, a political problem existed: 'Do self-employed workers always have the same interests/aspirations with employed workers?' (COSATU, 2013). Nevertheless, COSATU declared that, by working with SAMWU, the working-class character of street trader organisations would be maintained and defended (see Part II of this chapter).

Ultimately, the South African Informal Traders Alliance, mentioned previously, was launched independently of COSATU in April 2013, a year after the establishment of the VWTT.

Outside of the traditional unions, innovative forms of organisation were emerging among precarious workers. Some of these organisations, such as SAITA and the Migrant Workers Association (MWA), had been invited to participate in VWTT meetings.

The MWA works with migrants in South Africa. It is not a union but a registered non-profit organisation (NPO) focused on assisting foreign nationals to obtain documentation and take up employment. Documentation difficulties are formidable especially for informal workers who, among other things, struggle to open bank accounts. Xenophobia compounds their difficulties, intensified by politicians uttering anti-foreigner statements in the run-up to elections. Many migrants are desperate, but fear association with a union or worker association. MWA aims to provide a complementary service to unions, and hopes that progressive policies will emerge from its activism around documentation. It operates an office in the Johannesburg inner city and asks a ZAR 40 joining fee (approximately €2.50 in June 2022). At the time when it had dealings with the VWTT, governance structures and a constitution were in place, and it held an Annual General Meeting in 2014 to elect a committee comprised of migrant members (VWTT, 2014d).

Assessing the impact of the Vulnerable Workers Task Team

The VWTT's impact was limited. It contributed directly to discussions on the ILO's (2015) R204 on the Transition from the Informal to the Formal Economy, and brought informal and formal workers together for the first time in COSATU. However, few affiliates engaged with the VWTT pamphlet titled *Join the Drive to Organise All Vulnerable Workers!* (VWTT, 2014a). This reflected the gap between rhetoric and practice which had characterised COSATU's engagement with vulnerable workers over the years. The federation had not fundamentally shifted its organising strategy to incorporate precarious workers. A growing disconnect was evident between members and leadership of individual COSATU affiliates and with the COSATU leadership as the politics of the Tripartite Alliance – COSATU, the South African Communist Party (SACP), and the African National Congress (ANC) – was reproduced within COSATU. Its leadership was preoccupied with influencing Alliance politics and largely indifferent to representing more vulnerable workers (Craven, 2016: 66).

What emerges from the discussions at VWTT meetings is the complex nature of precarious work, and the different demands these workers were making to those in standard employment. This is illustrated by the content of the VWTT pamphlet mentioned previously, which was designed as an educative tool for unionists. A key demand was the removal of obstacles for own account workers to earn a living income rather than a wage. This new way of framing remuneration demands took into account changing workplace and employment relations. The VWTT case study also demonstrates that organisational experimentation around precarious or vulnerable work was mainly happening outside of COSATU affiliates, which was reflected in VWTT discussions, where non-COSATU affiliate structures like SAITA, SADSAWU and the MWA were taking a lead.

The VWTT demonstrated that when established unions engage with more vulnerable workers, new ideas and organising strategies can emerge – but they need to be supported by union leadership and structures. The low impact of the campaign highlighted the danger of unions and their federations aligning with the dominant political party as an overriding strategy to solve worker problems and build worker power. Unions can get sucked into political battles and leadership political ambitions to the detriment of basic organising work. In the process a representational gap emerges and unions become alienated from their worker base. The VWTT experience demonstrates that the growing gap between workers and unions makes it difficult for unions to develop and implement new and creative organisational strategies to represent and build the power of more precarious workers. This is especially the case with vulnerable and informal workers where multiple employers, or the absence of an employer and the need to engage with state institutions, necessitates new organisational approaches.

Part II: Organising informal traders

In this part of the chapter, we examine the struggle of informal traders to organise themselves. This struggle took place outside of traditional union structures, and ultimately resulted in the organisation of street and informal traders into SAITA in 2013, supported in particular by the global union StreetNet International.

Building local recognition

Under democracy, informal street traders have organised themselves in single and umbrella organisations to advance their concerns and demand changes from municipal authorities. Unlike South Africa's trade unions in the formal sector, which in the early days had a clear bargaining partner at enterprise level or through bargaining institutions, informal traders turned to local government to change their conditions. In the same way that the unions of the 1970s and 1980s met obdurate employers reluctant to give workers an equal say in wages and conditions, informal workers have been confronted with hard-nosed city authorities who have obstructed their attempts to be heard or assisted. In such interactions street vendors identified themselves primarily as traders and not as workers eking out a living on the city streets. In turn, municipal authorities had a vision of world-class South African cities with pristine sidewalks unsullied by the clutter that African cities elsewhere were identified with, and along which people would briskly make their way to their places of employment. They imagined hawker and street trading activity being contained in small, medium and micro enterprises (SMMEs) which would develop into sustainable businesses employing local labour.

Confronted with these contradictory visions, street traders' interactions with municipal officials were difficult from the start. However, at times, especially in the early days of democracy when a spirit of *Ubuntu* (goodwill) prevailed, city authorities moderately tolerated street trader activity. But as numbers of vendors increased, municipal attitudes hardened and trader associations were often greeted with hostility or inertia. Responses were uneven, however, and the individual city manager's approach would often determine whether or not traders' demands were heard, and whether some kind of negotiating forum was established. In Johannesburg and Durban immediately post 1994, the authorities demonstrated an initial willingness to engage with street vendors, but this soon hardened into a more autocratic form of governance. Some negotiating forums were established. In Durban, for example, the Department of Informal Trade and Small Business Opportunities (DITSBO) was given the mandate to meet and consult regularly with street vendors (especially women). However, the forum was quickly appropriated by the municipality to rubber-stamp policy with little consultation. Thus, in 1995 the eThekwini (Durban) Municipality passed new street trade by-laws with minimal discussion with street traders. In Johannesburg clashes soon erupted on the streets between street vendors and the Johannesburg Metro Police Division (JMPD) over permission to trade on its sidewalks. Instead of developing effective administrative structures to manage this, the City passed the responsibility to the Metro Trading Company (MTC), a municipal technical entity unsuited to the task (Horn, 2016).[4]

Informal trader organisation was constantly renewed, often in response to a crisis, and would again confront city authorities, sometimes with a single-issue success. However, such informal organisation, and the negotiating platforms they prompted, were seldom sustained. Nevertheless, with each setback or advance informal workers entrenched their existence as a sector that was not going to disappear and with which local government was going to have to interact. Thus, following a near insurrection by vendors in 2007 when the eThekwini council attempted to close the Warwick Road market, the municipality opened its doors to consultation with street vendor organisations which they had previously excluded from the eThekwini Municipality Informal Economy Forum (EMIEF). These periods of transparency were persistently followed by the council seeking to take back control. The Business Support Unit (BSU), which absorbed DITSBO, then side-lined the multi stakeholder EMIEF and invited

WIEGO and other researchers to advise it. Later it turned to the ILO to act as a broker and advisor in its dealings with informal traders, but in all cases it ignored recommendations and continued along a unilateral path (Horn, 2016).

In their reluctance to consult street vendors, municipalities created high levels of tension, which at times erupted into violence. Divide–and–rule tactics were common, and clashes between, for instance, permit and non-permit holders provided councils with further reason to remove traders from the streets. Politics, too, fed into the municipal management of vendors. When elections approached in 2015, a period of political turmoil surfaced in Durban, including tense internal provincial leadership conflicts in the ruling ANC. Regional and municipal political leadership was paralysed, and meetings with street trader representatives fell away (Horn, 2016).

This brief overview of the failure to sustain social dialogue between informal traders and local government belies the indirect associational power that was being incrementally built by informal traders. It implies that informal workers had little agency, while in fact over the years they were relentlessly pushing back boundaries and establishing themselves as a city partner that could not be ignored. Smaller committees combined to approach the council in a united manner; traders fought back both physically and with determination when their stands were threatened or their goods confiscated; and in crisis periods, when city councils attempted to enforce hostile by-laws, they forced municipalities to hear their objections. They have shown a sustained willingness to bargain, consult and work with city representatives, and they have drawn up demands and Charters to communicate their needs (Horn, 2016: 46).[5]

Street vendors have also used the legal organising tool, institutional power, to good effect. In 2013 they took the Johannesburg mayor to court to challenge the city's 'Operation Clean Sweep' aimed at clearing Johannesburg's pavements of traders' stalls; traders were regularly, often violently, evicted from their spaces and had their goods confiscated. "All the goods were jumbled together onto the back of a truck; no receipts were given and it was impossible to find and claim your things later", commented Lulama Mali, a Johannesburg street trader (Mali, 2019). The issue reached the Constitutional Court, South Africa's highest court, which ruled that trader evictions violated city by-laws. It ordered the city to allow traders to return to their places of work. Evoking the spirit of Nelson Mandela, Acting Chief Justice Dikgang Moseneke condemned the operation as an act of 'humiliation and degradation' which rendered thousands of people, and their children, destitute (Zondo, 2014). A further court challenge in the Durban High Court in 2015 held that the eThekwini municipality's confiscation of traders' goods under the 2014 Informal Trading By-law was unconstitutional and unlawful (Benjamin, 2015). These judgments had a disciplining effect on municipalities, who feared that if they tampered with traders' rights they might find themselves entangled in expensive and humiliating court cases.

Street vendors have also been resourceful in utilising both local and international organisations to help reach their goals. "We'll work with anyone who can push our struggle forward and teach us something and working with WIEGO and StreetNet ... has helped us", commented Mali (2019).

In 2002 the StreetNet International alliance of street vendors was launched in Durban. It included membership-based organisations (unions, cooperatives and associations) organising street vendors, market vendors and hawkers across Africa, South America and South East Asia. Its aim was to promote an exchange of information and ideas on issues impacting informal workers, as well as to discuss practical organising and advocacy strategies. StreetNet and WIEGO provide technical support through workshops to augment the voice and visibility of informal workers, and to conduct research where findings, data, case studies and lessons learned are disseminated (WIEGO, n.d.). These organisations brought a critical new perspective to organising informal traders: they were seen as both traders and workers. Previously, many traders had seen themselves as entrepreneurs and did not consider themselves as workers entitled to the rights that all workers have in South Africa. This change of perspective unleashed a whole new way of organising and framing demands. Through a worker lens, WIEGO and StreetNet helped to deepen and build more sustainable organisation among street traders, waste pickers and other own account workers (Barrett, 2019b; Horn, 2019).

Some WIEGO and StreetNet organisers (mainly women) had worked in the South African trade union movement in the 1980s, and had the flexibility and foresight to bring their organising experience to the informal sector. They brought with them useful understandings of how to build worker power. These included: the construction of unity and solidarity; the centrality of worker control and independence; basic organising tools, including tactical and strategic engagement combined with hard work, attention to detail and use of the legal strategy; the importance of influencing ILO task teams and forging international recommendations and conventions which in turn could be used by workers; and the centrality of negotiations and building bargaining institutions. Engaging with these principles and ways of operating bolstered confidence and gave informal workers a progressively stronger voice. Old trade union tropes were still being utilised but in different ways with a different class of worker.

Both organisations entered a terrain where informal workers were already organising and bargaining. Negotiating with local government was widespread; and because WIEGO and StreetNet understood the power that worker control brings to organising, they were able to provide assistance once the organisational capacity of informal worker associations had been assessed. StreetNet's international coordinator Pat Horn explained:

'This is why we're ahead as bargaining partners. We work with what people know but also see limitations and this is where we can help. There is something going on organically, but street traders are competing and conducting parallel negotiations, and this is a divide-and-rule situation for municipalities. We streamline, coordinate and discuss how to sustain unity for follow-up negotiations, and how to record and monitor agreements, and improve the quality of negotiations.' (Horn, 2019)

In this process workers' agency was encouraged through self-representation and independence.

Such coordination had a direct impact. The South African Informal Traders Alliance, a national organisation representing street traders, launched in April 2013 and registered as an NPO five months later. It had not opened a bank account, and had no membership records (VWTT, 2014b). In Johannesburg street traders were fragmented into three different associations (VWTT, 2014c). However, working with StreetNet and WIEGO, by 2018 SAITA had united eight of South Africa's regions. In the ninth region, Gauteng, SAITA's gatekeeping was preventing traders from representing themselves. In 2018 Jowedet, a small organisation based in Alexandra, a poor Black suburb in Johannesburg, began to apply StreetNet's principles and ways of operating. It called Johannesburg trader organisations together to construct solidarity. This united challenge, or Johannesburg platform as it is known, has now permitted Gauteng traders to represent themselves locally and nationally. The umbrella body has appointed trader representatives to handle marketing, public relations, safety and security, recruitment and so on, together with regular meetings where mandates and report backs are given (Mali, 2019). Joint StreetNet and WIEGO workshops have also brought waste pickers and street traders together so they can more powerfully proffer their demands to the municipality.

Both WIEGO and StreetNet play the role that a trade union education department would traditionally perform. Informal workers learn about their rights, labour and administration law, negotiation skills, and how to access useful organisations such as the Socio-Economic Rights Institute of South Africa (SERI) to assist with attacks on vendors and other needs. StreetNet and WIEGO, acknowledging the need for unity and the vulnerability of the sector, have worked widely with other actors in their sectors such as Groundwork, the KwaZulu-Natal (KZN) Fisherperson's Forum, KZN community health care workers, the South African National Civic Organisation (SANCO), the South African Self-Employed Women's Association, the South African Domestic Services Union, and the Food and Allied Workers Union (Horn, 2018). They also work nationally with organisations such as SAITA and the South African Waste Pickers Association

(SAWPA) with an eye to national negotiations and building the voice and power of the sector. WIEGO, SAWPA and Groundwork are currently driving the Waste Integration in South Africa (WISA) project to strengthen waste reclaimers' organisation in cities like Johannesburg, Sasolburg and Tshwane, and to demand their formalisation and integration into municipal cleaning services. Local government frequently complain about the lack of negotiating partners in the informal sector, so the combining and strengthening of organisation to speak with one voice has been an important organisational thrust (Pillay, 2017).

These forms of representation are in the process of building power in the informal sector, but none are new to traditional union organisation. However, they have been innovatively applied to the informal economy, enabling some significant victories for workers to be won, and for the emergence of a much stronger informal worker presence in municipal planning and consultation. However, until recently an informal trader's voice was mainly being built at a local level. The following section looks at how the sector is building representational power at national level in tandem with ongoing local initiatives.

National engagement with International Labour Organization Recommendation 204

In a significant moment in 2015 the ILO adopted Recommendation 204 (R204) on the Transition from the Informal to the Formal Economy. In essence, R204 acknowledges that most people enter the informal economy owing to a lack of opportunities in the formal economy and the absence of other means of livelihood. It recognises that workers in the informal economy are neglected in terms of their rights as workers, including rights at work, social protection, decent working conditions, inclusive development and the rule of law. It further recognises that the sector suffers from a lack of governance and other structural issues, and that public policies could speed up the process of transition to the formal economy in a context of social dialogue (ILO, 2015). South Africa, through the Department of Labour, had been important in framing R204. It gave input into its content and pushed hard for its adoption at the ILO's 107th International Labour Conference in June 2018. Subsequently it established a National Task Team to promote R204 with the intention of engaging in NEDLAC's Decent Work Country Programme. However, the National Task Team never engaged with serious intent at NEDLAC; instead the implementation of R204 continued in a number of different forums which still hold out hope. The Department of Cooperative Governance and Community Affairs and the South African Local Government Association now coordinate R204 implementation at local government level. Meanwhile WIEGO has begun the process of promoting negotiating forums between workers in the informal economy and local government authorities as the first step to implementing R204, and workers in different sectors of the informal economy are exerting bottom-up pressure on authorities to implement R204, initially by introducing them to the recommendation and its contents (WIEGO, 2018). Informal trader representation tends to be ahead of the game. According to Pat Horn (2022), the informal worker representative at NEDLAC, "In the early days we engaged mainly with campaigns and tried to improve traders' conditions at a local level". Chief among these campaigns was the ILO's Decent Work Country Campaign, and more latterly its Future of Work campaign. More recently, however, still using the ILO campaign themes as an organising tool, StreetNet has begun to work on a strategy which has implications for raising informal workers' conditions nationally through discussions at NEDLAC. NEDLAC is a by-product of the campaign surrounding the LRA, waged in the 1980s by COSATU, and is a forum to co-determine economic and social policies. The various parties concerned with the informal economy convene in the Development/Community Chamber of NEDLAC to reach consensus on matters pertaining to social and economic policy and developmental programmes. The informal sector is looking to repurpose this institution in order to make gains for informal workers.

Bizarrely, the informal sector is not permitted to sit in the Labour Chamber but is represented in the Community Chamber, unlike at the ILO where informal workers are represented in the labour sector. The NEDLAC Community Constituency has become overtly supportive of the demands of workers in the informal economy, promoting them in all NEDLAC structures. This support increased after the Presidential Job Summit in October 2018, and highlighted the integration of waste pickers into solid waste management as a national employment-promotion strategy. The focus has been on engaging in a national tripartite social dialogue in NEDLAC's Labour Market Policy area where organised business, government, organised labour and community chambers meet.

The tripartite NEDLAC structure has given the traditional unions a voice and the institutional power to negotiate special privileges for standard employees (most recently the national minimum wage was codetermined here) but has historically excluded the voice of workers in the informal economy. These workers are also excluded from the major laws providing protection and rights to workers – most notably the LRA. Recognition as workers, and representation in labour law, is thus a major organisational thrust for informal traders who will engage the various NEDLAC partners on its reform. The LRA was negotiated at NEDLAC and adopted in 1995, is considered one of the most progressive pieces of labour legislation in the world. The law, however, defines workers as 'employees' and in so doing excludes many in the informal sector who are own account workers. This definition of a worker renders many other clauses of the LRA inapplicable to informal sector workers. The LRA, and its partner the BCEA, permit access to a range of rights and benefits which are denied informal workers. These include: unemployment, old age and maternity benefits; compensation for workplace-related injury and ill-health; prohibition of child labour; the right to bargain collectively, and access to bargaining and dispute resolution and conciliation institutions; access to government training institutions; and codes of good practice. Redefining the LRA is complex, as informal workers may be both own account workers and micro employers. Yet as WIEGO and StreetNet opine, such 'small economic units' (so-called in R204)

'can be considered workers as the power of the authorities is loaded against them. Historically government has tended to view them as entrepreneurs, capitalist units which will grow rich and employ labour in their own right. A tiny minority who have succeeded in doing this get access to government grants. But most of these workers will never achieve this. So making their lives more decent and giving them access to infrastructure, benefits and rights is important to improving their daily lives and increasing their margins.' (Barrett, 2019a)

Organising informal workers is a complex strategy of combining struggles from both above and below, nationally and locally. Lulama Mali, an own account worker, stressed the difference that infrastructural provision from local government would make in her life:

'We have to use public toilets, which get blocked, and we wait in long queues, and all the time I'm worrying about my store. I'm losing customers and I'm worried things will get stolen. ... There's no proper overnight storage. It's a bit better than before because we can now store at the top of a building. But stuff gets wet, and rots out in the open. We have to pay two boys to look after our stuff and carry it up and down to our stores on the street. If you leave your stuff in illegal places the JMPD quickly confiscates it. I also need a small safe space under my table to restock. Now I have to go upstairs to the roof to fetch more things.' (Mali, 2019)

Mali sells bracelets, necklaces, arm bands, hats and scarves so her margins are small and every cent matters. She is clear on what local government needs to provide, and with the help of WIEGO recently submitted a document on traders' needs to a Johannesburg Integrated Development Plan (IDP) meeting.

'We need training, we need skills, we need facilities. We need a building for storage, a crèche, with a day care centre for little kids so our kids can be with us and we can also work. We want a lunch and soup kitchen, a small canteen for a cup of coffee and *vetkoek* [deep-fried dough] in the morning, and a post-school supervised homework centre. We want a building with two floors with lockers to store our stuff but also rooms to meet in, a hall with chairs and tables, fridges for water, ice and food. And a few beds so if you have to you can sleep over. A couple of offices for Johannesburg Informal Traders Platform to work from. We can use the hall for functions and make some money to maintain the building and create work for people. We are willing to contribute but we need the city as partners. We strategise, we are dreamers. We have not had any department on our side to transform our sector but we have a turnaround strategy.' (Mali, 2019)

Mali is keen to negotiate with the municipality in a sustainable forum where traders are taken seriously. "Government pays lip service. They invite you to meetings to make your lives better but nothing will be implemented. The Department of Small Business Development has a budget for the informal sector. But we never see its benefits. It's just promises and officials change all the time."

But she is optimistic: "At the IDP meeting they were interested in the proposal. They were happy to have a negotiating partner in the Johannesburg Platform. They said, 'You are organised so we will work with you as a collective'" (Mali, 2019).

A national impetus through negotiations at NEDLAC is essential if local government is to implement at least some of Mali's dreams. The national Treasury needs to allocate funds and send the message that street traders are an asset to the economy and essential to livelihoods and the economic stability of South Africa. This differs from the trade union struggles of the 1970s and 1980s where power was built incrementally from the workplace or factory upwards, until sufficient strength was mustered to achieve national negotiations in various sectors and ultimately at NEDLAC, which was launched in 1995, to plan the economy. But NEDLAC is now a source of strength for the informal economy where its voice can finally be heard.

Horn (2019) comments, "The informal sector is way in advance of other sectors at NEDLAC in terms of thinking through possibilities and how this could happen. The ILO takes us seriously and whatever forums we are in we are lead contributors". The sector's advanced thinking, however, has frustrated it in negotiations as its bargaining partners at NEDLAC are weak. Although the South African government has played a role internationally, it has few ideas and even less knowledge of the informal sector. Business Unity South Africa (BUSA) is also weak, although it is keen to learn from informal representatives at NEDLAC, and has engaged its affiliates in capacity building on formalisation issues concerning laws and tax contributions. The traditional unions have little interest in representing informal workers and have largely blocked them from combining in the labour chamber (Horn, 2019). NEDLAC affords protection and special privileges to standard employment workers, and so there is little impetus for these traditional unions to cross the formal/informal divide. The informal sector will inevitably have to play a large role in educating its bargaining partners, a role it has already assumed.

"South Africa, and perhaps Senegal, are the only countries which have successfully engaged with the idea of formalising informal workers and which have stopped working in silos", commented Horn (2019). Although South Africa has fewer informal workers than other African countries with large informal sectors, its informal workers have more potential to be absorbed into the formal labour relations system. Labour institutions built over years of struggle in Africa's most industrialised economy are allowing informal workers to access national corridors of power. Street traders are experimenting with new forms of representation at both national and local levels, and as the formal economy falters it will become more urgent for these institutions to align standard employment benefits and rights with those of informal workers.

The street trader case study holds lessons for both traditional trade unions in South Africa and for unorganised vulnerable and informal workers. Trade unions are faced with growing retrenchments and unemployment while redundant workers turn to own account survival activities. If the established unions do not adapt their role in working people's lives, they will become increasingly irrelevant. Engagement with the informal sector and with growing numbers of vulnerable workers is key to fulfilling unions' historical role, and moving from obsolescence into renewed relevance, as the case study of the Amalgamated Transport and General Workers' Union (AGTWU) in Uganda, discussed in Chapter 6, illustrates. In turn, informal worker organisation would receive a huge boost from the established unions' associational power, experience and strategic approaches. While they cannot rely on traditional unions to fight their battles, they simultaneously need to engage them and demonstrate new ways of organising and bargaining which involve the state. In the South African case, precarious workers need to continuously insert their voice and ideas into labour laws and institutions in order to demonstrate to established unions that labour solidarity is the only way to build the power of all workers in order to deliver changes in their conditions.

Conclusion

Two initiatives in experimenting with new forms of representation among precarious workers have been analysed in this chapter: COSATU'S

Vulnerable Workers Task Team and its attempts to develop a campaign to organise vulnerable workers, and the efforts by informal traders to build representational power in local and national government. Both these studies are about new ways of organising and representing the most vulnerable workers in South Africa. The VWTT's deliberations provide a valuable record, while the study of street traders demonstrates how these workers are experimenting with strategic ways of getting their voices heard and acted upon.

What emerges from the VWTT analysis of traditional unions' attempts to organise precarious workers is that they have largely failed, and that these workers remain largely unorganised. The VWTT, however, provided a forum where organisers could share their ideas of experimental new models of organising precarious workers. Migrant workers have not established a traditional union but a non-profit organisation, and their central demands are around citizenship rights rather than wages and working conditions. The weak bargaining position of domestic workers and the distinctive nature of their work, means that they have to target the state as an ally rather than individual employers to win rights. The failure of traditional unions such as FAWU and farmworkers and SAMWU and street traders to facilitate organisation lies in the model of organising and bargaining that they continue to rely on.

As Jan Theron argues in a paper presented to the VWTT:

> There is a need for tolerance and support on the part of trade unions toward other forms of organisation which are, in some sectors, organising workers in non-standard employment, or in sectors which are difficult for trade unions to organise in, such as agriculture and domestic work. Examples are cooperatives and associations bringing together self-employed workers, and NGOs. (Theron, 2014:12)

In arguing for an experimental approach, Theron (2014: 13) suggests establishing workplace forums that 'would provide representation to workers who currently have no voice in the labour relations system'. There is also a need 'to re-conceive the workplace, by focusing for example on the retail mall, or a transport hub such as O.R. Tambo [airport]' (Theron, 2014: 13–14).

The informal traders' study demonstrates that experimentation organising vulnerable workers is underway outside of the traditional unions. This is not, however, through established trade union structures, except in the case of the global union StreetNet, but through associations, platforms, umbrella organisations, NGOs and so on. Their demands are not those associated with formal unions; they are not demanding higher wages but a secure space, infrastructure and facilities that will allow them to earn a living income. Their demands are not to an employer but to local and national state authorities. Shifting the attitude to informal street workers at a national level is crucial for transforming local government attitudes and acceptance of street traders as a permanent feature of working life.

Vendors are also demanding that they be considered as both traders and workers. This is a radical assertion with which unions and state authorities are still grappling. It entails new ways of viewing vendors, with implications for the amendment of a range of labour and other laws, and the implementation of rights and responsibilities that assert the dignity of informal work, in the way R204 frames it. Bargaining is a two-way process with benefits for both sides. In acknowledging the needs and rights of informal workers, municipalities will create a stable economic environment in a society riven by high unemployment, and it will also benefit from local taxation and payment for services.

Informal traders as workers see the traditional unions as their natural allies. They believe that crossing the divide, breaking down the silos between formal and informal work, is critical in the process of changing laws and policies which will benefit all workers. Building an alliance is also important in preventing the established unions from resisting changes to the status quo where they now comfortably reside.

Yet established unions stand to benefit from lending solidarity to precarious workers. The example in Chapter 6 of the Ugandan ATGWU demonstrates how a union under pressure, through experimentation and incorporating informal workers, was able to rebuild a powerful union that won considerable victories for its membership. Traditional unions in South Africa are rapidly losing members as the formal economy weakens. Combining with the informal economy will ensure their survival while strengthening the hand of all workers.

If the established union movement is to overcome the representation gap, our research suggests that it needs to begin by gathering information on the nature and magnitude of precarious work in Africa. Instead of assuming that every worker will get a full-time job with benefits, established labour needs to acknowledge that the world of work has irrevocably changed, and that adopting an experimental approach to representation and bargaining is the only way in which it can secure a future.

We turn now to an examination of precarious work in five other sectors – local government, manufacturing, the platform economy, transport and the educational sector. We begin in Chapter 3 with the challenge of precarious work in the Johannesburg Metro.

Notes

[1] See Chapter 1 for a discussion on the meaning of 'vulnerability' in labour terms.

[2] Eventually implemented in January 2019 (Valodia and Francis, 2018).

[3] To claim UIF benefits, a person must have been previously employed, with the employer and employee respectively contributing 1 per cent of monthly wages to the

UIF. Application for UIF benefits must be made within six months of termination of employment and is a finite cash pay-out depending on length of service. Unemployed members of society are not eligible.

4   In this document Horn gives a detailed account of local government interactions with informal traders between 1990 and 2015 in Durban and Johannesburg.

5   For example, the Save the Hawkers Campaign Charter demands included: taking stock of the African informal trader reality; recognising and resourcing an independent Informal Traders Forum where traders could make inputs into policies and implementation; establishing a multi-stakeholder Informal Trading Committee to build consensus and find solutions with traders themselves; clarifying responsibilities and mandates with an accountable municipal department in charge of street trading, including area-based management committees to end governance opacity and delegate local issues to area-level.

Interviews

Barrett, J. (2019a); (2019b) Jane Barrett, Director WIEGO Organisation and Representation Programme, interviewed 13 March (2019a) and 22 March (2019b).

Horn, P. (2019); (2022) Pat Horn, StreetNet International, interviewed 21 March 2019 (2019) and 25 May 2022 (2022).

Mali, L. (2019) Lulama Mali, street trader, interviewed 8 March.

Masemola, K. (2019) Katishi Masemola, general secretary, Food and Allied Workers Union, telephone interview, 29 March.

References

Ally, S. (2010) *From Servants to Workers: South African Domestic Workers and the Democratic State*, Pietermaritzburg: University of KwaZulu-Natal Press.

Barrett, J. (2018) Comment made at the 'Crossing the Divide: Innovative Organising in Public Transport in Africa' workshop, University of the Witwatersrand, Johannesburg, 21–23 November 2018.

Benjamin, C. (2015) 'Municipality impounding informal traders' goods "unlawful"', Mail & Guardian, [online] 17 February, Available from: https://mg.co.za/article/2015-02-17-municipality-impounding-informal-traders-goods-unlawful [Accessed 9 June 2022].

Bernstein, H. (2007) 'Capital and labour from centre to margins'. Paper prepared for the 'Living on the Margins' conference, University of Cape Town, 26–28 March 2007.

Bischoff, C. (2015) 'COSATU's organisational decline and the erosion of the industrial order', in V. Satgar and R. Southall (eds) *COSATU in Crisis: The Fragmentation of an African Trade Union Federation*, Sandton: KMMR Publishing, pp 217–45.

Bischoff, C. and Tame, B. (2017) 'Labour aristocracy or labour elite? COSATU members' income, other sources of livelihood and household support', in A. Bezuidenhout and M. Tshoaedi (eds) *Labour beyond COSATU: Mapping the Rupture in South Africa's Landscape*, Johannesburg: Wits University Press, pp 62–84.

Buhlungu, S. (ed.) (2006) *Trade Unions and Democracy: COSATU Workers' Political Attitudes in South Africa*, Cape Town: HSRC Press.

Congress of South African Trade Unions (COSATU) (1997) *The Report of the September Commission on the Future of Unions*, [online] August, Available from: http://www.cosatu.org.za/show.php?ID=5123 [Accessed 9 June 2022].

Congress of South African Trade Unions (COSATU) (2013) 'Launch of informal traders' alliance in South Africa', Kimberley, Northern Cape province, 15–16 April 2013, Edward Webster Personal Archive, University of the Witwatersrand, Johannesburg.

Craven, P. (2016) *The Battle for COSATU: An Insider's View*, Johannesburg: Bookstorm.

Gallas, A. (2016) 'There is power in a union: a strategic-relational perspective on power resources', in A. Truger, E. Hein, M. Heine and F. Hoffer (eds), *Monetary Macroeconomics, Labour Markets and Development*, Berlin: Metropolis, pp 195–210.

Heery, E. (2009) 'Representation gap and the future of worker representation', *Industrial Relations Journal*, 40(4): 324–36.

Horn, P. (2016) *Collective Bargaining in the Informal Economy: Street Vendors*, Durban: WIEGO.

Horn, P. (2018) 'NEDLAC community constituency', National Dialogue on the Informal Economy and the Future of Work, Durban, 26–28 March 2018.

International Labour Organization (ILO) (2015) Recommendation 204 on the Transition from the Informal to the Formal Economy, [online] Available from: https://www.ilo.org/ilc/ILCSessions/104/texts-adopted/WCMS_377774/lang--en/index.htm [Accessed 9 June 2022].

Kenny, B. and Webster, E. (1998) 'Eroding the core: flexibility and the re-segmentation of the South African labour market', *Critical Sociology*, 24(3): 216–43.

Paret, M. (2015) 'Precarious labor politics: unions and the struggles of the insecure working class in the USA and South Africa', *Critical Sociology*, 41(4–5): 757–84.

Pillay, V. (2017) 'Amplifying voice visibility and validity: wastepickers in Jo'burg city', *South African Labour Bulletin*, 41(4): 4–6.

Theron, J. (2005) 'Intermediary or employer', *Industrial Law Journal*, 26: 618–48.

Theron, J. (2014) *Non-standard Employment and Labour Legislation: The Outlines of a Strategy*, Working paper, Cape Town: Labour & Enterprise Policy Research Group, University of Cape Town.

Valodia, I. and Francis, D. (2018) 'A minimum wage for South Africa: challenging labour market inequalities'. Draft paper prepared for the UNRISD Conference 'Overcoming Inequalities in a Fractured World: Between Elite Power and Social Mobilisation', Geneva, Switzerland, 8–9 November 2018.

Von Holdt, K. and Webster, E. (2005) 'Work restructuring and the crisis of social reproduction', in E. Webster and K. von Holdt (eds) *Beyond the Apartheid Workplace: Studies in Transition*, Pietermaritzburg: University of KwaZulu-Natal Press, pp 3–40.

Vulnerable Workers Task Team (VWTT) (2013a) 'Vulnerable workers general campaign', *Report of the COSATU Workshop on Vulnerable Workers*, 27 June 2013, Johannesburg: COSATU.

Vulnerable Workers Task Team (VWTT) (2013b) 'Minutes, 27 August 2013', in *Agendas and Minutes*, Edward Webster Personal Archive, University of the Witwatersrand, Johannesburg.

Vulnerable Workers Task Team (VWTT) (2013c) 'Minutes: 10 September 2013', in *Agendas and Minutes*, Edward Webster Personal Archive, University of the Witwatersrand, Johannesburg.

Vulnerable Workers Task Team (VWTT) (2013d) 'Minutes: 8 October 2013', in *Agendas and Minutes*, Edward Webster Personal Archive, University of the Witwatersrand, Johannesburg.

Vulnerable Workers Task Team (VWTT) (2014a) *Join the Drive to Organise all Vulnerable Workers!* Johannesburg: COSATU.

Vulnerable Workers Task Team (VWTT) (2014b) 'Minutes: 6 February 2014', in *Agendas and Minutes*, Edward Webster Personal Archive, University of the Witwatersrand, Johannesburg.

Vulnerable Workers Task ceam (VWTT) (2014c) 'Minutes: 26 June 2014', in *Agendas and Minutes*, Edward Webster Personal Archive, University of the Witwatersrand, Johannesburg.

Vulnerable Workers Task Team (VWTT) (2014d) 'Minutes: 8 October 2014', in *Agendas and Minutes*, Edward Webster Personal Archive, University of the Witwatersrand, Johannesburg.

Webster, E. (2005) 'Making a living, earning a living: work and employment in Southern Africa', *International Political Science Review*, 26(1): 55–71.

Webster, E. and Bischoff, C. (2011) 'New actors in employment relations in the periphery: Closing the representation gap amongst micro and small enterprises', *Industrial Relations/Relations Industrielles*, 66(1): 11–33.

Webster, E. and Nkosi, M. (2013) 'You entered through that gate and you will leave through that gate: the decent work deficit amongst farm workers', in C. Scherrer and D. Saha (eds) *The Food Crisis: Implications for Labor*, Munich: Rainer Hampp-Verlag.

Webster, E. and Englert, T. (2020) 'New dawn or end of labour? From South Africa's East Rand to Ekurhuleni', *Globalizations*, 17(2): 279–93.

Webster, E., Britwum, A. and Bhowmik, S. (2017) *Crossing the Divide: Precarious Work and the Future of Labour*, Pietermaritzburg: University of Kwa-Zulu Natal Press.

Women in Informal Employment: Globalizing and Organizing (WIEGO) (n.d.) *Street Vendors*, [online] Available from: https://www.wiego.org/street-vendors [Accessed 21 June 2022].

Women in Informal Employment: Globalizing and Organizing (WIEGO) (2018) Public Dialogue on Forging a Path towards Recognition and Inclusion of Informal Workers in South Africa, [online] Available from: https://www.wiego.org/public-dialogue-forging-path-towards-recognition-and-inclusion-informal-workers [Accessed 25 June 2022].

Zondo, N. (2014) 'ConCourt slams JMPD's Operation Clean Sweep', PoliticsWeb, [online] 9 June, Available from: https://www.politicsweb.co.za/politics/concourt-slams-jmpds-operation-clean-sweep--seri [Accessed 9 June 2022].

3

Neo-liberalism Comes to Johannesburg: Changing the Rules of the Game

In February 2002 something strange happened to 46-year-old Maria, employed by the University of the Witwatersrand to clean the offices on the third floor of what was then Senate House (and is now Solomon Mahlangu House). Suddenly, Maria's salary dropped overnight by a third, she lost her benefits, her workload increased and her employment status changed from being a long-standing employee of the University to an outsourced contract worker attached to a cleaning company (Bezuidenhout and Fakier, 2006: 462–85).

Through the recently launched Wits 2001 Strategic Plan, the restructuring of the university had begun. Simultaneously, iGoli 2002, a strategic plan by the Johannesburg Metropolitan Council (JMC) to commercialise, privatise, outsource and retrench its employees had been introduced. To explore this new thinking on corporate governance the University partnered with the JMC to host a major international conference on Urban Futures; it took place in the Johannesburg City Hall (Mabin, 2001). The highlight was a panel discussion by leading international urban scholars, Manuel Castells and Saskia Sassen.

The choice of Castells as a keynote speaker proved to be particularly prescient. He had recently published three highly acclaimed volumes arguing that the world had entered a new phase of capitalism, informational capitalism, 'organised around new informational technologies' (Castells, 1996: 29). Labour unions, he argued, were products of the past. In the first volume, on the rise of the network society, Castells writes of how 'capital and labor increasingly tend to exist in different spaces and times. ... At its core, capital is global. As a rule, labor is local' (Castells, 1996: 476). The network society, he wrote, results in labour becoming localised, disaggregated, fragmented, diversified and divided in its collective identity (Castells,

1996: 475). For Castells (1997: 361), 'The labour movement seems to be historically superseded. ... [It] does not seem fit to generate by itself and from itself a project identity able to reconstruct social control and to rebuild social institutions in the Information Age'. Above all, he said, labour unions were unable to represent the new workers, act in the new workplaces and function in the new forms of organisation (Castells, 1996: 278). Castells' ideas were well received by sections of the audience and he was rushed off to spend time with Thabo Mbeki, recently appointed President of South Africa. Mbeki was keen to discuss Castells' ideas on the information society, as Mbeki was about to launch the Presidential International Advisory Council on Information Society and Development.

While Castells was concerned with pointing out the challenges for organised labour under what he was terming the network society, the City Council saw his analysis as an opportunity to weaken organised labour.[1] The end of labour thesis was music to the ears of the architects of iGoli 2002. Johannesburg was about to become the testing ground for structural changes in the local government sector. The strategic relevance of Johannesburg was expressed by a shop steward in the main trade union in the municipal sector, SAMWU, in these terms: "Everything in South Africa is tested here, in Johannesburg. We are in a boiling pot here. So once we lose the battle here, you must know that you have lost the battle for the whole South Africa" (Metrobus shop steward, cited in Ludwig, 2019: 105).

Castells' analysis of how IT was transforming the world of work was an important contribution to the debate on the future of work. Its weakness lay in its failure to recognise the continuities with the past. For the bulk of those employed by the City Council, the nature of their work was not about to change; instead iGoli 2002 was about to change the rules of the game by reintroducing apartheid-style contract labour.

At the centre of iGoli 2002 was a strategy to transform the role of the state from directly providing services to facilitating and monitoring service delivery through a multiplicity of contracts. Barchiesi (2001: 23) describes this reduction in the capacity of the state as a shift to a 'contracting state'. As Ludwig argues, this shift in the role of the state served two purposes. First, contracting out was seen as a way of reducing costs. She cites a city councillor who admitted that "grass cutting costs eight times higher than a contracted-out operation; this is not to do with wages alone but hours, technology, motivation, teams, management, skills and unit costs" (SAMWU, 1999, cited by Ludwig, 2019: 78). Second, outsourcing services was seen as a way of promoting Black Economic Empowerment (BEE) by giving preference to Black-owned companies when awarding state tenders and in the formulation of sectoral targets in terms of the transfer of ownership and control.[2]

Essentially, iGoli 2002 can be seen as the local implementation of a national programme, which committed government to the privatisation of state assets and to the application of public–private partnerships (PPPs) based on cost recovery (DoF, 1996: 17). The introduction of the Growth, Employment and Redistribution (GEAR) policy in 1996 had signalled a shift of national government's economic policy towards neo-liberalism. The new intellectual influences had a powerful effect on the thinking of key policy makers in the ANC. As Padaychee observed: "It was not unusual in the early 90s to hear senior ANC spokespersons arguing that the world had totally changed, and that those arguing for more radical or alternative economic solutions in this new globalised context were simply living in a bygone age" (Padaychee, 1997, cited in Webster and Adler, 1999: 370).

These perspectives corresponded well with the interests of a growing professional middle class and business group emerging out of the liberation movement that stood to gain materially from the rightward shift in economic policies (Webster and Adler, 1999: 371).

In this chapter we show how, in response to the changes introduced by the JMC, labour rediscovered its power and resisted iGoli 2002. But these gains were eroded when the union leadership succumbed to corruption and SAMWU split. The chapter is divided into two parts: in Part I we reflect on different cycles of municipal workers' resistance in Johannesburg and SAMWU's response to iGoli 2002. In Part II we show how these local government workers in Johannesburg rediscover their power and attempt to resist the casualisation of their work through strike action. We argue that by failing to extend their struggle to the community the union lost an opportunity to broaden its power resources. We conclude by showing how, in the age of globalisation, neo-liberalism has captured the state, labour's historical ally. This has drawn sections of the union leadership into corrupt practices. If sustainable worker organisation is to be built, unions must become autonomous actors.

Part I: Building counter power in the workplace and in society

Johannesburg is a very contradictory city. Built on the back of cheap Black migrant gold miners, it developed a highly sophisticated financial sector to provide the money to mine the gold. It is also a deeply unequal city, arguably the most unequal in the world (Bond, 2014). Its high-walled, uneasily gated communities co-exist with a decaying inner city surrounded by informal settlements inhabited by migrants from all over Africa. As Luli Callinicos writes in her book *Who Built Jozi?*: 'Today we still find mock Tuscan houses behind high walls, blocking off the view of the burgeoning informal settlements outside. The rich (now Black and white) and the poor remain worlds apart, as they did under apartheid' (Callinicos, 2012: 167).

It is also a city with a history of sharp conflict – strikes by white workers around the issue of the colour bar on the mines in the first decades of the twentieth century, and strikes by the Black workers who service the city. The majority of Black workers were migrants who were vulnerable under apartheid to deportation to their rural 'homelands'. In terms of the system of influx control, they were in the 'white man's city' on fixed-term contracts and their movements were tightly controlled by the pass system.

We identify three cycles of resistance by municipal workers over the past four decades.[3] The first cycle, 1980–1995, was a period of militancy that began with a mass strike of municipal workers in Johannesburg in July 1980 and culminated in the formation of SAMWU in 1987. SAMWU focused on dismantling racial discrimination in the workplace and the contract labour system. The period ended with municipal workers winning significant institutional power in the form of progressive labour laws that eliminated racial discrimination in the labour market and gave workers a voice at workplace, sector and national levels (Webster and Ludwig, 2017: 170–1).

The second cycle covers the shift to privatisation, 1996–2000, when intense ideological contestation took place around opposition to the governments' policy shift. As discussed earlier, the Johannesburg Metropolitan Council adopted iGoli 2002 to transform and restructure the municipality. In contrast, SAMWU's post-apartheid strategy was to pursue a double track of opposing the privatisation of municipal services, while building labour–community links with the aim of establishing a democratically controlled public service. In its struggle against iGoli 2002, SAMWU was initially able to build societal power by working together with community-based organisations.

While union–community links had been at the core of the unions' strategy in the 1980s, social movement unionism, as we came to call it (Webster, 1988), was limited in the 1990s by the alliance of COSATU with the ruling party, the ANC.[4] As Ludwig (2019: 119) argues, 'SAMWU's campaign against privatisation was constrained by an underlying tension between loyalty to the ANC and loyalty to the labour movement'. The failure of COSATU to seriously challenge its Alliance partner on the issue of privatisation impacted negatively on SAMWUs campaign 'and led to its failure to exploit political opportunities, such as the local government election in 2000' (Webster and Ludwig, 2017: 173).

Their strategy of combining mass mobilisation – strikes, sit-ins, disruption of road traffic – with strategic engagement with the JMC proved ineffective when the Council did not agree to a moratorium on the implementation of iGoli 2002 for the period of negotiations (Musi, 2010). The fact that the City did not agree to a moratorium put SAWMU at a disadvantage. As we argue, 'by focussing on negotiations, SAMWU increasingly gave preference to containing forms of protest, agreeing even to temporarily abstaining from protest action' (Ludwig and Webster, 2017: 144).

By the end of 2000, SAMWU had lost the fight against iGoli 2002. With the creation of Pikitup in 2001, the solid waste sector in Johannesburg had

Figure 3.1: Increasing fragmentation of the workforce in solid waste in Johannesburg

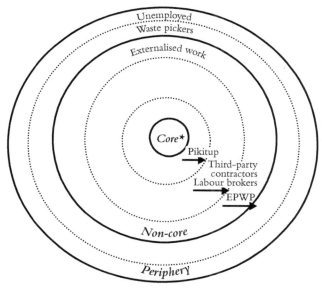

* The core refers to the remaining municipal workforce which has been drastically reduced through the externalisation of the City's municipal services into 14 municipal-owned entities, including Pikitup, City Power and Joburg Water.

Source: Developed by Carmen Ludwig and Edward Webster and first published in Webster and Ludwig (2017: 175).

moved away from being located in the core of municipal work, as illustrated in Figure 3.1.

Ten years after its creation, Pikitup employees were in the minority in the workplace; 60 per cent of the workforce were now outsourced, with the majority employed by labour brokers. As Ludwig (2019) argues, a 'flexibility buffer' had been created not to handle peak workloads but rather as a strategic instrument to reduce labour costs by replacing permanent workers. Pikitup also made use of the national government's public employment scheme, the Expanded Public Works Programme (EPWP). EPWP workers were employed on short-term contracts and were paid at a much lower rate than regular employees.

We have also seen the growth of informal waste pickers on the periphery of Figure 3.1. In 2013 they formed SAWPA, which engages with their counterparts in national government departments and local government. These own account workers cannot register as a trade union because they are self-employed, and the LRA only covers employees. The waste pickers aim to develop a bargaining forum which would include the big waste buyers like Mondi (Impact) who take no responsibility for pickers, who often sleep under plastic in the veld. Waste picker integration into the city's solid waste system and threats to outsource waste collection are high on the agenda (Schmidt et al, 2023).

This outsourcing of permanent employment to labour brokers was part of a broader process from the late 1990s to the early 2000s, of what we called at the time 'eroding the core' (Kenny and Webster, 1998). We argued that new forms of labour control were emerging in democratic South Africa as a means of evading the new labour dispensation in the workplace. This had the effect of exacerbating the vulnerability of some workers, further dividing the labour force and reducing the capacity of trade unions to counter such measures.

But the Urban Futures conference had not only been an opportunity to launch the restructuring of the municipality; the conference was also the catalyst for the launch of the Anti-Privatisation Forum (APF), a collective of community-based organisations mobilising against privatisation of state services. The weakening of workplace bargaining saw the political emergence of 'new social movements' around state services providing electricity and water, HIV and AIDS, housing and land redistribution. 'Thus an upsurge of protests', Kenny and Webster (2021) observe, 'also linked the broader labour market changes around externalization of employment to issues of the commodification of reproductive life in the context of democratic transition where the majority of South Africans expected to see changes marking more equitable inclusion' (Kenny and Webster, 2021: 22).

The trigger for the third cycle, 2001–2011, was found in the conditions arising out of restructuring. The union started to confront the consequences of privatisation and precarious work. This was a decade devoted to mobilising precarious workers and rebuilding union power in the workplace.

Part II: 'We rediscovered our power': the 2011 strike

SAMWU embarked on a two-pronged strategy to rebuild union power in the workplace. The first component was to make all casual workers permanent employees of Pikitup by intensifying organising among all employees working directly or indirectly for the company (Webster and Ludwig, 2017: 178–9). The second component was to confront the Pikitup management and challenge it to end corruption in the entity. When negotiations deadlocked in April 2011, workers went out on a one-week go-slow and then a two-week strike. Importantly, permanent and temporary workers came out on strike in solidarity with each other (Webster and Ludwig, 2017: 179).

As Stephen Faulkner, a union official at the time, remarked, "We rediscovered our power" (Faulkner, 2021). During the strike no refuse collection took place and "the city began to stink". The women street cleaners stood firm: "Council must settle this dispute", they said, "or rats will", Faulkner reported. They "trashed" the streets, emptying bins and throwing the rubbish on the streets. "It is almost as if these women", Faulkner remarked, were "undoing their work" in order to make what is usually invisible and unacknowledged visible.

The ANC responded to SAMWU's anti-corruption campaign by victimising those who were exposing corruption. In Kally Forrest's interview with a SAMWU official, he remarked:

> The city appoints those loyal to the ANC and people deployed by the ANC remain loyal and compromise their beliefs. ... The ANC wants to weaken us as we are the only COSATU union organising in local government. ... The ANC prefers IMATU [Independent Municipal and Allied Trade Union; a rival union affiliated to another union centre] which is not strong and does not threaten them. (Forrest, 2011: 7)

The workers were exercising what we have called logistical power, but they were doing more than disrupting a public space; they were asserting the importance of their work and communicating it to the broader public. This is illustrated in the interview by Ludwig with a Pikitup shop steward:

> [If] we were just marching, after that the next person that comes can't see anything; he won't recognise that there was something which was taking place. If it's clean there is no need for them to say that this strike should come to an end, but if it's not clean they will see the need of those people, that these people are important. [They will say:] Let us listen to them so then they must go and do their job. (Webster and Ludwig, 2017: 180)

A key part of the union's strategy in the strike was to 'blow the whistle' on corruption in Pikitup. "We showed that the fight against corruption is a union issue", the media officer Tahir Sema said when interviewed by Faulkner shortly after the strike: "If you allow corruption to take place, it will impact on working conditions, not least because money goes into private pockets instead of providing a service to be delivered by our members" (Faulkner, 2011: 26).[5] Sema went on to explain:

> [Our] members watch in horror as private contractors are brought in by the same tenderpreneurs[6] to do work which should be done by the municipality. Not only is this work sub-standard, but it is undertaken by labour broker workers who are not paid the municipal minimum and who have little protection. Like all broker workers they are super exploited. (Faulkner, 2011: 26)

SAMWU responded to these attacks by abstaining from campaigning for the ANC in the local government elections. "It is impossible at present, given the attacks our members are experiencing in many provinces", Tahir Sema remarked bitterly, "for us to actively campaign for the ANC while our grievances are not being met" (Faulkner, 2011: 27). Sema believed that the attacks on SAMWU were worsening. "There are more brazen attacks on whistle blowers and the employer and politicians are more open. There is a tussle between the employer, union and the political party. Fights have taken on a more politically violent nature" (Forrest, 2011: 7).

The outcome of the 2011 strike was a victory for SAMWU, as the parties agreed to absorb contract workers involved in the core cleaning service. The public were sympathetic to the strikers because the union was blowing the whistle on corruption in Pikitup. The issuing of tenders at the core of the 'contracting out' state had fostered corruption. SAMWU was vindicated when the managing director and all but one board member resigned over corruption (Pikitup, 2011).

SAMWU had drawn on two additional sources of power that were crucial to the success of the strike – logistical and societal power. In sum: 'The iGoli 2002 project had been framed by the JCC [sic] as an increase in public efficiency. In the Pikitup strike SAMWU exposed privatisation and "tenderisation" as a source of corruption and self-enrichment' (Webster and Ludwig, 2017: 180–1).

The rise of the tenderpreneurs

In a provocative analysis of corruption, Karl Von Holdt has lifted the veil on what has been seen as primarily a moral crusade by forcefully arguing that corruption is a mechanism of class formation, using the rhetoric of BEE. 'The defining social process in post-apartheid South Africa is the formation of a new black elite' (Von Holdt, 2019: 3). This process, he argues, has given rise to a pervasive informal and often violent political–economic system that pre-dated Zuma's succession to the Presidency. Importantly, Von Holdt (2019: 7) argues, 'this empowerment elite remains small, economically weak and politically dependent on the ANC, and compromised by the increase in inequality over the same period in which they were empowered'. It is, he believes, a precarious elite.

In an interview with a union official on this process of class formation, the official remarked on how "quickly it happened" in the City Council (Faulkner, 2021). The government turned a blind eye. They did not have to provide services. Council officials ran the show for a 'facilitation fee'. Indeed, the wife of the mayor was on the board of one of these companies (Cox, 2012).

Spencer Malongete (2021), managing director of a company called the Waste Group,[7] is an example of a wealthy Black entrepreneur who was drawn into waste management. He helped set up Pikitup and was appointed General Manager of Operations in 2001. However, Malongete was uncomfortable with "people lining their own pockets" through the system of preferential procurement for "disadvantaged people" and left Pikitup to begin his own business. His company, Waste Group, is a partnership with a white man, Dirk van Niekerk, who holds 74 per cent of the equity; Malongete holds 24 per cent (Malongete, 2021).

Ironically, in spite of his financial success, Malongete feels his situation is insecure: "To a person who sees me driving a BMW, he says I have succeeded. But if the person realises that the BMW is owed by Standard Bank and that it is a financed vehicle, the story changes. Access to credit does not necessarily mean success" (Malongete, 2021). He remains sceptical that an independent Black business class is being created:

'We have created a dependency relationship where people are depending on grants. We celebrate a black bourgeois who don't even know how to make money because they have not worked for it. They make money out of shares and speculations; they don't know how to create value. We have black billionaires sitting in resource extraction but they are not reinvesting into beneficiation programmes and getting young people into the jewellery industry.' (Malongete, 2021)

Malongete concluded the interview by expressing his bitterness. He alluded to Cyril Ramaphosa, whom he sees as part of the "insiders" who benefitted by easy access to white capital in the early stages of the transition to democracy. Johnny Steinberg (2021: 9) refers to this 'driving narrative force' as the 'idea of an original sin – a sordid transaction, conducted in broad daylight at the dawn of democracy, between the holders of white capital and those blessed with insider status in the first two ANC governments'.

Labour's original sin?

The issue of union corruption became a national public issue when former chief executive officer (CEO) of Bosasa, Angelo Agrizzi, gave evidence at the Judicial Commission of Inquiry into Allegations of State Capture, Corruption and Fraud (the Zondo Commission) on how union leaders were bribed to secure contracts worth millions of rand for Bosasa in the companies where they organised. He suggested that this practice went back to the 1980s when outsourcing was introduced for catering on the mines. The National Union of Mineworkers (NUM) fought for a say in the appointment of the service providers, stating that it wanted to influence everything that affects workers, including the quality of food (Mahlakoana, 2019: 3).

A lively debate took place in the 1990s on how COSATU should respond to the creation of union investment companies. Although these companies were notionally separate from the union, they soon came under fire for promoting business values (Special Correspondent, 1996). For their protagonists, the investment companies provided a vehicle for progressive social change, worker power and Black empowerment. The counter-argument proposed that union investment companies were likely to de-politicise and de-mobilise workers, distract unions from fighting for better wages and jobs, invest in morally dubious enterprises, and favour the interests of union leaders over those of the membership at large (Collins, 1997; Faulkner, 1999; McKinley, 1999).

Union investment companies now have major stakes in key companies on the stock market: in television, in casinos, in luxury hotels, in the media, in banking, in car rental firms, in property insurance, in outsourcing companies, and so on (Tangari and Southall, 2008). Tangari and Southall conclude their useful analysis of union investment companies by pointing to 'major concerns' raised, not only about 'how union investment finance is becoming entangled with established corporate capital and to what end, but how this has enabled some former trade unionists to become extremely wealthy. There are many, too, who think that investments in such activities as gambling are peculiarly inappropriate' (Tangari and Southall, 2008: 700).

This engagement in the stock market led Buhlungu and Tshoaedi (2012: 14) to identify 'a new culture of individualism and accumulation' among COSATU members. The authors point to a fundamental disconnect between what the leaders say and what they do: 'The radical Marxist rhetoric is at odds with the private beliefs and practices of the federation's members today. They participate actively in the consumerism of post-apartheid society and, when presented with opportunities for upward social mobility, they enthusiastically make use of them' (Buhlungu and Tshoaedi, 2012: 13).

The result of these changing values in the union, the former COSATU president Sidumo Dlamini (2016: 5) suggests, is that union leaders are pursuing 'a BEE-type business unionism on the basis of workers' collective power'. Union investment companies are part of what he sees as a form of business unionism operating through:

> [its] control over worker funds, totalling multi-millions of rand in subscriptions and agency shop fees, pension and provident funds, medical aid schemes, sick pay funds, union investment companies, and so on, as well as service providers such as financial services administrators and providers, banks, property developers and administrators, all other services that have to do with money in unions, and the corrupt use of procurement of other goods. (Dlamini, 2016: 5)

It could be argued that, through embracing individualism, accumulation and an increasingly top-down structure, many union leaders have taken on business values. Could these pacts with capital be a major contributing factor to union decline?

The decline of the traditional union

In 2014 new leadership took over in SAMWU and many of the existing staff were retrenched. The head office was moved from Cape Town to Johannesburg. By 2015 SAMWU had completely reversed its position, writes Ludwig (2019: 97), making it one of the unions within COSATU that vigorously expressed support for the Alliance. The new leadership sold many of the union offices and, within a few years, were under investigation by the police after allegations arose that they stole R178 million from the union's bank account. Staff and shop stewards who called publicly for a forensic investigation into the theft were dismissed or expelled. They formed the 'Save Our SAMWU' coalition, before registering the Democratic Municipal and Allied Workers Union of South Africa (DEMAWUSA) as a rival union (Majavu, 2020).

The formation of a new union has not been easy, remarked Stephen Faulkner, the general secretary of DEMAWUSA, when we interviewed him. Although they have succeeded in recruiting 17,000 paid-up members, drawn largely from former SAMWU members and precarious EPWP workers, the Department of Labour tried to de-register the new union on trumped-up charges after they had led a successful strike in 2019 (Faulkner, 2021).

The decline of traditional union power in the municipality since its high point in the 1990s and the split inside SAMWU in 2014 are illustrative of broader trends within labour, both in South Africa and beyond. In trying to explain the decline of the union, critics have focused on the union's political alliance with the ANC and the lack of autonomy this relationship gives them, especially in their struggle against the privatisation of municipalities (Barchiesi, 2011). Arguably a deeper, more socio-political explanation for decline focuses on the internal dynamics and changes in the structure of unions in post-apartheid South Africa (Buhlungu, 2010; Ludwig, 2019). These internal processes led to a slow and gradual decline, which accelerated after 2012 (Ludwig, 2019: 96).

Ludwig's point of departure in explaining the decline of SAMWU is the fact that the union had developed significant financial resources. 'Trade unions', she argues, 'have become relevant financial players, increasing conflicts the trade unions have about access to those resources' (Ludwig, 2019: 101). Although SAMWU does not have an investment arm, it has a medical aid scheme and benefits from agency fees, which provide unions with financial resources independent of membership fees.

These financial resources strengthened two problematic processes that facilitated union decline. First was 'the centralisation of union structures, the limited autonomy of the lower union structures and a decline in worker control' (Ludwig, 2019: 101). The union has become much more hierarchical and lacks worker control, which in principle ensures checks and balances in the union. Second, this has led to a neglect of the workplace. This is partly because more attention is paid to the political party and party-related processes. But it is also because unions are well covered by institutional arrangements. 'SAMWU, like many other unions', Ludwig (2019: 216) argues, 'had become complacent and reliant on the established and institutionalised mechanisms of organising in the municipal sector'. Basically, municipal employees decide between two trade unions, and the employers have agreed on an agency shop fee for those workers who decide not to join a union, which is administered by the bargaining council and paid over to the trade unions. As one of the national organisers explained in an interview with Ludwig:

> Unions have become almost in a sense the victims of their own success because they managed to secure all of these rights and they've grown; they've put themselves into new offices. The focus has changed of what the union was in the 80s and I think that has contributed to the inability to organise new vulnerable forms of work that does exist. (SAMWU national official, cited in Ludwig, 2019: 217)

Revisiting the power resources approach

We have shown how it was through major strikes – structural power – that SAWMU was able to build associational power. But for a strike to succeed, workers also need the support of their communities – what we have called societal power. However, if these sources of power are to be consolidated, certain 'rules of the game' need to be established through legislation (labour law), through institutions and, in the case of SAMWU, through its alliance with the ruling party. These new rules of the game we call institutional power (see also Chapter 1).

If a union relies too much on institutional power, as SAMWU did, the strength of their associational power is weakened (Dörre et al, 2009). Institutional power is, we argue, a 'double-edged sword' as it has a two-fold nature – although it may grant rights to trade unions, at the same time it restricts the union's power to act. Reconnecting associational power to institutional power, we would argue, is at the heart of building sustainable and democratic union organisation. Institutional power embeds past social compromises through the incorporation of associational, structural and societal power into institutions. As McGuire (2012) argues, this source of power continues to be applied during ongoing economic cycles, even where power relations within society may have changed. It may take the form of labour law, wage-setting and bargaining arrangements, or institutionalised forms of social dialogue, such as NEDLAC (McGuire, 2012: 43). The important point about institutional power is that it grants rights but it can also make unions complacent.

But power resources are a potential: they need strategic capabilities to detect power resources in order to make use of them, and the organisational flexibility to optimise associational power. In post-apartheid South Africa, unions such as SAMWU which created the new labour regime have become disconnected from the institutions they created. Schmalz and Dörre (2014: 227) describe institutional power as a secondary source of power – the dependent variable – which distinguishes it from the other sources of power. Institutional power is usually the result of struggles and negotiation processes based on structural power and associational power. As 'a secondary form of power', such institutions constitute 'a coagulated form of the two other primary forms of power' (Brinkmann and Nachtwey, 2010: 21; on the concept of secondary power see Jürgens, 1984: 61).

It is only through interaction between associational and institutional power that leadership can keep in contact with its members, and maintain or expand the unions' gains.

Attempts were made by SAMWU to build grassroots alliances but unlike the 1980s, when community organisations formed alliances with the trade union movement, the union locals have atrophied (Faulkner, 2021). Faulkner observed about intervening at the time: "I was attending two meetings a month in certain townships such as Heidelberg. We had joint protests between the union and the community. The EFF [Economic Freedom Fighters] even pitched up. But the widespread and intense community protests since 2005 did not lead to a joint union–community alliance" (2021).

In spite of a decline in the delivery of services, participation in community service delivery protests has declined, according to surveys of COSATU members. In an analysis of this data, Sarah Mosoetsa (2012: 163–4) explains this lack of labour–community links as being due to 'COSATU members' prioritization of shop floor and labour market concerns – better wages, job security and employment creation – over the issues of service delivery by the government'. Different tensions between SAMWU and the community existed in Cape Town, where suspicion existed towards the union because of its alliance with the ANC. (This is covered in detail in Ludwig, 2019: 297–302.)

Implicit in Mosoetsa's observation is a critique of the growing distance between members of trade unions and the numbers of working people outside the ranks of trade unions. In the 2004 COSATU Workers Survey, 91 per cent of COSATU members were drawn from the core of permanent, full-time workers (Buhlungu, 2006). It was argued at the time that the federation was facing a 'crisis of representation' (Webster, 2005: 23). Increasingly the institutional arrangements set up at the dawn of democracy were being challenged by those who felt left out – the precarious workers such as the EPWP workers who are now demanding union representation. In Chapter 2 we explored attempts by COSATU to recruit precarious workers into the federation and the imaginative experiments with new forms of representation outside traditional unions.

Despite temporary successes in organising precarious workers in the 2011 Pikitup strike, in terms of Vissers' (2019) typology SAMWU is an example of dualisation, where unions defend existing strongholds and focus on those workers in stable jobs. This opens up a growing representational gap as more and more precarious workers are left without a voice.

We turn now to the manufacturing sector, where we see the entrenching of dualised workplace regimes based on hegemonic control over unionised, permanent workers and despotic forms of control over workers under precarious forms of employment.

Notes

[1] We are not suggesting that Castells was advocating measures to weaken organised labour; he was analysing how the network society was making it increasingly difficult for labour to organise along traditional lines.

[2] Companies that want to tender for a government contract not only have to demonstrate that they are partly Black-owned and managed, but also work with BEE-compliant supplier firms (Seekings and Nattrass, 2015: 219).

[3] This chapter draws from two articles (Ludwig and Webster, 2017; Webster and Ludwig, 2017), as well as Ludwig's PhD thesis, now published as a book (Ludwig, 2019).

[4] The third partner in the Tripartite Alliance, as it was known, was the SACP.

[5] For a detailed discussion of press coverage of the strike and its impact on public opinion, especially the exposure of corruption, as an example of societal power see Ludwig (2019: 180–7).

[6] Tenderpreneurs are persons who use their political connections to secure government contracts for personal advantage. The word is formed by combining 'tender' and 'entrepreneur'.

[7] Faulkner (2019) is critical of the Waste Group. He argues that the company hired hundreds of workers, paid them irregularly and below what was agreed, and then outsourced further to locally developed projects of their friends.

Interviews

Faulkner, S. (2021) Stephen Faulkner, General Secretary, Democratic Employee Workers Union of South Africa (DEWUSA), interviewed by Edward Webster, Johannesburg, 1 February.

Malongete, S. (2021) Spenser Malongete, Managing Director, Waste Group, interviewed by Kally Forrest, Johannesburg, 22 February.

References

Barchiesi, F. (2001) 'Fiscal discipline and worker response: the restructuring of Johannesburg's solid waste management, in M. Qotole, M. Xali and F. Barchiesi (eds) *The Commercialisation of Waste Management in South Africa*, Municipal Services Project, Occasional Papers 3, Kingston, Ontario: Municipal Services Project, pp 21–48.

Barchiesi, F. (2011) *Precarious Liberation: Workers, the State and Contested Social Citizenship in Post-apartheid South Africa*, Pietermaritzburg: University of KwaZulu-Natal Press.

Bezuidenhout, A. and Fakier, K. (2006) 'Maria's burden: contract cleaning and the crisis of social reproduction in post-apartheid South Africa', *Antipode*, 38(3): 462–85.

Bond, P. (2014) *Elite Transition: From Apartheid to Neoliberalism in South Africa*, London: Pluto Press.

Brinkmann, U. and Nachtwey, O. (2010) 'Krise und strategische Neuorientierung der Gewerkschaften', *Aus Politik und Zeitgeschichte*, 13–14: 21–9.

Buhlungu, S. (ed.) (2006) *Taking Democracy Seriously: A Survey of Cosatu Members*, Cape Town: HSRC Press.

Buhlungu, S. (2010) *A Paradox of Victory: COSATU and the Democratic Transformation in South Africa*, Pietermaritzburg: University of KwaZulu-Natal Press.

Buhlungu, S. and Tshoaedi. M. (eds) (2012) *Cosatu's Legacy: South African Trade Unionism in the Second Decade of Democracy*, Cape Town: HSRC Press.

Callinicos, L (2012) *Who Built Jozi? Discovering Memory at Wits Junction*, Johannesburg: Wits University Press.

Castells, M. (1996) *The Rise of the Network Society, The Information Age: Economy, Society and Culture*, Volume 1, Oxford: Blackwell.

Castells, M. (1997) *The Power of Identity, The Information Age: Economy, Society and Culture*, Volume 2, Oxford: Blackwell.

Collins, D. (1997) 'An open letter to Johnny Copelyn and Marcel Golding', *South African Labour Bulletin*, 21(1): 79–80.

Cox, A. (2012) 'Mayor's wife linked to R2bn Joburg fund', The Star, 9 October.

Department of Finance (DoF) (1996) *Growth, Employment and Redistribution: A Macroeconomic Strategy (GEAR)*, Pretoria: Ministry of Finance.

Dlamini, S. (2016) 'Unite against the primary opponents of our struggle and their collaborators, the enemy within', Advance the National Democratic Revolution, SACP discussion document, Benoni, 13 February.

Dörre, K., Holst, H. and Nachtwey, O. (2009) 'Organizing – a strategic option for trade union renewal?' *International Journal of Action Research*, 5(1): 33–67.

Faulkner, S. (1999) 'Investing in ourselves: a cautionary tale', *South African Labour Bulletin*, 23(4): 18–22.

Faulkner, S. (2011) 'Municipal union in the firing line: Stephen Faulkner talks to Tahir Sema', *South African Labour Bulletin*, 35(2): 26–7.

Forrest, K. (2011) 'Silencing union that will not be silenced', *South African Labour Bulletin*, 35(3): 5–9.

Jürgens, U. (1984) 'Die Entwicklung von Macht, Herrschaft und Kontrolle im Betrieb als politischer Prozess – eine Problemskizze zur Arbeitspolitik', in U. Jürgens and F. Naschold (eds), *Arbeitspolitik. Materialien zum Zusammenhang von politischer Macht, Kontrolle und betrieblicher Organisation der Arbeit*, Opladen: Westdeutscher Verlag, pp 32–45.

Kenny, B. and Webster, E. (1998) 'Eroding the core: flexibility and the re-segmentation of the South African labour market', *Critical Sociology*, 24(3): 216–43.

Kenny, B. and Webster, E. (2021) 'The return of the labour process: race, skill and technology in South African labour studies', *Work in the Global Economy*, 1(1–2): 13–31.

Ludwig, C. (2019) *Politics of Solidarity. Privatisation, Precarious Work and Labour in South Africa*, Frankfurt and New York: Campus.

Ludwig, C. and Webster, E. (2017) 'Changing forms of power and municipal workers' resistance in Johannesburg', in M. Paret, C. Runciman and L. Sinwell (eds) *Southern Resistance in Critical Perspective: The Politics of Protest in South Africa's Contentious Democracy*, Abingdon and New York: Routledge, pp 137–52.

Mabin, A. (2001) 'Contested urban futures: report on a global gathering in Johannesburg, 2000', *International Journal of Urban and Regional Research*, 25(1): 180–84.

Mahlakoana, T. (2019) 'Agrizzi's testimony exposes how union leaders score huge bribes', Business Day, 23 January.

Majavu, A. (2020) 'Saftu's municipal union scores against government', New Frame, 13 March.

McGuire, D. (2012) Global and local union struggles against the GATS: an assessment of the opportunity and capacity for unions to influence international trade policy, Unpublished PhD dissertation, University of Kassel, Germany.

McKinley, D. (1999) 'Union investment strategy: socialist unionism or "social capitalism"', *South African Labour Bulletin*, 23(6): 85–90.

Mosoetsa, S. (2012) 'What would you do if the government fails to deliver? Cosatu members' attitudes towards service delivery', in S. Buhlungu and M. Tshoaedi (eds) *Cosatu's Contested Legacy: South African Trade Unions in the Second Decade of Democracy*, Cape Town: HSRC Press, pp 147–66.

Musi, M.M. (2010) Evaluating IMATU and SAMWU policy responses to iGoli 2002, Unpublished Masters dissertation, University of the Witwatersrand, Johannesburg.

Pikitup (2011) *Annual Report 2010/11*, Johannesburg: Pikitup.

Schmalz, S. and Dörre, K. (2014) 'Der Machtressourcenansatz. Ein Instrument zur Analyse gewerkschaftlichen Handlungsvermögens', *Industrielle Beziehungen*, 21(3): 217–37.

Schmidt, V., Webster, E., Mhlana, S. and Forrest, K. (2023) *Negotiations by Workers in the Informal Economy*, ILO Working Paper 86, Geneva: ILO.

Seekings, J. and Nattrass, N. (2015) *Policy, Politics and Poverty in South Africa*, Basingstoke and New York: Palgrave Macmillan.

Special Correspondent (1996) 'Union investment: new opportunities, new threats', *South African Labour Bulletin*, 20(5): 33–9.

Steinberg, K. (2021) 'We reap bitter consequences of the ANC's original sin', Business Day, 12 February.

Tangari, R. and Southall, R. (2008) 'The politics of black economic empowerment in South Africa', *Journal of Southern African Studies*, 34(3): 699–716.

Visser J. (2019) 'Can unions revitalise themselves?', *International Journal of Labour Research*, 9(1–2): 17–48.

Von Holdt, K. (2019) *The Political Economy of Corruption: Elite Formation, Factions and Violence*, Working Paper 10, Johannesburg: Society, Work and Politics Institute, University of the Witwatersrand.

Webster, E. (1988) 'The rise of social movement unionism: the two faces of the black trade union movement in South Africa', in P. Frankel, P. Pines and M. Swilling (eds), *State Resistance and Change in South Africa*, North Ryde, NY, and Kent, UK: Croom Helm, pp 20–40.

Webster, E. (2005) 'New forms of work and the representational gap', in E. Webster and K. von Holdt (eds) *Beyond the Apartheid Workplace: Studies in Transition*, Pietermaritzburg: University of KwaZulu-Natal Press.

Webster, E. and Adler, G. (1999) 'Toward a class compromise in South Africa's "double transition": bargained liberalization and the consolidation of democracy', *Politics and Society*, 27(2): 347–85.

Webster, E. and Ludwig, C. (2017) 'Sword of justice or defenders of vested interest? The struggles of Johannesburg's municipal workers', in E. Webster, A.O. Britwum and S. Bhowmik (eds) *Crossing the Divide: Precarious Work and the Future of Labour*, Pietermaritzburg: University of KwaZulu Natal Press, pp 165–86.

4

Divided Workers, Divided Struggles: Entrenching Dualisation and the Struggle for Equalisation in South Africa's Manufacturing Sector

Lynford Dor

Introduction

The growth of manufacturing industries in South Africa during the mid-1900s was central to the apartheid accumulation model of racial capitalism. After emerging as support sector for mining, a range of manufacturing industries established themselves at the centre of the Minerals Energy Complex (Fine and Rustomjee, 1996). By 1950, manufacturing overtook mining in its contribution to the country's GDP and continued to outstrip it for the rest of the century (Fine and Rustomjee, 1996: 72). Manufacturing grew by turning towards mass production, capitalising on the regime of cheap Black migrant labour that had developed on the mines a half-century earlier (Wolpe, 1972; Webster, 1985). Unskilled and semi-skilled Black workers would be brought together in large manufacturing workplaces, where they were highly exploited by white managers for the benefit of a white capitalist class.

As Webster (1985) initially identified, the contradictions inherent in the manufacturing labour process in that period laid the basis for Black workers to build power at the point of production, while the contradictions of the apartheid political economy generated struggle against it from the reproductive sphere of the townships and hostels. After a wave of strikes in the early 1970s that began in the manufacturing sector, an independent trade union movement was born. As it grew and began to bargain at industry level in the post-Wiehahn period,[1] it won better conditions for Black workers. During this process, the social weight of the industrial working class grew and began to move beyond the factory to assert itself at the heart of the struggle against apartheid.

The manufacturing sector has declined in the post-apartheid period. In 2021, the sector contributed 11.7 per cent to the share of GDP, making it the fourth-largest sector in the economy behind trade, personal services and finance – finance contributed 23.5 per cent (Stats SA, 2021). The power of the trade unions in manufacturing and the social weight of this layer of the working class has mirrored the declining economic weight of the sector – 70.2 per cent of workers in manufacturing were union members in 1990, but by 2012 this figure was just 31.2 per cent (Macun, 2014: 44).

It is unsurprising that scholars and activists have often looked elsewhere in their efforts to build working-class power and search for a counter-movement. But in the first quarter of 2022, over 1.5 million people were still employed in manufacturing (Stats SA, 2022). Despite the weakened state of labour in the sector, this is too significant a number of workers to ignore. To pursue the central theme of this book, which is to interrogate what the future of labour might look like, we argue that it is necessary to re-enter the 'hidden abode of production' (Webster, 1985; Marx, 1990 [1867]) and reiterate the calls for a research agenda that interrogates what labour process changes mean for workers and worker organising (Kenny and Webster, 2021; Dor and Runciman, 2022).

This chapter argues that the restructuring of the manufacturing labour process around advances in productive technologies and new forms of 'externalised' and 'casualised' employment has contributed to the weakening of worker organisation (Theron, 2005). It shows how capital has re-established dualistic workplace regimes of labour control in the post-apartheid period – that is, 'hegemonic control' by means of collective bargaining for a shrinking section of permanent unionised workers and more 'despotic' forms of control for the rest (Burawoy, 1982). The result of these dualistic regimes of control, we argue, is the degradation of work on the whole. Far from generating a stable workforce of well-paid permanent jobs with some flexi-workers on the margins, these dualistic regimes have instead made precarious work the centrepiece of capital's valorisation strategy.

Although we show in detail how dualistic regimes throw up extensive (and potentially unacknowledged) obstacles to worker organising, they simultaneously generate collective grievances that lay the basis for new and continuous organising efforts from below. Although countless grievances are generated by the highly abusive practices involved in casualised or externalised forms of employment, two demands that are common at most workplaces are the demands for 'permanent jobs' and 'equalisation' of wages and benefits. These demands are linked to the provisions contained in section 198 of the LRA, which 'deems' labour broker workers and certain fixed-term contract workers to be permanent employees of a 'client' company after three months of work, and compels employers to treat them 'no less favourably' than permanent workers doing 'the same or similar work'. They are rights that resonate with workers not only because they have the potential to improve their livelihoods, but also because they ultimately strike at the heart of a labour control regime that rests upon creating arbitrary lines of division between workers.

This chapter argues that the established industrial unions have undertaken a political and organising orientation that has generally entrenched the dualistic forms of control that manufacturing capital's favoured valorisation regime rests upon. In response to manufacturing capital's extensive restructuring of the labour process in recent decades and in response to the decline of the industrial unions in the sector, workers have begun to experiment with a range of tactical approaches that include seeking representation from various forms of organisation in order to access the different power resources that are at their disposal. We argue that this sets the tone for the future of labour in the manufacturing sector. While capital's fracturing of the labour process in recent decades has allowed it to overcome past impediments to accumulation, it simultaneously deepens the age-old wage labour contradiction which lays the basis for the re-emergence of struggles from below, although under increasingly more precarious and difficult conditions.

This chapter details the findings from four case studies of manufacturing workplaces in Ekurhuleni – a municipality east of Johannesburg, and the centre of South Africa's manufacturing sector. It ultimately shows how a previously unionised layer of workers under standard employment relationships (SERs) have been 'unmade' through processes of casualisation and externalisation and 're-made' under highly precarious conditions. In some cases, we also see the 'making' of a whole new layer of younger workers under these conditions, who come into production without previous experiences of worker organising.

A multi-sited mapping of the manufacturing labour process

This chapter presents the findings of four workplace case studies. Individual and group interviews were conducted with workers, and group mapping exercises were undertaken to piece together a comprehensive picture of the labour process in each factory. This included: mapping workflows; identifying the types of machinery and technologies in use; identifying the tasks carried out by different groups of workers; assessing the skill levels and training required to carry out each task; identifying the forms of employment for different groups of workers; identifying wages, conditions and shift patterns for different groups of workers; assessing the various forms of control management employed throughout the workplace; and tracking the organisational responses from workers.[2] This data is complemented by insights into worker experiences in the manufacturing sector at a more general level, which were acquired through participant observation by the researcher, who spent five years volunteering and working at the Casual Workers Advice Office (CWAO).

Fracturing the labour process and the dualisation of control

Of the four manufacturing workplaces studied, two are in the chemical industry and the other two fall under food processing. Simba Chips is owned by PepsiCo, which bought it in 1999. Its factory in Isando is a relatively well-known landmark, bordering the highway between Johannesburg and O.R. Tambo International Airport. Reckitt Benckiser is a multinational company that produces well-known household hygiene and medical products at its factory in Jet Park. PFG Building Glass produces glass at its plant in Springs, primarily for use in construction. Finally, Pioneer Foods is a large local producer that was bought out by PepsiCo in 2019. We undertook research at one of its factories in Clayville where it mainly produces its range of pre-mixed desserts.

The labour process at each workplace can be broken down into four main phases: receiving, production, warehousing and distribution. Figures 4.1 to 4.3 demonstrate how management at Simba, Reckitt and PFG all use different companies to supply labour for each phase of the process. Only at Pioneer did we find no externalisation, although we did find that labour broking is prevalent at their other nearby factories. At their Clayville plant, Pioneer relied on a labour pool to carry out 'project work' as their dominant form of precarious employment. Figure 4.4 shows how, on just one production line, they have workers under a variety of different short-term contracts.

This section of the chapter provides a window into the ways in which manufacturing firms organise labour power in their factories, highlighting the centrality of precarious forms of employment as a control mechanism under the contemporary manufacturing workplace regime. What emerges is a picture of complex arrangements of labour in each workplace, with the workforce atomised by its geographical distribution, employment status, shifts and more. Despite the multiplicity of divisions generated by workplace restructuring in recent decades, we identify the clear trend towards the dualisation of forms of labour control. Our findings confirm the re-emergence of workplace regimes based on hegemonic control for a minority

Figure 4.1: Externalisation in Simba's labour process

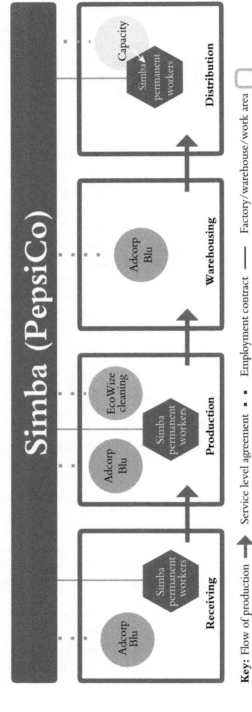

Key: Flow of production ➔ Service level agreement ▪ Employment contract —— Factory/warehouse/work area ▢

Source: Interviews, mapping exercise; figure created by Lynford Dor.

Figure 4.2: Externalisation in Reckitt's labour process

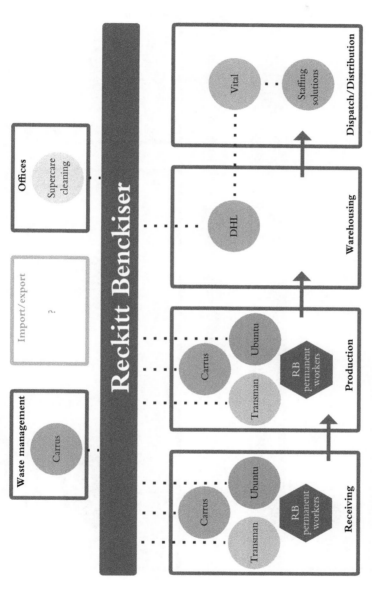

Source: Interviews, mapping exercise; figure created by Lynford Dor.

Figure 4.3: Externalisation in PFG's labour process

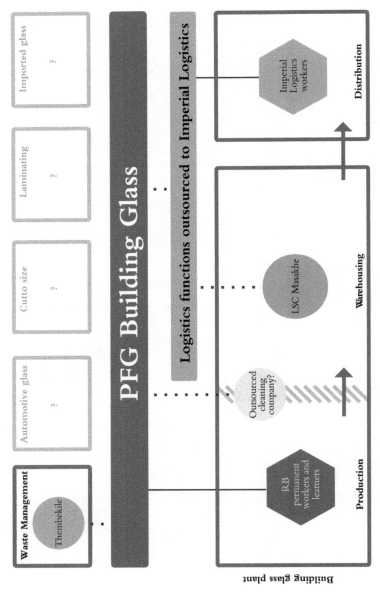

Source: Interviews, mapping exercise; figure created by Lynford Dor.

Figure 4.4: Englert's representation of externalisation at Heineken

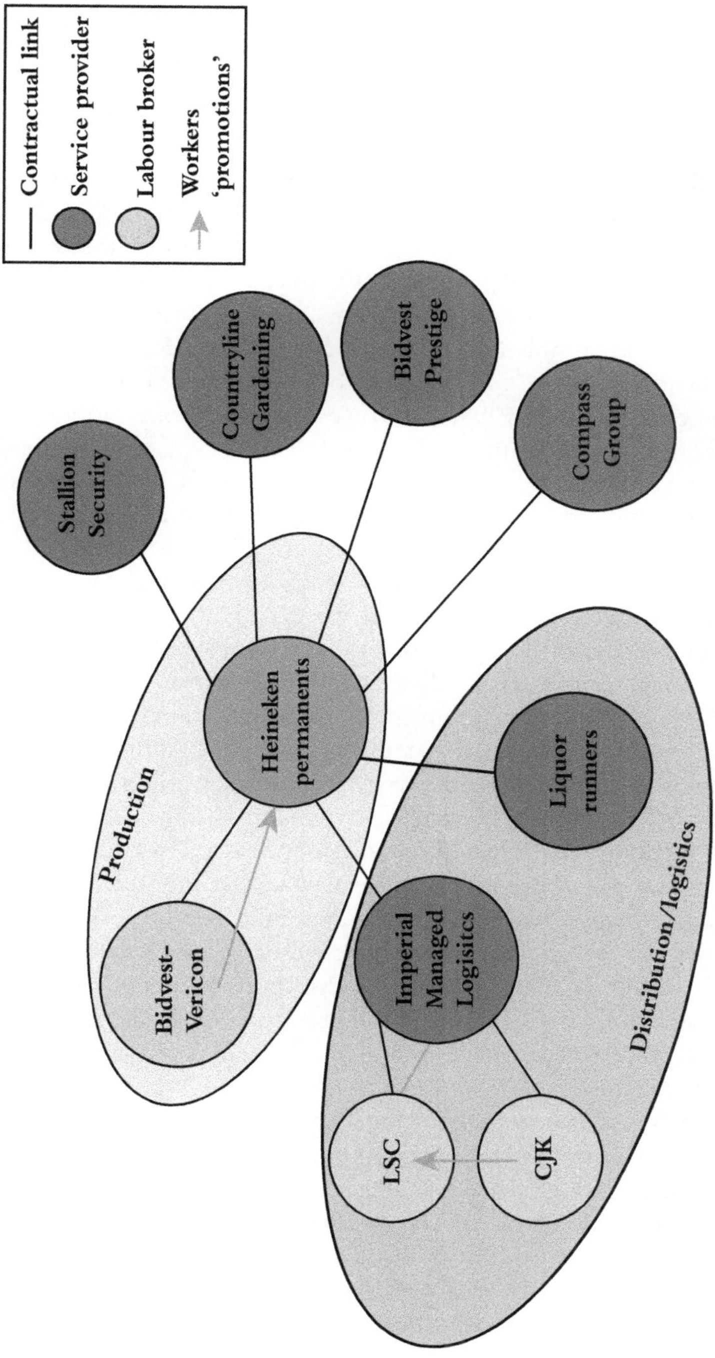

Source: Englert (2018).

of workers, often in permanent positions and with union representation, and despotic control for the majority, often under precarious or non-standard forms of employment with no formal recognition as a bargaining agent.[3]

Simba Chips

Over the last three decades, Simba has restructured its factory on several occasions, leading to significant changes in both the size and character of the workforce. In the early 1990s, almost the entire workforce at the Isando factory, well over 1,000 workers, were employed directly by Simba on permanent contracts (John, 2019). By early 2015, permanent workers made up only a fraction of a reduced workforce of just over 600. Vehicle maintenance was the first to be outsourced in 1996, followed by merchandising in 1998. The turn towards labour broking began in distribution with the introduction of LSC Masakhe in 2004, which was later replaced by Capacity in 2007. By 2010, Simba management began to use labour broker workers in receiving, production and in the warehouse (John, 2019).

Figure 4.1 details the organisation of labour at Simba's factory just prior to the victory of 467 labour broker workers who won permanent jobs in September 2018. All those workers were employed under a temporary employment service (TES) called Adcorp Blu. In production and receiving, 402 Adcorp Blu workers, most of whom were women, worked alongside approximately 40 of Simba's permanent workers. Although their payslips categorised them as general workers, they did the same work as the permanent machine operators, packers and forklift drivers. Cleaning work in production was contracted out to EcoWize. In warehousing, 65 Adcorp Blu workers were employed as packers, pickers and forklift drivers. By early 2018, distribution was the only function of the labour process in which the majority of workers were permanent Simba employees. However, of the 102 drivers and driving assistants in distribution, 94 had previously been employed under the labour broker Capacity. In 2015, Simba management began a process of gradually insourcing all these workers, a process which took three years.

Nevertheless, by externalising the employment of the majority of workers in its Isando factory and retaining only a minority of workers on a permanent basis, Simba created a clearly delineated two-tier workforce. The small layer of permanent workers was represented by the FAWU, and had their wages and working conditions regulated through plant and company-level bargaining agreements.[4] Brokered workers, on the other hand, were treated as a source of cheap labour; they were forced to resort to a legal case which included a long process of collective mobilisation as well as the threat of a strike just to bring Simba management to the negotiating table. This demonstrates how manufacturing firms like Simba have used externalisation to recreate the dualised dynamic of the old apartheid workplace regime, where management exerts control over a small group of better-off workers by 'manufacturing consent' (hegemonic control) while it reserves sheer class force to keep the majority in a submissive position (despotic control) (Burawoy, 1982).

The workers under Adcorp Blu undertook a three-year struggle for permanent jobs, by pursuing a case at the CCMA under section 198 of the LRA. On 28 June 2018, management signed a settlement agreement to take all Adcorp Blu workers on permanent contracts. Just 24 hours later, workers were told that Simba would be retrenching 142 packers from production due to operational requirements, which included a plan to purchase new machinery such as automated palletisers (Bassier and Potlaki, 2018). Eventually, 467 Adcorp Blu workers were made permanent on 1 September 2018. Of that group, 75 packers from production were retrenched in December 2018. On top of this, almost the entire workforce in warehousing and distribution was moved to a new distribution centre in Elandsfontein, called PepsiCo Park. The new palletising machinery never arrived. By January 2019, Simba had replaced the retrenched packers in production with 90 new workers employed under a learnership programme, which is regulated by the Skills Development Act (SDA). It is important to note that these are largely unskilled positions. Adding learnership work to the mix throws up the potential for the subsidisation of learners' remuneration (in the form of stipends) from Sectoral Education and Training Authorities (SETAs), tax incentives and an alternative mode of labour control for Simba management.[5]

Reckitt Benckiser

Figure 4.2 captures the layout of the Reckitt factory in Jet Park. The receiving, production, warehousing and distribution departments are housed in physically separate facilities, with a biometrics system of fingerprint scanners that restrict or regulate the movement of workers between them. Apart from the four main functions of the Reckitt labour process, the graphic also identifies a waste management department, import/export function and management offices that are found on the premises of the plant. All in all, seven different subcontracted companies employ the labour power necessary to carry out the work of the factory.

In production alone, we estimate that there are 200 workers across different shifts who feed 15 production lines (refillers), relieve them (forklift drivers and general workers) or operate machines on the lines (machine operators and general workers). Up until 2018 all of these workers were employed by labour brokers – either Carrus, Transman or Ubuntu. After the Constitutional Court ruled in favour of the 'sole employer' interpretation of section 198 of the LRA in the *Assign v Numsa* (2018) case,[6] Reckitt management promptly 'insourced' only a small number of workers in operating positions. This action allowed it to argue that all other externalised workers, whether they were in the production department or elsewhere in the factory, were employed by 'outsourced service providers' and not by 'temporary employment services'. This meant that it was able to evade the ramifications of section 198A[7] of the LRA which only deems workers to be permanently employed by a client company if they work under a temporary employment service. A temporary employment service is the LRA's definition for what are colloquially referred to as 'labour brokers' or 'agents'. Here we see how manufacturing firms have managed to persist with externalisation as a form of labour control, despite the 2015 LRA amendments to regulate labour broking.

The entire warehousing function on the Reckitt premises is outsourced to DHL. DHL subsequently contracted Vital Distribution Solutions to run the dispatch function. Vital then hired a labour broker called Staffing Solutions to provide it with workers to load and drive their trucks. Figure 4.2 provides a visual representation of the extent to which multiple layers of externalisation, coupled with the control of workers' movements, can fracture the workforce in a given workplace. This gives us an important insight into the degree to which manufacturing firms have succeeded in atomising workers inside the workplace.

Despite the extremely fragmented nature of the workforce, it is one's employment status of being either 'permanent' or 'casual'[8] that workers use most regularly to establish their location in the workplace hierarchy. Before the insourcing of machine operators, the only permanent workers in the company were employed as supervisors and line leaders – which are viewed as semi-management positions by the workers who take orders from them. The nature of their employment contracts and job grades meant that they had greater bargaining power to regulate their employment relationship with Reckitt directly. Externalised workers, on the other hand, found that their employment conditions were established in a far more unilateral manner.

In the chemical industry collective bargaining takes place at sub-industry or subsector level, under the watch of the National Bargaining Council for the Chemical Industry (NBCCI). Reckitt has been a party to agreements signed in the Fast-Moving Consumer Goods (FMCG) subsector since at least 2011, after withdrawing from 2005 to 2008 (FMCG Substantive Agreements, 2005–2007 and 2011–2019). The latest available FMCG Substantive Agreement sets a minimum wage of R7,020.35 per month for the subsector for 2019, which would increase by the greater of 6.75 per cent or average Consumer Price Index (CPI) plus 1.5 per cent for the next two years. It also sets minimum conditions for the subsector in relation to annual bonuses, leave, shift allowances, hours of work and more. Neither the minimum wages or minimum conditions are extremely favourable to workers, yet the Substantive Agreement restricts their application to only 'employees in the Bargaining Units as defined in existing Agreements between employers and unions at company level' (NBCCI, 2019). This means that workers must bargain at company or plant level just to gain access to the protections won at sectoral level. At Reckitt, union power has been decimated over the last decade, which means that most workers are not covered by the FMCG Agreements. Their minimum wages and working conditions are established largely unilaterally by the company, and are only protected by the National Minimum Wage Act (NMWA) and the BCEA.

What was once a Chemical, Energy, Paper, Printing, Wood and Allied Workers Union (CEPPWAWU) factory now has no significant union presence. The General Industries Workers Union of South Africa (GIWUSA) had a small number of members in production in 2018 when most of this research was conducted, while the National Transport Movement (NTM) had members in distribution. Reckitt's workplace regime can ultimately be said to rest upon the extreme fracturing of the labour process to secure a high level of despotic control over the majority of workers, who are kept out of the 'bargaining unit' that is covered by the FMCG Substantive Agreement.

PFG Building Glass

The PFG workplace in Springs houses several factories, each with their own distinct processes. The building glass and automotive glass plants manufacture glass from raw materials. The smaller plants on the premises process glass in various ways: cutting it to size as per customer request; lamination; warehousing and cleaning imported glass for local distribution; and recycling, which is outsourced to a company called Thembekile Waste Management. The research focused on piecing together a picture of the labour process at PFG Springs' largest plant, where it produces its building glass.

In the building glass plant, two large production lines produce flat sheets of glass using a float process. In the receiving phase, the suppliers' trucks deposit the raw materials into two silos that feed directly into furnaces at the start of the production lines (Dor and Runciman, 2022). In the production phase, molten glass is produced at the 'hot end' of the lines, which is then 'floated' along a bed of molten tin (PFG, 2019; Dor and Runciman, 2022). The glass is cooled in a controlled manner and is then rolled along the line to the 'cold end' where it is cut and stacked. Unlike in our previous two cases, the warehousing function is located inside the factory, on the opposite end to production. In warehousing, the glass is moved from the cold end of the line and stored in preparation for distribution.

All the work currently done on the production line is carried out by PFG's permanent workers. All the other work done in the factory is classified as logistics work and is carried out by workers employed by a labour broker called LSC Masakhe. LSC itself does not have a contractual relationship with PFG. All logistics functions, including distribution, have been outsourced to Imperial Logistics. LSC is one of its subsidiaries and has been contracted by Imperial to supply labour in the warehouse. See Figure 4.3 for a graphical representation of this.

Prior to the amendments to the LRA in 2015, permanent and labour broker workers were scattered somewhat randomly throughout both production and logistics. The decision to reorganise the division of labour between production and logistics along the lines of employment status has allowed PFG to claim that all logistics work is in fact an 'outsourced service'. Like Reckitt, PFG evades the ramifications of section 198A of the LRA which only deems the workers of the TES companies to be permanent employees of the client after three months. As a result, both companies are ultimately able to continue to externalise the most labour-intensive functions of their labour processes.

This bifurcation of the manufacturing labour process into production and logistics is similar to the Heineken example that Englert (2018) details (see Figure 4.4). At Heineken's brewery in Sedibeng, logistics has also been outsourced to Imperial, which again uses LSC to supply workers. Englert suggests that the distinction between the jobs and tasks that fell under production and those that were categorised as logistics was often arbitrary, since some logistics workers contributed to the work done on the production lines – often either feeding or relieving them. This arbitrary distinction between work processes is similar to the Reckitt case. At PFG, however, the feeding of the lines is carried out automatically from the silos and controlled by skilled permanent workers, while the relieving of the lines is carried out by automated stacking machines that are monitored by less-skilled permanent workers. The glass is stacked in batches of 50 sheets, at which point the LSC logistics workers move it into the warehouse section of the factory. These workers operate in teams of four – one forklift driver, one crane driver and two handlers. The distinction between production line work and logistics work is, therefore, a bit clearer. The fact that the float glass production process is highly automated means that the majority of the actual labour in PFG's factory is carried out in the factory's warehousing area.

The dominance of the tasks that can be classified as 'logistics work' inside the manufacturing workplace means that externalisation remains a viable primary source of control for many manufacturing employers. This is so because it has been all too easy for employers to convince the CCMA and the courts that logistics functions are carried out by service providers and not labour brokers. Case law on section 198A places the onus on workers who claim to be under a labour broking relationship to prove that their day-to-day work and their employment conditions are controlled by the client company. The 'control test' was established in *Victor and Others v Chep SA* (2020) and clarifies how the courts should distinguish between labour broking and service provision. Ultimately, client employers are arguing that contractors supply more than just labour, but rather a logistics process that is controlled by a 'service provider'.

Externalisation remains central to the workplace regime at PFG by entrenching different forms of control over the two groups of workers in the factory. At first, LSC workers were told by both shop stewards and management that they were not allowed to join the union, which was CEPPWAWU at the time. When the permanent workers decided to replace CEPPWAWU with NUMSA, the LSC workers joined, too. At the time of conducting the research, however, the LSC workers felt that they had not benefitted from their union membership and had been excluded from participating fully in collective bargaining processes at the workplace, not least because they were considered to work for a different employer.

Pioneer Foods

The plant in Clayville is made up of three departments, each housed in a physically separate part of the factory. The first produces Safari and other snack bars. The second produces Bokomo corn flakes as well as no-name-brand corn flakes packaged for Pick n Pay (a major South African retailer). The third department produces Moir's powdered desserts, such as jellies, custards and cake mixes, as well as other powder-based products like baking soda and instant mashed potatoes. Pioneer management hires 'independent contractors' to supply raw materials for each of the three departments and to distribute their products. The independent contractors load and offload their own trucks, which allows Pioneer to operate without large receiving and distribution functions.

In the Bars department, under 50 permanent workers run two production lines. Although they have permanent status, the majority of these workers are paid less than the workers in the rest of the factory, including the contract workers. The Corn Flakes department houses one highly automated production line that produces corn flakes, which is run by fewer than ten permanent workers per shift and under 30 in total. An automated palletiser does the job that teams of end-of-line packers do in the other two departments. The workers in Corn Flakes are better paid and hold a higher status than those in the Bars department.

In the Moir's department, over 100 workers are divided by job grade and contract type. There are less than 15 permanent workers, of which four are ordinary workers that operate machines while the rest are process controllers who operate machines and oversee the running of ten production lines. Although process controllers do some work on the lines, they are nevertheless viewed by other workers as an arm of management. Another 20 workers are currently employed on six-month contracts, which started in June 2019. Prior to this, these 20 workers had spent two years in a 'learnership programme'. Instead of studying, they worked in the positions of machine operators and general workers. Finally, over 80 workers are employed on one-month revolving contracts, and had been for over two years at the time the research was conducted. This number remains stable for the most part, but increases during peak season before Christmas. These workers are referred to by management as C4Cs (Casuals for Company) – an employment scheme that started in 2016. They are employed as mixers, line packers, end-of-line packers and forklift drivers but they are also often required to operate machines on the line. Figure 4.5 demonstrates how Pioneer management organises its labour power on the Moir's production line, using a combination of permanent and short-term contract/project workers. Permanent workers and six-month contract workers operate the same machines while one-month contract workers mostly work along the conveyor belts as packers. They do, however, also operate machines when the other workers are not present.

Pioneer management justifies the use of revolving one-month contracts by telling workers that they are only employed to carry out 'project work'. In other words, each batch of a particular product supposedly counts as a new project. This allows Pioneer to vary production in relation to market demand (a form of just-in-time production). More importantly, however, this contract/project work scheme is used as an everyday control mechanism to drive up the intensity of labour and to prevent workers from organising or unionising. In fact, the permanent workers in the Moir's department are members and shop stewards of FAWU but have played an active role in keeping the C4C workers out of the union. In one instance, a shop steward refused to accept signed membership forms from C4C workers, suggesting that union representation is reserved for workers in permanent employment. In a response that parallels the approach that brokered workers took at Simba, these workers have had to pursue their interests through a legal case in an attempt to win permanent jobs but also to bring the employer to the negotiating table.

Skill, power and precarity in the manufacturing workplace

Common to the four workplaces, we would argue, is that all manufacturing work can be roughly separated into two types: production line tasks and auxiliary tasks. This is of course a major abstraction, but a useful framework

Figure 4.5: The organisation of labour along a Moir's production line

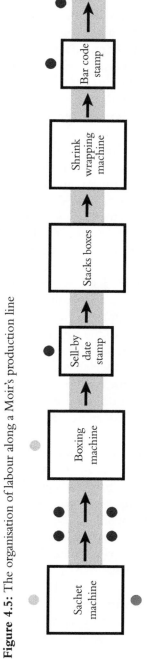

Key: Permanent worker ● Workers on 6-month contract (former learners) ● C4C workers on one-month contracts ● Conveyor belt ↑

Source: Interviews, mapping exercise; figure created by Lynford Dor.

to contribute to the debates on the nature of work in the contemporary manufacturing labour process. Broadly speaking, in each of the four workplaces there is a smaller group of workers that operate or monitor the machines that actually manufacture goods on the production lines, and a much larger group of workers who do all sorts of other important auxiliary work that contributes to the full functioning of the factory. This latter group includes all those job grades or positions in which workers feed or relieve the lines as well as those where workers move raw materials or finished products around the rest of the plant as production and logistics flows dictate. It also includes workers involved in cleaning, waste management and other similar functions that contribute towards the sustenance of the labour process.

There is some irony in referring to this second group of workers as auxiliary, since our argument is in fact that they are the dominant contributors towards the labour component of the manufacturing production process. Our reasons for distinguishing between production and auxiliary work are twofold. First, manufacturing firms have themselves entrenched this very line of divide to respond to the amendments to section 198A of the LRA that regulated labour broking. Management at both Reckitt and PFG, for example, have looked to categorise all auxiliary work inside their own factories as 'non-core functions' in order to continue to externalise them by outsourcing them to 'service providers'. Second, we choose to explore the distinction between production line and auxiliary tasks precisely to argue that there is little that actually separates these two types of work in each factory in terms of the qualitative nature of the labour power required. This allows us to address some persistent commonplace assumptions that workers closer to 'the point of production' are inevitably more highly skilled, less easily replaceable and wield greater structural power in the workplace. Or that workers who perform tasks that do not involve the actual manufacturing of goods are inevitably less skilled, more easily replaceable and wield less structural power.

At Reckitt today, unskilled general workers often operate the machines when the operators take lunch breaks or are off sick. The almost total deskilling of this work also means that it was possible for Reckitt to employ low-paid, unskilled labour broker workers as operators for many years. At Pioneer, the C4C project workers also operate machines when the permanent operators take lunch, go for a smoke or use the toilet. They also often have to operate the lines during the night shift when there are fewer permanents around. The skill required to operate one of these machines was explained by one worker as matter of simply knowing when to press start and stop. At Simba, machine work has been deskilled to the point where management, in an effort to restructure the workplace in April 2018, could remove all the brokered workers from machine operating positions and replace them with permanent workers from packing positions without any significant pause in production. At PFG, one worker insisted that operating the stacking machines on the cold end of the line was so straightforward that the operator merely had to monitor and reset the machine when needed. He also suggested that even the supposedly skilled position of process controller on the hot end of the line could be learned simply by job shadowing for a short period. Of the four factories, only PFG had higher skill jobs in production that required real training which the externalised workers felt unable to do, such as the engineering positions in the control room.

Our research findings suggest that the generally high levels of mechanisation in production work, which is linked to the high rates of fixed capital investment in the South African manufacturing sector (Black et al, 2017), appear to have resulted in a rise in the relative importance of auxiliary labour in the factory. Some auxiliary positions require workers to have undergone training or carry certification to operate cranes and forklifts, for example. Many other auxiliary tasks, even those that do not require much taught skill, nevertheless require a greater variety of tacit skills and dexterity to carry out (see Leger, 1992). These might include a knowledge of the layout of goods in the warehouse or 'tricks of the trade' that are developed on the job, such as those required by handlers in the PFG warehouse whose jobs are dangerous and require high levels of concentration when manoeuvring the glass to ensure that there are no breakages. Auxiliary work generally remains labour-intensive because it is more expensive to automate, since it is difficult to build machines that appropriate the tacit skills and variety of movements required by this work. Production work, on the other hand, has been so thoroughly deskilled as a result of mechanisation that workers in each factory commented repeatedly on how little training is required to run the line.

These findings contradict the understandable assumption that there exists a major difference in skill between machine operators at the centre of production and auxiliary workers elsewhere in the factory. They instead suggest that, on the whole, there is a negligible difference between operators in production and auxiliary workers in terms of skill and training required (or in terms of the value of labour power that is required). As a result, they provide evidence in support of Marx's (1990 [1867]) homogenisation of labour thesis and Braverman's (1974) degradation of labour thesis. In other words, it can be argued that one of the defining features of the industrial labour process in South Africa today is the division of different types of basic tasks between a mass of workers that are not required to exhibit a wide variety of specialised knowledge to carry out their work. This is especially so in the light manufacturing industries such as food processing (Simba and Pioneer) and in chemical's fast-moving consumer goods industry (Reckitt). At each of the firms we studied, it is only the collective labour of all the workers' 'homogenised labour powers' that allows for the smooth functioning of the labour process. These insights into the question of skill are important because they have a direct bearing on the future of work and workplace regimes as well the future of labour in the manufacturing sector.

The process of 'eroding the core' (Kenny and Webster, 1998) of standard, permanent work is made possible by a number of factors, including a legislative framework that opens the space for the proliferation of 'non-standard' forms of employment and the growth of a massive reserve army of unemployed workers willing to accept lower wages and employment conditions. But these factors only come into play as a result of the low demands of manufacturing labour processes in relation to skill and training requirements. Each case in this study shows that capital no longer depends on a stable, permanently employed workforce as may have been the case in the past. The case study findings also reveal that precarious workers are no longer simply found on the periphery of the workplace. Instead, manufacturing firms are choosing to use cheaper, unskilled, precarious workers wherever they can, including in positions at the heart of production, such as machine operators. The nature of skill and training levels required in the contemporary manufacturing labour process and the power that this affords employers over workers must, therefore, be linked to the rapid growth of precarious forms of employment in the sector.

It is, however, crucial to point out that although the process of eroding the core is made possible by the previously mentioned factors (which are driven by the state and capital), it is nonetheless a process that is regulated by collective responses (or lack thereof) of workers and their organisations. In the sections that follow, we show how the tactics of the unions that were traditionally dominant in each industry have ultimately contributed to the process of eroding the core in the long run, by buying into capital's refashioned 'dualistic system of labour control' for the post-apartheid era (Kenny and Webster, 1998). We then show how precarious workers have been waging struggles for 'permanent jobs' and 'equalisation' in recent years, which challenges the duality upon which capital's workplace regime rests. In these struggles, precarious workers often look to exploit sources of institutional power (such as the CCMA) while they experiment with building their associational power in different forms (such as oscillating between traditional unions and workplace committees).

Union responses: entrenching dualisation

Despite the negligible difference in skill required for production and auxiliary work, which allows capital to employ cheaper, unskilled, precarious workers almost anywhere they like, each workplace in this study still had a small layer of relatively better-paid permanent workers occupying positions such as machine operators, process controllers, line leaders or supervisors at the heart of production. This dynamic can be explained in part by the way that manufacturing firms have reacted to the amendments to the LRA in 2015. They have created a clearer division of labour between permanent workers in production as the company's supposedly 'core function' and externalised workers in auxiliary tasks which are supposedly 'non-core functions' and therefore outsourceable to service providers. But the survival of a relatively small number of permanent and often better-paid jobs in these manufacturing workplaces can also be explained by looking into the ways that unions have responded to capital's restructuring of the labour process in the post-apartheid period.

Webster (1985) originally showed how under apartheid the white craft unions defended the categorisation of their members' jobs as 'skilled' despite their objective deskilling. This effectively reserved better-paid positions for white workers in the face of an influx of cheap Black labour into the metal industry at the time. Webster (1985) argues that the white craft unions employed two strategies to achieve this. The first was to oppose the Black unions and the second was to try to control these new workers by establishing parallel unions. In the post-apartheid context, unions like FAWU and CEPPWAWU have responded to the influx of precarious workers into their industries by prioritising the interests of their permanent members. Precarious workers across the four workplaces all share similar stories about being overlooked by the union at their workplaces. In some cases, we found that the unions even opposed the organising efforts of precarious workers, which rather uncomfortably resembles one of the strategies employed by the old white craft unions. The bargaining power that FAWU and CEPPWAWU amassed in their heyday has, for a finite period, allowed them to reserve job grades such as machine operators for their members and to defend the grading system which privileges these positions. Over time, however, there has been an almost total collapse of their structures at the four factories, as management eventually found ways to replace unionised, permanent workers with cheaper, precarious workers that these unions do not organise.

In the first decade or so after the democratic transition, much industrial sociology was focused on the question of the role of trade unionism in the potential democratisation of workplace regimes (Dickinson, 2005; Von Holdt and Webster, 2005). The despotic nature of the apartheid workplace regime, it was suggested, could potentially be transformed through collective bargaining under powerful unions into regimes based on consent or codetermination (Dickinson, 2005; Von Holdt and Webster, 2005). Our findings suggest that that those unions that have bought into the project of codetermination (by harnessing their institutional power to represent workers in workplace- or sectoral-level bargaining forums) have ultimately only managed to do so at the expense of precarious workers in their factories (see also Dickinson, 2017a, 2017b; Englert, 2018). What we see in each workplace in this study is that over recent decades capital has been able to effectively recreate its 'dualistic system of labour control', which Kenny and Webster (1998) identify as the bedrock of its factory regime under apartheid. In other words, capital has returned to a factory regime based on varying degrees of hegemonic control for workers who have their wages and working conditions regulated through collective bargaining and despotic control for workers whose conditions are generally established by management in a more unilateral manner (Kenny and Webster, 1998).

In Englert's (2018) study of Heineken, he argues that:

> FAWU acted – consciously or not – as a guardian of the status quo and is perceived as such by the workers and management alike. ... The workers' relationship with the union is thus very much shaped by FAWU falling on 'the double-edged sword' of institutional power. FAWU's behaviour illustrates Gallas' (2016: 200) point that under specific circumstances institutional power can lead a union to behave against workers' interests. (Englert, 2018: 75)

These findings can be repeated for each case in our study. The status quo that CEPPWAWU and FAWU buttressed in each factory were essentially workplace regimes based upon the dualisation of forms of labour control. It is telling that the CEPPWAWU and FAWU structures have eventually all but collapsed at the four workplaces as a result of their over-reliance on institutional power and their decisions to wield such power in favour of only one section of the workforce.

The more recent attempts of unions like GIWUSA at Reckitt and NUMSA at PFG to recruit and organise precarious workers is a welcome break from the trajectory that the previously mentioned unions have taken. However, at Reckitt the attempts to organise externalised workers was thoroughly defeated by an intransigent employer through mass dismissal, while at PFG the approach that NUMSA has taken to organising externalised workers separately from permanents has only served to entrench the workplace divide upon which management's valorisation regime rests. Although NUMSA did not set up a parallel union for these workers, the parallel workplace structures are reminiscent of the old white craft unions' second strategy to deal with new workers in their workplaces (Webster, 1985) – that of creating parallel unions.

Runciman (2019) has previously highlighted the 'paternalistic' attitudes adopted by some unions that have begun to recruit and organise precarious workers: union officials and even some shop stewards appear to believe that the only way to advance the interests of these workers is to mobilise the union's institutional power *on the workers' behalf*. Such attitudes do not value the potential structural and associational power that lies with these workers. Indeed, very often, precarious workers do not see the potential in mobilising these sources of power in themselves. But in their desire to win better conditions and wages, precarious workers at each of the factories in this study (and beyond) have taken up the demand for permanent jobs and equalisation in the years following the amendments to the LRA, although they have done so with different degrees of success. These two simple demands pose a challenge to the dualistic systems of labour control that post-apartheid factory regimes continue to depend upon. The next section shows how, in the process of pursuing these demands, workers have attempted to harness different forms of power by experimenting with different forms of organisation and representation.

Precarious worker responses: fighting for equalisation

The amendments to section 198 of the LRA, which came into effect in 2015, gave important new rights to workers under different forms of precarious employment (Labour Relations Amendment Act, 2014). According to 198A (3)(b), TES (or labour broker) workers are 'deemed' to be employed by the 'client' company on an 'indefinite basis' after three months of work (Labour Relations Amendment Act, 2014). Similarly, 198B (5) says that the employment of workers on fixed-term contracts is 'deemed to be of indefinite duration' after three months of work (Labour Relations Amendment Act, 2014).[9] The introduction of these so-called deeming provisions resonated with workers because they reflected a demand that has long existed among those who toil under all sorts of non-standard forms of employment – that is, a demand for permanent jobs directly under the company at which they work. 'Permanent status' under the direct employer offers workers a greater sense of job security, but it does not in itself denote better wages and conditions. The popularity of the demand can and should also be linked to the ways in which workers view questions of power and control in the workplace (see Dickinson, 2017a). In other words, workers often view the acquisition of permanent status as a route towards being included in collective bargaining processes and as a shield from the more despotic forms control that result from their status as 'casuals'.[10]

Along with the deeming provisions, the 2015 amendments include clauses that prohibit deemed employees from being treated 'less favourably' than permanent workers 'performing the same or similar work' (Labour Relations Amendment Act, 2014). This became known as the right to 'equalisation' and resonated with the very basic demand that workers had for equal treatment. This right proved to contain significant mobilising potential because it was viewed by many workers as a one-stop shop to resolve almost all their grievances over low wages and poor working conditions.

The promulgation of the deeming and equalisation provisions and their popularisation by organisations like the CWAO (Rees, 2019) convinced some workers to begin to organise at factory level. At Simba and Pioneer, workers eventually advanced their demands for permanent status and equal treatment through section 198 cases in the CCMA, while PFG workers did the same through the NBCCI. In each case, workers combined the sourcing of support from established organisations with self-organising efforts under nascent factory-based structures that were generally led by small but determined groups of active workers. At both Simba and Pioneer, these nascent factory committees approached the CWAO for advice and support in their attempts to organise other workers in their factories and for taking up CCMA cases. At PFG, the workers' case was taken up through NUMSA, but workers pursued it actively by organising and meeting in their own informal structure that was not directed by union officials or even shop stewards.

The LSC workers at PFG met in the township of KwaThema on weekends when they began to feel that they needed to advance their own interests inside the factory despite having union representation. By organising through both the informal factory committee structure and the formal union structure, these workers embarked on a protected strike, pursued a section 198 case, and began to place their demands to management over a period of three years. The relationship between the workers' formal and informal organising efforts was neither harmonious nor purely antagonistic. The tension that existed between the worker-led committee and the union reflected a reliance on the formal union structure as a recognised form of representation at both workplace level and in the NBCCI, as well as these workers' perceptions of the shortcomings of either this form of representation or their individual representatives. By creating their own loosely structured committee, workers had identified the potential pitfall of relying purely on the union's institutional power and looked at times to complement it, at times hold it to account, and at times defy it by mobilising their own forms of structural and associational power. The PFG example goes some way to show how workers in precarious forms of employment are experimenting with different forms of organisation or representation as they search for ways to mobilise the different sources of power at their disposal.

At Simba, 467 workers eventually won permanent jobs and got rid of their labour broker after a three-year struggle that married self-organising efforts with legal and organisational support from the CWAO. A significant number of workers were union members, but this struggle was waged outside of any of the unions that had been organising at Simba. The institutional route of the CCMA was complemented by workers mobilising their associational power to force management to bargain directly with their committee, which the workers called the Simba Workers Forum. When management moved brokered workers out of production in an attempt to avoid the ramifications of section 198 in the lead-up to the CCMA arbitration, workers also threatened to mobilise their structural power by calling a protected strike over a unilateral change to their terms and conditions of employment. Management quickly reversed the changes to prevent a strike. Soon after, management signed an agreement at the CCMA with the leaders of the Simba Workers Forum to settle the section 198 case. It is interesting to note that once workers were made permanent, a large number collectively joined a new union called the Agricultural Food and Allied Democratic Workers Union (AFADWU).[11] This parallels the trajectories that workers took at Dischem and Luxor Paints (Englert and Runciman, 2019), where they have turned towards more traditional forms of representation once they won win their struggles for permanent jobs in order to advance their interests via the institutionalised channels of recognised workplace bargaining. Joining AFADWU, however, coincided with the demobilisation of rank-and-file workers who had previously participated actively in the Simba Workers Forum. In 2021, after two years in the union with no tangible gains made as a result of union representation, workers at Simba began to call for the re-formation of the Forum in order to rebuild their associational power.

Conclusion

The rise of externalisation and casualisation in the manufacturing sector has the effect of unmaking an older industrial workforce that was well unionised and generally employed in a standard employment relationship. At the same time, it is making and remaking a newer layer of workers under more precarious conditions. As these processes unfold, struggles continue to emerge from both the old and the new.

In general, unions rely primarily on institutional power associated with the established channels of collective bargaining to defend the interests of the older layer of permanent workers. The effect of this is unfortunately to buttress capital's dualised workplace regimes, which we have seen eventually leads to the marginalisation of these unions.

Newer layers of precarious workers often choose to rely on the institutional route of the CCMA to advance their struggles for permanent jobs and equalisation. Wielding this source of institutional power allows these workers to wage a struggle against management and its despotic forms of control without the risks associated with mobilising their structural power (for example, by striking). But in the process of pursuing their demands through regulatory institutions, these workers are looking for support from established organisations such as unions and NGOs as well as simultaneously building their own nascent workplace structures. Once again, this reflects a process of significant experimentation that is under way as these workers search for the best organisational forms and practices to build or rebuild their associational power.

Overall, what the examples of worker organising at firms like Reckitt Benckiser, PFG, Pioneer and Simba suggest, we would argue, is that the trajectory that precarious worker struggles are taking is by no means unilinear. Labour in the current period of prolonged retreat is characterised by uneven development, where there are emerging contestations over organisational form, over organising practices and tactics, and over the orientation towards different sections of the workforce. Workers in manufacturing have been experimenting with different forms of organisation and representation (often jumping repeatedly between organisations) to harness the different power resources available to them. The future for labour in this sector is, therefore, clearly alive, but yet uncertain of its own direction and form.

Notes

[1] In 1977 the apartheid government set up the Commission of Enquiry into Labour Legislation, which became known as the Wiehahn Commission. The Commission was set up in response to the 1973 Durban Strikes, the 1976 uprisings and the growth of Black (independent) trade unions. Its recommendations led to amendments to labour legislation aimed largely at bringing Black unions into the official labour relations regime.

[2] This approach was an adaptation of previous iterations of workplace mapping (Brooks et al, 2017; Englert, 2018).

[3] The information that follows is derived from a number of interviews, details of which are given in the interview list that forms part of the Reference list. Where the workers' actual words are used, a citation providing those details is given.

[4] There is no bargaining council or sectoral determination covering the food processing industry.

[5] SETAs were established for different industries and are responsible for providing vocational and skills training for their respective industries. They are regulated by the Skills Development Act of 1998.

[6] The Labour Appeal Court initially interpreted section 19AA of the LRA to mean that a worker becomes the employee of both the labour broker and the client company after three months of work. This was known as the 'dual employer interpretation' of section 198. The Constitutional Court ruled that the worker instead becomes the employee of only the client company and that the labour broker falls away. This is the 'sole employer' interpretation.

[7] Section 198A applies to TES (labour broker) workers, 198B applies to workers on fixed-term contracts, and 198C applies to part-time workers.

[8] Workers often use the term casual to interchangeably refer for workers under externalised or casualised conditions. It can be compared with the way that sociological literature uses the term 'precarious'.

[9] Employers can, however, fix the term of a contract for longer but only under very specific conditions listed in 198B (3) and (4)).

[10] Workers in both externalised and casualised forms of employment are both colloquially regarded as 'casuals'.

[11] AFADWU is a breakaway from FAWU; the former remained inside COSATU when the latter left the federation.

Interviews

Note: For all interviews, the author is in possession of digital recordings; pseudonyms have been used.

Alfred, 2 April 2019, Germiston.

Eric, 26 August 2019, Germiston.

Eric and Siya, 11 June 2019, Germiston.

Jacob, 9 August 2019, Germiston.

John, 17 June 2019, Germiston.

Matthews, 13 June 2019, Germiston.

PFG group interview, 14 May 2019, Germiston.

Pioneer group interview 1, 2019a (27 April 2019), Germiston.

Pioneer group interview 2, 2019b (25 May 2019), Thembisa.

Pioneer group interview 3, 2019c (13 June 2019), Germiston.

Sihle and Vuyo, 18 April 2019, Germiston.

Thando, 16 May 2019, Germiston.

References

Bassier, I. and Potlaki, J. (2018) 'From 198 to 189: Simba workers face retrenchments after huge insourcing victory', *The New Worker*: 6(2): 2–3.

Black, A., Craig, S. and Dunne, P. (2017) 'Capital intensity, employment and sustainability in the South African manufacturing sector', paper presented at the 2017 TIPS Annual Forum, 13–14 June 2017, University of Johannesburg [online] Available from: file:///Users/lynforddor/Desktop/CapitalZintensityZemploymentZandZsustainabilityZinZtheZSouthZAfricanZmanufacturingZsector_1.pdf [Accessed 22 October 2019].

Braverman, H. (1974) *Labor and Monopoly Capital*, New York and London: Monthly Review Press.

Brooks, C., Singh, S. and Winslow, S. (2017) *Trainers Guide: Secrets of a Successful Organiser*, New York: Labour Notes.

Burawoy, M. (1982) *Manufacturing Consent: Changes in the Labor Process under Monopoly Capitalism*, Chicago, IL: University of Chicago Press.

Dickinson, D. (2005) 'Beyond marshmallow mountain: workplace change in the new South Africa', in E. Webster and K. von Holdt (eds) *Beyond the Apartheid Workplace: Studies in Transition*, Pietermaritzburg: University of KwaZulu-Natal Press, pp 187–212.

Dickinson, D. (2017a) 'Institutionalised conflict, subaltern worker rebellions and insurgent unionism: casual workers' organisation and power resources in the South African Post Office', *Review of African Political Economy*, 44(153): 415–31.

Dickinson, D. (2017b) 'Contracting out of the constitution: labour brokers, Post Office casual workers and the failure of South Africa's industrial relations framework', *Journal of Southern African Studies*, 43(4): 789–803.

Dor, L. and Runciman, C. (2022) 'Precarious workers and the labour process: problematising the core/non-core', *Global Labour Journal*, 13(1): 20–40.

Englert, T. (2018) Precarious workers, their power and the ways to realise it: the struggle of Heineken labour broker workers, Unpublished Master's dissertation, University of the Witwatersrand, Johannesburg.

Englert, T. and Runciman, C. (2019) 'Challenging workplace inequality: precarious workers' institutional and associational power in Gauteng, South Africa', *Transformation: Critical Perspectives on Southern Africa*, 101(1), 84–104.

Fine, B. and Rustomjee, Z.Z.R. (1996) *The Political Economy of South Africa*, Johannesburg: Witwatersrand University Press.

Gallas, A. (2016) 'There is power in a union: a strategic-relational perspective on power resources', in A. Truger, E. Hein, M. Heine and F. Hoffer (eds) *Monetary Macroeconomics, Labour Market and Development*, Marburg: Metropolis-Verlag, pp 195–210.

Kenny, B. and Webster, E. (1998) 'Eroding the core: flexibility and the re-segmentation of the South African labour market', *Critical Sociology*, 24(3): 216–43.

Kenny, B. and Webster, E. (2021) 'The return of the labour process: race, skill and technology in South African labour studies', *Work in the Global Economy*, 1(1–2): 13–32.

Labour Relations Amendment Act (2014) No. 6, Available from: https://www.gov.za/sites/default/files/gcis_document/201501/37921gon629.pdf [Accessed 7 March 2023].

Leger, J.-P. (1992) Talking rocks: an investigation of the pit sense of rockfall accidents amongst underground gold miners, Unpublished doctoral dissertation, University of the Witwatersrand, Johannesburg.

Macun, I. (2014) 'The state of organised labour: still living like there's no tomorrow', *New South African Review*, 4: 39–55.

Marx, K. (1990 [1867]) *Capital*, Volume 1, London: Penguin Books.

Rees, R. (2019) *Becoming Permanent: Taking Section 198 Up*, Johannesburg: National Labour and Economic Development Institute.

Runciman, C. (2019) 'The "double-edged sword" of institutional power: COSATU, neo-liberalisation and the right to strike', *Global Labour Journal*, 10(2): 142–58.

Theron, J. (2005) 'Employment is not what it used to be', in E. Webster and K. von Holdt (eds) *Beyond the Apartheid Workplace: Studies in Transition*, Pietermaritzburg: University of KwaZulu-Natal Press, pp 293–316.

Von Holdt, K. and Webster, E. (2005) 'Work restructuring and the crisis of social reproduction: a Southern perspective', in E. Webster and K. von Holdt (eds) *Beyond the Apartheid Workplace: Studies in Transition*, Pietermaritzburg: University of KwaZulu-Natal Press Press, pp 3–40.

Webster, E. (1985) *Cast in a Racial Mould: Labour Process and Trade Unionism in the Foundries*, Johannesburg: Ravan Press.

Wolpe, H. (1972) 'Capitalism and cheap labour-power in South Africa: from segregation to apartheid', *Economy and Society*, 1(4): 425–56.

Other documents

Assign Services (Pty) Limited v National Union of Metalworkers of South Africa and Others (CCT194/17) [2018] ZACC 22; [2018] 9 BLLR 837 (CC); (2018) 39 ILJ 1911 (CC); 2018 (5) SA 323 (CC); 2018 (11) BCLR 1309 (CC) (26 July 2018).

National Bargaining Council for the Chemical Industry (NBCCI) (4 July 2003) Fast Moving Consumer Goods Sector: Substantive Agreement, 1 July 2003 – 30 June 2004, [online] Available from: https://www.nbcci.org.za [Accessed 14 December 2021].

National Bargaining Council for the Chemical Industry (NBCCI) (27 July 2005) Fast Moving Consumer Goods Sector: Substantive Agreement, 1 July 2005 – 30 June 2006, [online] Available from: https://www.nbcci.org.za [Accessed 14 December 2021].   ʼ

National Bargaining Council for the Chemical Industry (NBCCI) (3 August 2006) Fast Moving Consumer Goods Sector: Substantive Agreement, 1 July 2006 – 30 June 2007, [online] Available from: https://www.nbcci.org.za [Accessed 14 December 2021].

National Bargaining Council for the Chemical Industry (NBCCI) (8 August 2007) Fast Moving Consumer Goods Sector: Substantive Agreement, 1 July 2007 – 30 June 2008, [online] Available from: https://www.nbcci.org.za [Accessed 14 December 2021].

National Bargaining Council for the Chemical Industry (NBCCI) (7 September 2011) Fast Moving Consumer Goods Sector: Substantive Agreement, 1 July 2011 – 30 June 2012, [online] Available from: https://www.nbcci.org.za [Accessed 14 December 2021].

National Bargaining Council for the Chemical Industry (NBCCI) (15 August 2012) Fast Moving Consumer Goods Sector: Substantive Agreement, 1 July 2012 – 30 June 2013, [online] Available from: https://www.nbcci.org.za [Accessed 14 December 2021].

National Bargaining Council for the Chemical Industry (NBCCI) (27 July 2013) Fast Moving Consumer Goods Sector: Substantive Agreement, 1 July 2013 – 30 June 2014, [online] Available from: https://www.nbcci.org.za [Accessed 14 December 2021].

National Bargaining Council for the Chemical Industry (NBCCI) (25 July 2014) Fast Moving Consumer Goods Sector: Substantive Agreement, 1 July 2014 – 30 June 2015, [online] Available from: https://www.nbcci.org.za [Accessed 14 December 2021].

National Bargaining Council for the Chemical Industry (NBCCI) (11 August 2015) Fast Moving Consumer Goods Sector: Substantive Agreement, 1 July 2015 – 30 June 2016, [online] Available from: https://www.nbcci.org.za [Accessed 14 December 2021].

National Bargaining Council for the Chemical Industry (NBCCI) (19 August 2016) Fast Moving Consumer Goods Sector: Substantive Agreement, 1 July 2016 – 30 June 2017, [online] Available from: https://www.nbcci.org.za [Accessed 14 December 2021].

National Bargaining Council for the Chemical Industry (NBCCI) (22 June 2018) Fast Moving Consumer Goods Sector: Addendum to the Substantive Agreement, 1 July 2017 – 30 June 2019, [online] Available from: https://www.nbcci.org.za [Accessed 14 December 2021].

National Bargaining Council for the Chemical Industry (NBCCI) (13 September 2019) Fast Moving Consumer Goods Sector: Substantive Agreement, 1 July 2019 – 30 June 2021, [online] Available from: https://www.nbcci.org.za [Accessed 14 December 2021].

National Bargaining Council for the Chemical Industry (NBCCI) (20 July 2020) Fast Moving Consumer Goods Sector: Addendum to the Substantive Agreement, 1 July 2019 – 30 June 2021, [online] Available from: https://www.nbcci.org.za [Accessed 14 December 2021].

Statistics South Africa (Stats SA) (2021) *Gross Domestic Product, Fourth Quarter,* Pretoria: Stats SA.

Statistics South Africa (Stats SA) (2022) *Quarterly Labour Force Survey, First Quarter,* Pretoria: Stats SA.

Victor and Others v Chep South Africa (Pty) Ltd and Others (JA55/2019) [2020] ZALAC 59; (2020) 41 ILJ 2802 (LAC); [2021] 1 BLLR 53 (LAC) (16 September 2020).

5

Authoritarian Algorithmic Management: The Double-edged Sword of the Gig Economies

With Fikile Masikane

In this chapter we look at location-based platforms,[1] in the period 2019–2022. Their use has increased significantly since their first entry into Africa in 2016. We focus specifically on the rider-hailing sector in Johannesburg, which we will refer to as food courier delivery riders. We draw much of the data in this chapter from our research report titled 'I just want to survive: a comparative study of food courier riders in three African cities' (Webster and Masikane, 2021). That report points to the emergence of a new type of worker in the digital economy, who is subject to a new business model based on a form of authoritarian algorithmic management.

This new form of work is controlled by a few corporations, popularly known as tech giants, such as Uber and Amazon. Promising freedom, flexibility, self-employment, and shared business ownership (SBO), these multinational tech conglomerates claim to be creating new economic opportunities in Africa. In reality, as is evident from our study, these opportunities are predicated on precarious work, deepening worker insecurity, undermining worker rights, and increasing inequality between extremely wealthy senior managers and a growing reserve of precarious workers. These forms of control make management figures invisible, as they become hidden and inaccessible. Nevertheless, by technologically linking riders together, companies have increased workers' bargaining power, opening the possibility of riders exercising structural, associational, and societal power.

We begin by discussing the rise of platform capitalism and the platform labour process, and how the rider-hailing sector entered Africa. We then look at who the food courier riders are, in order to understand the nature of this type of work, drawing from the findings of the research report. We have found in our research among food courier riders that despite the individualisation, dispersal and pervasive monitoring that characterises work in the 'gig economy' – that is, short-term freelance work where digital platforms connect freelancers with customers or clients (ILO, 2021) – digital technology is generating forms of counter-mobilisation. By technologically linking platform workers, the gig economy tends to link their working bargaining power, thus contributing to the emergence of self-organised, hybrid forms of union-like associations (associational power) and new partnerships with traditional unions and NGOs (societal power). The chapter concludes by suggesting that the new digital technology is a double-edged sword. On the one hand, it is leading to an extension of authoritarian managerial control over workers, increasing their insecurity and deepening inequality. On the other hand, by technologically linking workers, the technology has increased their workplace bargaining power by providing them with the ability to develop collective solidarity and even strike action.

The rise of platform capitalism

Over the past decade there has been a dramatic expansion of digital platforms which have reshaped the world of work by introducing platform work. Platform work is paid work mediated by a software application (the App) used by the platform, using a new business model that is based on authoritarian algorithmic management. This business model allows platforms such as Uber to organise work without having to invest in capital equipment or to hire employees. The labour process or the structure of the work is such that instead of traditional clocking-in with a timecard, gig workers log in to an App, and in so doing become subject to an external authority: the algorithm (Webster and Masikane, 2021). Simply put, the algorithm is a process or set of rules to be followed in calculations or other problem-solving operations, especially by a computer (Maphukata et al, 2021).

This algorithm translates consumer demand into tasks that food courier riders need to execute, specifies where and when those tasks must be performed, and directly or indirectly determines how much money workers will be paid for the execution of such tasks, regardless of the distance between the restaurant and the customer's home. The App directly or indirectly controls the execution of the work and the worker's performance at work – there is no worker autonomy (Maphukata et al, 2021). Essentially, the companies perform the intermediation by integrating reviews, rating systems, global positioning systems (GPS) and electronic payment systems (Sànchez and Mcdonaldo, 2022).

The model creates a highly segmented labour market comprising a small core of high-value-added activities and a non-core of outsourced and franchised activities. The core workers enjoy enhanced salaries, pensions and other benefits. Their founders and CEOs such as Jeff Bezos, Bill Gates and Mark Zuckerberg are among the richest business owners in the world. In late June 2020, Jeff Bezos added US$12 billion to his net worth in a single day, which illustrates the extraordinary wealth of such tech giants (Shapiro, 2020). The workers at the peripheral or outsourced outlets, on the other hand, must make do with far inferior and often precarious pay and working conditions. We refer to this as the 'uberisation' of work (Webster, 2020).

These new business entities concentrate on high-value-adding activities while divesting themselves from 'downstream' employment liabilities. They do this through technology-enabled outsourcing and subcontracting practices that manage their fragmented supply chains remotely. The practices of tech giants such as Uber and Amazon rest upon three key characteristics. First, they display 'monopoly tendencies' as exemplified by the trillion-dollar valuations many of them have achieved, as well as their drive to undercut other producers (Srnicek, 2016: 48; see also Nocke et al, 2007). Second, they are willing to by-pass standard corporate governance norms, and they have an appetite for dual class shares which deliver their founders huge salaries and very extensive share options (Govindarajan and Srivastava, 2018).[2] Third, their employment policies show certain characteristics: the 'riders' are misclassified as 'partners' and designated as 'independent contractors' with a 'self-employed' status; the rider partners provide the tools of their trade and are paid on a piecework basis, but they are not paid for their actual working time. Lastly, due to their so-called self-employed status, the company can by-pass the rights of workers covered by standard employment relationships.

Platform capitalism has created a new work paradigm in which workers are managed through online platforms, monitored indirectly and expected to produce measurable outputs (Huws, 2016). Work is 'logged in', Huws (2016: 15) explains, in three distinct ways: it is divided into standard and quantified components; it is subjected to continuous surveillance and monitoring, and it requires a worker to be connected to an online platform to obtain work.

This new paradigm of gig work exemplifies new market-based principles where precarious employment relations, along with algorithmic controls of the labour process, are used to great effect in shifting risk from capital to labour. Furthermore, gig work favours individual freedom over collective freedom, which further puts pressure on the ability of workers to control their wages and working hours. As a result, the alleged freedom in gig work, which offers workers flexibility to schedule their working and personal lives freely, is heavily constrained (Huws, 2016; see also Anwar and Graham, 2020: 16). The main reason why we say that this freedom, which has become the selling point for the platforms, is pseudo-freedom is because of the rating system, which is the core feature of the algorithm. Embedded in that system is customer feedback, where riders are ranked and rated. This we will discuss in detail in the sections that follow.

Location-based platforms enter Africa

In 2012, Uber was the first ride-sharing service to launch on the African continent, followed by its competitor Bolt (now Taxify). Uber is the largest ride-sharing service in Africa, with over 60,000 drivers across the continent. It displaced local transport operators, taxis and metered cabs in the process (Kute et al, 2021).

Mr Delivery had already been launched in Cape Town in 1992, and Uber Eats was launched in 2016. Mr Delivery was fully acquired by Takealot, an e-commerce company, in 2014. In 2015, a merger between Takealot and Kalahari, a Naspers-owned firm, was completed. In 2017, Naspers increased its investment in Takealot by 96 per cent. By implication, Naspers, a South African firm, now owns Mr D Foods.

There are two reasons for the rapid entry and growth of Uber on the African continent, according to Kute et al (2021). First, relaxed regulations in Africa significantly lowered Uber's barriers to entry, thereby enabling its rapid expansion into the South African market under the guise of job creation. Second, Uber made a shrewd and agile adjustment to its business model to adapt to Africa's unique operating environment. This aided its continued growth and expansion in the continent (Kute et al, 2021).

It is often forgotten that a gig economy requires extensive foundational infrastructure, including massive investment in subsea cables. There is a high concentration of trans-Atlantic and trans-Pacific subsea cables connecting North America to Europe and North America to Southeast Asia, but very few connections with Africa (Qiu, 2019).

In 2019, platform work represented only 1 per cent of employment in South Africa, divided between online web-based work performed largely at home (100,000 workers) and location-based work such as food couriers (35,000 workers). The categorisation itself leads to a digital divide, since not everyone can participate in this line of work depending on where they are located geographically.

Globally, online food courier riders are operating at a net loss as they attempt to increase their market share by spending large portions of their revenue on advertising, promotions, bonuses, and exclusive partnerships with big brands such as McDonalds. McDonald's makes up just under 9 per cent of all outlets on Uber Eats globally (Hawkins, 2018). The percentage of food delivered by Uber Eats from restaurant to customer in South Africa was 16.1 per cent in 2020. Projections are that it will reach 20.4 per cent by 2024 (Curry, 2022). As of 2018, Mr Delivery saw an order growth of 210 per cent (De Villiers, 2018).

Food courier company revenue

Uber Eats, and most food courier delivery companies, are only profitable in one quarter of the markets in which they operate (Hawkins, 2018). However, lower losses have been reported by online food platforms each year (Beckett, 2020). Uber's earning release indicates that ride hailing significantly decreased globally during the pandemic, but food couriering dramatically increased. However, although there were more Uber Eats customers than Uber taxis drivers, the taxi drivers are still the dominant contributor to the company.

South Africa's level of food courier growth is higher than in most other countries (Statista, n.d.-a). Globally, restaurant-to-consumer delivery accounts for 9.6 million users and US$442 million revenue (Statista, n.d.-b). Mr Delivery has an estimated 2 million downloads and 700,000 active monthly users. Uber Eats has 2.1 million downloads but in 2020 did not make its sales data public (PYMNTS, 2020). Naspers CEO Larry Illg indicated that food delivery is still an under-penetrated market in South Africa and that Mr Delivery is attempting to expand (De Villiers, 2018). We turn now to our research strategies, and begin with the challenge of conducting ethnographic research during the pandemic.

Research strategy

We used a semi-structured questionnaire as our main research instrument and interviewed a total of 150 food courier delivery riders drawn equally from Accra in Ghana, Johannesburg in South Africa and Nairobi in Kenya.[3] We interviewed riders in and around shopping centres and malls where there is a high concentration of food courier riders. We used a snowball sampling technique to select 50 participants in each city. The survey questions were prepared in English and took between 30 and 45 minutes to complete. Interestingly, riders seemed to be divided by nationality in different geographical areas. In Johannesburg, for example, riders at Campus Square, Columbine Square and Cresta were originally from Uganda; at Rosebank Mall the majority of food courier delivery riders were from Zimbabwe, with a few from the Democratic Republic of Congo (DRC); and at Clearwater Mall most of the riders were from Zimbabwe.

In addition to the survey, we drew on several qualitative research strategies. The first involved in-depth interviews in Johannesburg and one in-depth interview with a woman rider in Nairobi. In addition, we constructed biographies of two riders in Johannesburg. We collected a diary entry from one rider who wrote of his experiences via WhatsApp over a period of two weeks. We engaged in participant observation by attending soccer matches that the riders host on public holidays in South Africa. To give us greater insight into platform work, in June 2021 co-researcher Fikile Masikane registered as an Uber Eats rider.

In the process of reporting back our findings to our respondents, an ongoing forum emerged. In essence, our research became a form of critical engagement.[4] The purpose of the forum is to create a structure where riders can air their grievances across the different work zones and collectively find ways to address grievances with the relevant authorities.

We have divided our findings into three main themes: In Part I we find out who the food courier delivery riders are. In Part II, we discuss the nature and conditions of their work. Then in Part III, we examine what power they have to challenge their working conditions.

Part I: Who are the food courier delivery riders?

The most striking feature of food courier delivery riders in these three cities is that they are overwhelmingly men, young, Black and relatively well-educated. They have been doing the job for some time, and predominantly live in rented accommodation. There are important regional variations, however. In Johannesburg, 90 per cent of the riders interviewed were cross-border migrants, while in Nairobi and Accra riders were local citizens. Cross-border migrants are more precarious, as platforms take advantage of their status and use the workers for cheap labour.

A surprising finding is that the workforce is relatively stable; riders remain in the job for relatively long periods of time. The most likely explanation is that app-based platform work is the best job available to them. As one respondent remarked, "I just want to survive". However, our Nairobi data suggests that for those 12 per cent of courier riders who have been in the job for over five years, food couriering may well be a career.

Food couriers are old-fashioned piece workers; they are only paid when they perform the task of delivering food to a customer. On average, 69 per cent of the total sample of riders wait between 30 and 60 minutes between calls. The result is a long working day, but a significant proportion of the time is unpaid. According to 46 per cent of the total sample, the length of the average working day was 12 hours – from 9 am to 9 pm. As a Ghanaian courier rider remarked, "I do not have off days. I work all days of the week. I only pause when there is an occasion" (Richard, 2021). Because remuneration is task-based, the more tasks – that is, the more deliveries – riders undertake, the more money they make. The riders refer to these long hours as an attempt at reaching a target. In other words, if the drivers earn a certain amount of money in a week, they can at least cover their daily expenses such as rent, petrol and groceries. In the words of a Johannesburg courier, "It's up to you. If you want to meet your target, you work more. If you want to make extra you must work harder" (Chris, 2020).

Of the total sample of riders, 37 per cent said they earned enough to cover their monthly expenses. The highest proportion of riders who said they earned enough was in Accra (48 per cent), followed by Nairobi (39 per cent) and Johannesburg (25 per cent). Although 32 per cent of riders said they could not cover their monthly expenses, a significant 31 per cent said they did not know. The high number of 'don't know' responses is likely because riders' earnings are unpredictable. As one rider in Accra remarked, "I live within whatever income I am able to make in the month, [enough that] I am able to pay rent and utilities" (Yussif, 2021).

However, it was clear that for many courier riders their work was a hand-to-mouth existence, as these two comments attest: "Some deliveries are calculated based on distance, so the income is not adequate" (Ali, 2021). And "My salary is not enough. I have siblings in school and parents to take care of. My dependents are more than my salary" (Emmanuel, 2021). Joseph, a food courier in Johannesburg, spoke about the difficulties of estimating his income because he does not have a fixed income:

'I know how the system works but sometimes we have challenges logging in. Sometimes one driver gets more trips than the other. We do not know how it works. Data only lasts for a week. If you go on Facebook and WhatsApp [to communicate with family and friends] your data will finish quicker. The Uber App takes up too much data. One GB of data is enough if you do not chat or use Facebook. One day, you wake up and make R200. Some days we make more and others less. There's no fixed amount that we get paid per day.' (Joseph, 2020)

We asked: If you do not cover expenses, where do you get the extra money? Family, friends and neighbours (24 per cent) seemed to be a common source of filling riders' expenses gap, but the largest category was other informal economic activities. Not surprisingly, few drew on their savings: only 4 per cent in Nairobi and Johannesburg did so; a significantly higher number of riders in Accra (23 per cent) drew on their savings.

Part II: What is the nature and condition of the work?

The most common problems riders faced in all three cities are shown in Table 5.1.

In ranking riders' responses by the most significant in each city, crime topped the list in Johannesburg (57 per cent). In Accra, 45 per cent of riders cited police harassment, while in Nairobi police harassment was at 41 per cent. The surprisingly low figure of 12 per cent of Johannesburg riders citing police harassment may be related to corrupt Metro Police officers accepting

Table 5.1: Common problems faced by food delivery drivers

Problem	Per cent
Police harassment	22
Unfair clients	20
Stress caused by work	19
Accidents	15
Illness caused by work	12
Crime	11

bribes. In an informal conversation with couriers, bribery was accepted as a norm, with a modest amount of ZAR20 per incident (about €1.20).

Employees or partners?

The employment status of platform workers has been a topic of debate in most studies on the platform economy. As evidence from our research shows, the working conditions of food courier delivery riders is characterised by low wages, irregular and long working hours, accidents including those leading to fatalities, the pressure of ratings and customer feedback, algorithmic management, lack of transparency, and an ambiguous employment status. This ambiguous status is our main point of departure in understanding riders' attempts to better their working conditions.

The misclassification of the riders as partners or independent contractors undermines their rights as workers and prohibits them from challenging their working conditions. It is important that this employment status be reviewed. We argue that the riders should be classified as dependent workers (Mhlana et al, 2022).

Most of the e-companies present the work as self-employment or a partnership opportunity. The majority of riders, however, saw themselves as self-employed: 76 per cent in Accra and 80 per cent in Nairobi. In Johannesburg, we discovered that only 18 per cent of riders described themselves as 'self-employed' and 56 per cent described themselves as 'partners'. When exploring this further, we interpreted their understanding of the term 'partners' as being similar to self-employed. When adding 18 per cent (self-employed) and 56 per cent (partners) we arrive at 74 per cent; which was very close to the data for Accra and Nairobi.

In Accra, some of the riders explained that their employment was "not under any control of an employer" (Abn, 2021). Another rider remarked, "I am not accountable to anyone" (Bright, 2021). Michael quipped, "I work for a third party, my boss" (Michael, 2021). Musala said he was happy because "Jumia gives you freedom to do other work" (Musala, 2021). A Nairobi respondent remarked, "I am self-employed because I own my bike" (Makena, 2021).

Riders' responses go to the very heart of the legal dispute over whether they are independent contractors (that is, self-employed) or employees. A dispute took place in 2018 when Uber B.V. deactivated the Uber drivers' App. Because Uber B.V. is a Netherlands-based company, South African courts do not have any jurisdiction over it. However, the drivers claimed unfair dismissal and took Uber B.V. to the CCMA in South Africa. Uber rejected the CCMA's jurisdiction on the basis that workers were independent contractors and not employees (Pagdens, 2020).[5] In their case, the drivers made reference to Section 200A and Section 213 of the LRA, contending that they were employees. Workers argued this because they were required to perform their duties personally, customers created contracts with Uber and not the drivers as individuals, and drivers are largely controlled by Uber specifically with regard to their performance being algorithmically monitored.

Uber's case was that drivers were not under any obligation to use the Uber App or drive Uber-registered vehicles; drivers could choose where to drive and which passengers to collect, and the drivers bore the risk of profit vs. loss. Uber SA also claimed that no contractual agreement existed between them and Uber drivers, as there was only a contractual agreement between drivers and Uber B.V.

The CCMA agreed with the applicants in the case, the drivers. But the decision was overturned on a technicality when Uber SA appealed to the Labour Court. The Labour Court held that the CCMA failed to consider the fact that Uber SA and Uber B.V. were separate, independent entities and that applicants should have also lodged a complaint against Uber B.V.

Uber B.V. provides the legal contracts and technology, and deals with the collection and payment of monies received from customers who hail the Uber drivers. However, Uber SA – being Uber B.V.'s local subsidiary – hires, controls and approves the Uber drivers. The Uber drivers predominantly, if not exclusively, engage with Uber SA daily and not with Uber B.V.

The Labour Court made it clear that the question of whether drivers were independent contractors or employees was left unanswered. It stated that the CCMA's decision was solely overturned on a technicality.

On 19 February 2021, the United Kingdom's Supreme court ruled in favour of Uber drivers who argued that they were workers, not independent contractors (Uber B.V. and Others (Appellants) v. Aslam and Others, 2019). The court ruling stipulated that while drivers have fewer job rights than employees, they are provided with more benefits and protection than independent contractors. This ruling catalysed further attempts to legally challenge the employment status of Uber riders in South Africa.

Figure 5.1: Employment in the informal economy

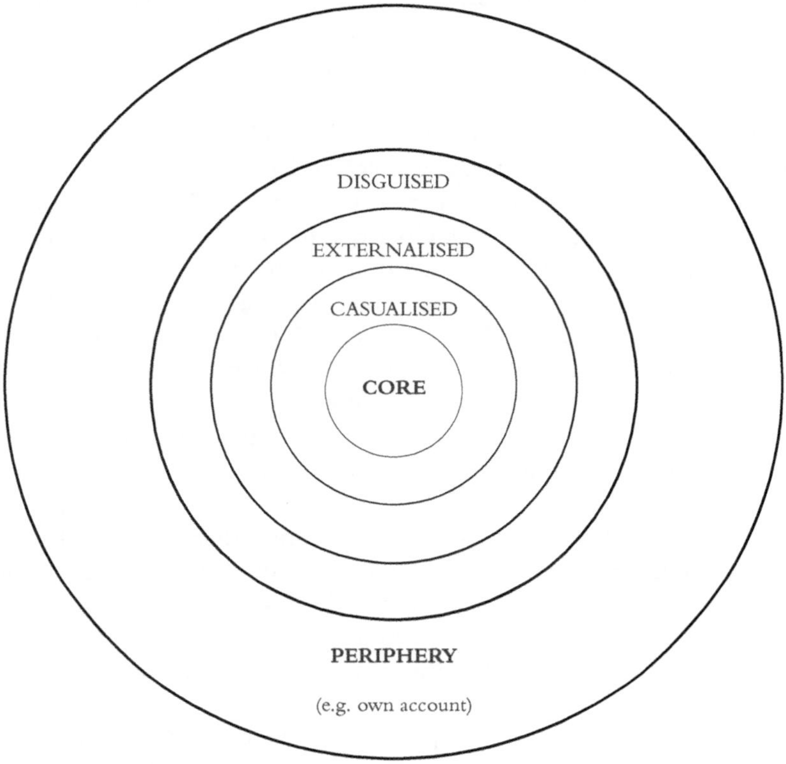

Source: Developed by Edward Webster.

The ILO (2021) defines food couriers as disguised employment or, more specifically, dependent contractors. In 2018, the International Conference of Labour Statisticians (ICLS) introduced the new category of 'dependent contractors' – workers who have contractual arrangements of a commercial nature (but not a contract of employment) to provide goods and services for or through another economic unit. They are not employees of that economic unit, but are dependent on that unit for organisation and execution of the work, for income or for access to the market. They are workers employed for profit, who are dependent on another entity that exercises control over their productive activities and directly benefits from the work performed by them (ILO, 2018: para 5). This is illustrated in Figure 5.1.

In Figure 5.1, the core consists of workers in relatively stable jobs in the formal sector – that is, in standard employment relationships. In contrast, each successive ring located outside of the core represents workers in non-standard and increasingly precarious work arrangements. The second and third rings, casualised and externalised, are examples of informal employees. In casualisation, the employment relationship between the employer and the employee is retained but is rendered insecure and unstable through temporary or part-time work and weak employee rights. Externalisation, through which the employment relationship is devolved to a third-party or nominal employer, renders employment even less secure and reduces the claims of employees on the de facto employer. The fourth ring – disguised employment – consists of dependent contractors such as location-based platform workers. Workers in this category are usually responsible for obtaining their own social security. Since many of them do not have the means to do this, or indeed social security plans may not be accessible to them, they are often part of the informal economy. Finally, the largest ring – the periphery – consists mostly of informal workers but also includes informal small enterprises.

Disguised employment is still thought of in binary terms – that is, an employer–employee relationship. It is important to note that this is a new kind of worker, one who has emerged through the digital economy, and therefore that there is a new relationship that needs to be understood in order to provide the worker with the necessary benefits needed in this line of work.

The nature of the new work order

Drawing on labour process theory, we identify three common features of digital work – the App; customer feedback; and a new form of managerial control.

First, there is a common point of production, the App, which is downloaded on one's smartphone using data. The App is where worker and customer encounter each other, and it is the App that operates as the central point of production. And, as the food courier delivery riders agreed, their smartphone is the workplace. As one respondent in Johannesburg remarked, "Without my phone, I have no work" (Steven, 2021).

The platform itself determines the worker's percentage of what the customer pays. This percentage is based on algorithmic elaborations, the specifics of which are blocked from workers. Workers – that is, riders – either accept or decline orders; they cannot intervene in the calculation. If they try to do so, the platform can deactivate the rider's App.

This leads to the second feature common to digital work, embedded in the worker's execution. This is customer feedback; customers rank and rate the riders. The platform translates this into a reputational score, a proxy of trustworthiness, which the riders believe gets them more work. Emotional labour, to use a sociological term, puts the riders under constant stress – to perform better, and to get the food delivered on time and in good condition. The vast majority of our respondents (83 per cent) said that the service rating system was important to them. Riders get stars via the App as a way of feedback on the quality of their service. The lowest rating score is 1 and the highest is 5. The rating scores are added to give the rider and the customer an idea of how many stars the rider has overall. For example, a rider might have about 4,000 stars and this is shown on the rider's details. Riders said that this motivates them to improve their service. "It pushes drivers to comply because they want higher ratings", said Josias (2020), a Johannesburg rider.

Riders' commission is a crucial reason why rating is important; ratings determine riders' income and it motivates them. The commission is the amount that Uber Eats charges per trip. When we asked the riders why the driver rating is important, they explained that a high rating was important to ensure their continued access to the Uber network and, by extension, a good rating helped protect their income stream generated on the App. Each city on Uber's global network has its own minimum rating level that drivers must maintain for them to stay active on the platform (Uber, 2016). This provides riders with an instrument to control income and further solidify the perceived 'flexibility' they enjoy.

This situation highlights the precarity of the work, as this tech giant company has the authority to deactivate the riders' accounts should they not perform satisfactorily. In Johannesburg, the riders are even more precarious because 90 per cent of them are migrant workers, some with no legal documents – a fact that the employer knows.

There is a key contradiction in the platform rating system (Sánchez and Maldonado, 2022). It lies in the way in which the algorithm determines riders' access to more trips. According to those behind its design and promotion, rating systems are open and democratised; they are embedded in transparency from customer feedback, and the riders are able to see customer satisfaction. However, rating systems feed algorithms to optimise and improve the performance of the platform. There is no interaction with riders, so they are unable to state their experience with the App itself or to lodge complaints about the contradiction between customer experiences and workers' interaction with the platform. This is perceived as part of the surveillance of the platform; there is a perception that a bad review can be traced by the platform and be punished by blocking the individual rider's account (Sánchez and Maldonado, 2022).

The third feature is that a new form of managerial control is introduced. Gandani (2018) calls this a form of techno-normative control over workers: '(a) platforms are akin to management by customers like call centres; (b) personal bests (PBs) are used to stimulate and reward workers. These forms of control make invisible the management figure; they become hidden and inaccessible'[6] (Gandani, 2018: 15).

By introducing an element of competition through rating and providing visible evidence of success, the couriers are drawn into 'playing the game'.

Sarah Mason (2018) calls this 'gamification' and it is the centre of the Uber business model. Mason, who took a job as an Uber driver to study the work model, described it in this way:

> Simply defined, gamification is the use of game elements – point-scoring, levels, competition with others, measurable evidence of accomplishment, ratings and rules of play – in non-game contexts. Games deliver an instantaneous, visceral experience of success and reward, and they are increasingly used in the workplace to promote emotional engagement with the work process, to increase workers' psychological investment in completing otherwise uninspiring tasks, and to influence, or 'nudge' workers' behaviour. (Mason, 2018: 4)

Most of the participants believed that customer ratings were important because ratings affected their chances of getting potential clients. Joseph (2020), a Johannesburg driver, remarked: "When you get poor ratings from clients, Uber Eats deactivates your account. When it [your rating] is as low as 85 they [Uber Eats] send you a message warning you about your ratings. If there are no improvements, they deactivate your account".

Part III: What power do riders have to challenge their working conditions?

In this section we explore what potential the food courier riders have to get the tech giant companies to respond to their demands, including opportunities to organise.

Networks and organisation

We asked riders whether they had a relationship with their co-workers. Although geographically isolated, the majority overall (88 per cent) said they had developed relationships with their co-workers. Country by country, 19 per cent in Accra said they had not, followed by 10 per cent of riders in Johannesburg and 8 per cent in Nairobi.

Regarding whether there were trade unions or union-like organisations for riders, of the overall sample only 12 per cent said 'yes', and 46 per cent said 'no'; 42 per cent of the riders said they did not know. One driver in Johannesburg said, "I would like to be unionised, as we take 100 per cent risk. We are exposed to diseases and are often robbed. Nyaope boys [drug addicts] take our phones every day; some people rob us" (Ronald, 2020).

While most of the drivers confirmed that there were no trade unions among food delivery riders, many said that the WhatsApp groups operate like a trade union. A rider gave the example of the Brothers of Melville

(BOM), an informal society of food couriers at Campus Square, a small shopping mall in Melville, Johannesburg. The chairperson of the Brothers of Melville is quite clear about their demands. First, they want to be permanent drivers. He believes there is negligence in Uber Eats, rider fatalities, work insecurity and very little support. "They do not give you anything, besides the paper bag when you go to collect an order" (Paul, 2020).

For these reasons, this rider started two main WhatsApp groups: Brothers of Melville and United Ugandans (UU). Because of the individualistic nature of the job, it is difficult to connect with drivers from elsewhere, so they all have separate groups; the Congolese and the Zimbabwean riders have their own groups as well. Unless riders work at Campus Square together, or are from the same country, it is difficult to connect.

The groups BOM and UU have rules and regulations. If a rider does not understand them, or agree with them, they are free to leave. BOM and UU function as mutual support groups. They contribute money and share information about several things. For example, they each put in ZAR100 (about €5.15) when something happens to a person, such as accidents, death or robbery. They also collect ZAR20 (about €1.20) every Sunday for informal savings and split the money at the end of the year. There are about 20 people in each group. One of the members of the Brothers of Melville said, "These groups help us. When you are alone you cannot go far, especially in South Africa; you always need support from people. It is better to be part of these groups" (Paul, 2020). In Accra, 9 per cent of riders said they were members of a group; in Johannesburg it was 25 per cent, and in Nairobi 21 per cent.

The purpose of riders' WhatsApp's groups was to share information about work (59 per cent) and working conditions (20 per cent). This represented a total of 79 per cent of riders sharing information about their work. Informal savings were mentioned as a reason by 11 per cent of the sample as a whole. Of the Nairobi sample, 25 per cent mentioned informal savings. This is likely the result of the widespread formalisation of saving groups in Kenya such as the Savings and Credit Cooperatives (SACCOs).[7]

Food couriers are not only organised at work. They also come together after working hours. In Johannesburg, this is especially so on public holidays, when riders gather to participate in their own soccer tournaments. It was quite intriguing to see the riders relaxing in a different setting. On the invitation of a Mr Delivery rider, Brian Chirwa, we visited Pieter Roos Park in Parktown, Johannesburg on 27 April 2021, Freedom Day, to watch their soccer tournament.

From our observations we drew these general insights:

- The couriers are already well-organised and even have a photographer. They are not organised into a trade union, although they do not seem hostile to the idea. They come together face-to-face. They use their phones to communicate through WhatsApp groups, each of which is run by a group leader. They see themselves as having common interests as an occupational group. As one rider said, "We are all facing the same problems, so we come together to help each other" (Lovemore, 2021).

- All the couriers in the group were from Zimbabwe, except for two people: one man from Uganda and a woman from South Africa.
- They do not have work permits, and seem to think permits are impossible to obtain. When the police stop them, couriers give them ZAR20 (about €1.20), and the police let them go on their way. But their lack of work permits seems to be one of the key problems that couriers face.
- Couriers value very highly the freedom they get from not having a direct boss; they can work whenever they want to, and take time off to, for example, take their children to school. But they also want some security and compensation for accidents. One courier at the tournament was still limping from a fractured ankle caused by a road crash.
- One interesting point is that the couriers reacted against the idea of being regulated. They seem to feel that regulations would jeopardise their already precarious situation. Although their work is dangerous, they earn considerably more than security guards. The couriers seemed quite proud of what they do.
- The couriers are well-educated, and some want to continue with their studies.
- They are determined to make a better living in South Africa.

The most common demand riders had was around payment, followed by police harassment. Safety was not a high demand; it did not appear in our sample in Accra, and was only mentioned by 2 per cent in Nairobi and 4 per cent in Johannesburg. A major food courier riders' strike with Uber Eats in Cape Town in 2018 was over the company cutting rates. The strike was unsuccessful because some riders from other work zones did not know about it. Apps can also isolate drivers and riders, as they do not reveal how many drivers and riders there are, or who they are.

However, in terms of organising, riders are often afraid to reveal their identities, as they are fearful of being algorithmically punished or kicked off the App. Since most couriers in Johannesburg are cross-border migrants, they are worried that by participating in acts of collective resistance they would increase their chance of being discovered by the company, such as Uber Eats or Mr Delivery, and become deactivated.

A meeting spot at Campus Square allows the Johannesburg riders to share their common grievances regarding the nature and the conditions of their work. As courier rider Brian (2020) states, "The poor working conditions is all we ever talk about when we meet". As discussed earlier, this led to online solidarity and the formation of WhatsApp groups such as the Uganda Bike Drivers Association. Although this association is not formally registered as a trade union, it functions in much the same way through acts of collective solidarity. Alex (2020), a Ugandan courier, recalled an occasion when a car drove into one of the bikers from Uganda, killing him. The group helped with the funeral arrangements and the return of the rider's body to Uganda. There is no joining fee for the group; money is only collected on a case-by-case basis. This WhatsApp group has 60 members, all from Uganda.

Brothers of Melville, reported on earlier in this chapter, organised a strike in February 2020. They demanded an increase in the amount of money they earned for each trip. They said the rate was too low compared to the kilometres they drove for each trip. They used their WhatsApp group to alert all drivers about the strike. If one driver was found working on the roads during this time, they took away his phone. "We take away your office", Alex (2020), a member of BOM, said. Due to the strike, Uber Eats was losing money as riders refused to deliver. "We withdrew our labour and we refused to take any trips. We collectively refused to take trips. Uber Eats did not victimise anyone" (Alex, 2020).

Many rider participants in our research were reluctant to venture an opinion about strikes, but of those who did 44 per cent said there had been rider strikes in response to their grievances, with a high response incidence in Nairobi (68 per cent) and in Johannesburg (58 per cent). Of those who said there had been strikes, 63 per cent said there had been as many as three strikes.

First city-wide strike of platform workers in South Africa

On 18 December 2020, in response to a fare decrease, roughly 2,000 couriers across Johannesburg collectively logged off the Uber Eats platform, forcing the company to halt operations across the city (Mokhoali, 2019).[8] Scores of couriers in other big cities – Tshwane, Durban and Port Elizabeth – also collectively logged off. Under pressure during the COVID-19 pandemic lockdown on restaurants, Uber Eats lowered the fare they were required to pay from a 30 per cent commission per order (plus 5 per cent to the rider) to a flat rate of approximately R9 (about €0.50) per meal. This change meant a loss of potential income for the rider. To cover the losses associated with these pricing changes, on Monday, 14 December 2020, without consulting any couriers, Uber Eats indicated their intention to lower the rates paid to couriers. While courier rates vary in different geographical areas, couriers claimed they were normally paid around R4 (about €0.25) per km. This was only the latest of many reductions in couriers' fares, with couriers receiving almost half the rate they were paid three to four years ago.

While localised food courier rider protests are relatively common occurrences, and generally ignored by management, a city-wide demonstration was widely viewed both by management and trade unions as something isolated; they believed that independently contracted couriers did not have the organisational capacity to achieve such an action. The couriers released a memorandum of 12 demands. They wanted, inter alia: increased delivery fees; safer routes; a halt to arbitrary suspension of courier accounts; improved safety and better in-trip support; labour brokers (company set up to supply labour to clients) to be banned; Uber Eats to supply delivery bags and other equipment; and to be able to choose not to accept cash trips.

The primary demand was increased fares. The riders organised strikes using WhatsApp groups. This enabled the strike organisers to overcome the attempts of the company platform to isolate them. Strikers set up communication networks and channels from which they could spread messages and communicate across multiple WhatsApp groups.

Ultimately, strikers were unable to achieve their demands because Uber Eats was unwilling to engage with them. They rejected the strikers' demands. This meant both the initial strike and the one-day follow-up strike on 22 January 2021 failed to achieve couriers' immediate intention of increasing income and levels of security.

Nevertheless, the strikers demonstrated their ability to overcome the hyper-individualised identities that platforms impose on them. They were able to organise coordinated provincial and nation-wide resistance to Uber Eats. Previous strikes and collective logoffs were very regionally specific. They did not receive much media attention and only lasted a few hours. Uber Eats easily stopped them by refusing to collectively bargain with couriers. However, never have courier strikes received as much media attention as these more widespread strikes, with extensive coverage in the media; for the first time, a food courier strike in South Africa was televised on a TV news platform. Although the strikers' demands were not met, they developed the power resources from which to capitalise in the future.

We turn in our last section to the possibilities of new forms of food courier workers' organisation emerging from below.

The emergence of union–like associations

Our research findings point towards the emergence of union–like organisations existing side-by-side with traditional trade unions to defend workers' needs and interests in the digital economy. In other words, those who speak of the 'end of labour' are, as Visser (2012) says, 'speaking of the end of a particular kind of worker organisation, in particular the traditional industrial union' (Visser, 2012: 45). Instead, what we see emerging in the digital economy are hybrid forms of organisation, including different types of associations that blur the distinction between traditional unionism and informal workers' associations or cooperatives.[9] 'Unions are reinventing themselves', argues the International Federation of App-based Transport Workers of India (IFAT); they are doing this by 'utilizing the newest technology to connect with the workers and collaborate with independent researchers and knowledge-based research organizations' (IFAT, 2020: 5).

As Gadgil and Samson (2017: 162) argue in their study of a trade union of waste pickers in India, 'increasing numbers of informal worker organisations are developing hybrid forms to address a range of needs far wider than those of formally employed wage workers'. They describe the politics of developing hybrid organisations as complex and dependent on the recognition 'that the union form can be simultaneously crucial and insufficient for meeting the needs of their members' (Gadgil and Samson, 2017: 160).

Traditional unions remain crucial in providing support and access to institutional power for the emerging organisations of precarious workers (Webster et al, 2021). It is misleading to characterise this approach as trade union fetishism, as Atzeni (2020) does, because it assumes that the organisational form of trade unions is static. This is demonstrated most clearly in the response by the Transport and Allied Workers Union of Kenya (TAWU-K), and the shift in their organising strategy to recruit and organise platform workers (Webster and Masikane, 2021).

Discovering power

If effective regulation of platform capitalism is to emerge, then collective representation and voice for workers in the digital economy will be necessary. Vandaele (2018: 15) points us in the right direction when he says that 'stopping machines in the twentieth century corresponds to collective logouts in the twenty-first century'. He goes on to stress the constraints facing digital workers going on strike, such as management's ability to 'disconnect' them and the difficulties of coordinating collective action. But he suggests three ways of enhancing digital workers' bargaining power through applying the power resources approach. This can be illustrated by drawing a distinction between actual and potential power.

First, digital workers can create worker-driven messaging apps and chat groups where they can share information, develop a shared identity and announce local direct action. Direct interaction at their work zones contributes 'to their self-organisation and associational power in the making' (Vandaele, 2018: 16). Riders have the potential for workplace bargaining power through being technologically linked through the app. Although their classification as self-employed weakens their associational power, the potential for associational power is drastically increased when workers meet face-to-face at work zones and begin to form a collective identity.

Second, platform workers can draw on associational power by forming alliances with trade unions or other organisations. These organisations can assist platform workers by taking test cases to courts, providing financial assistance to strikers and gaining support from the providers, such as the restaurants, and the customers.

Third, digital workers can influence the public discourse by debunking management's narrative about entrepreneurship, delegitimising the platforms' employment practices and building discursive or social power. This can translate into rulemaking and institutional power through setting minimum standards for wages and social protection.

However, couriers' major limitiation is that they have weak marketplace bargaining power. Entry requirements for the job are low and large reserves of unemployed labour from across Africa make riders easily replaceable. Riders in Johnnesburg are esepcially vulnerable as they are largely cross-border migrants who can be deported. A union strategy that requires management to limit the number of riders operating at any one time would undoubtedly improve riders' maketplace bargaining power.

Conclusion: Looking to the future

The disruption caused by the digital age and platform businesses exists in a regulatory vacuum. This presents both a challenge and an opportunity to the governments of African countries, to the e-commerce companies and to the people who work in these platforms. There has been an important initiative by an organisation called Fair Work to rate platform companies. Its goal is to show that better and fairer jobs are possible in the platform economy.

In the absence of an adequate regulatory framework for platform work, two broad pathways can be identified. One involves a deepening of the domination of foreign-owned tech giants with no national or global agreement on how to operate. With profits and taxes retained abroad, this could be described as a form of re-colonisation of the Global South (Couldry and Mejias, 2019). This would create more informal jobs, but workers would be stuck in low-wage drudgery with none of the protections or benefits of formal employment. Futhermore forcing cross-border migrants to work in the shadows makes it easier for those who employ them to ignore labour laws, lower their pay and perpetuate dismal conditions – which paradoxically makes hiring these workers more attractive. The ensuing 'race to the bottom' would not preserve jobs for South Africans but may do the reverse, all while immiserating immigrant workers.[10]

An alternative pathway could be a 'digital social compact' created with the active participation of platform workers and their organisations. This would involve coherent global and national policies, including legislation to protect such workers. This optimistic path opens the possibility of the extension of labour and social protections to informalised workers. In this scenario, the new technology of platform work creates opportunities – what Chacaltana and Leung (2019) call 'entry points' that facilitate access to social protection, simplify registration and support compliance with laws. It can, they suggest, create a trend to e-formality. The first step in this process of developing an alternative path is for the many union-like structures emerging in the gig economy to come together and to create a national coordinating structure.

Notes

[1] Location-based platforms include both rider-hailing and e-hailing; they cannot be separated (ILO, 2021).

[2] Some classes of shares give 'executive owners' the power to control a corporation's decision-making without having a voting majority, in exchange for taking a lower share of profit.

[3] Due to COVID-19 and the lockdown restrictions, we arranged local field researchers to assist with the surveys in Ghana and Kenya. Karim Saagbuk was our field researcher in Accra, and Agnes Tsheri was our field researcher in Nairobi.

[4] Critical engagement addresses the difficult challenge of producing knowledge in a collaborative way while advancing research that might be meaningful for both the social sciences and the constituencies with whom the research is undertaken (Lozano, 2018: 107). Instead of 'working on social movements', Lozano (2018: 103) suggests a collaborative approach which involves 'working and thinking together with social movement activists' in order to advance research that might be meaningful for both social science and the 'research subjects'.

[5] *Uber South Africa Technology Services (Pty) Ltd v National Union of Public Service and Allied Workers (NUPSAW) and Others* (C449/17) [2018] ZALCCT 1; [2018] 4 BLLR 399 (LC); (2018) 39 ILJ 903 (LC) (12 January 2018). See the text of the case at http://www.saf lii.org/za/cases/ZALCCT/2018/1.html and https://www.pagdens.co.za/legal_employ ment_status_of_uber_drivers/#:~ [Accessed 14 June 2020].

[6] Interestingly, the executive owners of tech giant companies are often very visible as philanthropists who contribute substantially to worthy causes, but they are largely invisible when it comes to questions of employment and workers' conditions of work.

[7] The cooperatives are registered with the Ministry of Cooperatives, which in turn authorises each SACCO to receive deposits and provide loans to its members. The group as a whole selects certain members to run the SACCO. The emergence of these cooperatives was a response to the long, bureaucratic processes associated with Kenyan banks.

[8] This portion of the chapter was researched and drafted by Jamie Rosenberg, a research assistant who followed the Uber strike in December, for this project and an undergraduate student at the University of the Witwatersrand.

[9] Visser identifies five different types of unions in the industrialised world: (1) the traditional industrial union that organised blue-collar workers in a particular sector, covering all skill grades including technicians, supervisors and white-collar staff; (2) a narrow industrial union that only organises non-manual workers or white-collar staff in a particular sector; (3) the classic blue-collar craft union; (4) the occupational white-collar union or staff association that organises particular occupations and professions irrespective of sector; and (5) general unions that cut across occupations and sectors (Visser, 2012: 136).

[10] Similar phenomena have been documented in other national contexts. See Daniel Costa (2019) and Stephen Clibborn (2015).

Interviews

Abn, 26 June, 2021, Nairobi Central
Alex, 17 March 2020, Campus Square, Johannesburg
Ali, 26 June 2021, Nairobi Central
Brian, 17 March 2020, Campus Square, Johannesburg
Bright, 21 June 2021, Ahafo Region, Accra
Brothers of Melville, 17 March, 2020, Campus Square, Johannesburg
Chris, 17 March 2020, Campus Square, Johannesburg
Emmanuel, 26 June 2021, Nairobi Central
Joseph, 19 June, 2020, Campus Square, Johannesburg
Josias, 18 June, 2020, Rosebank Mall, Johannesburg
Lovemore, 21 March, 2021, Pieter Roos Park, Johannesburg
Makena, 23 June, 2021, Nairobi
Michael, 23 June, 2021, Volta Volo, Accra
Musala, 23 June 2021, James Town, Accra
Paul, 17 March 2020, Campus Square, Campus Square
Richard, 24 June 2021, Tema, Accra
Ronald, 18 June, 2020, Columbine, Johannesburg
Steven, 20 June, 2021, Clearwater, Johannesburg
Yussif, 25 June, 2021, Madina, Accra

References

Anwar, M. and Graham, M. (2020) 'Between a rock and a hard place: freedom, flexibility, precarity and vulnerability', *Competition and Change*, 25(2): 237–58.

Atzeni, M. (2020) 'Worker organisation in precarious times: abandoning trade union fetishism, rediscovering class', *Global Labour Journal*, 11(3): 311–14

Beckett, E.L. (2020) 'Uber Eats lead steps down amid profitability struggles', Restaurant Dive, [online] 25 February, Available from: https://www.res taurantdive.com/news/breaking-uber-eats-lead-steps-down-amid-profit ability-struggles/572976/#:~:text=Even%20though%20Eats%20is%20a rguably,its%20lead%20in%20key%20markets [Accessed 14 June 2022].

Chacaltana, J. and Leung, V. (2019) *Transitioning to the Formal Economy through Technology: The Trends towards e-formality*. Geneva: ILO.

Clibborn, S. (2015) 'Why undocumented immigrant workers should have workplace rights', *Economic and Labour Relations Review*, 26(3): 465–73.

Costa, D. (2019) 'How well is the American economy working for working people?', Economic Policy Institute, [online] 27 August, Available from: https://www.epi.org/publication/labor-day-2019/#:~:text=Employ ers%20increase%20their%20profits%20and%20put%20downward%20p ressure,both%20immigrant%20and%20U.S.-born%20workers%20powerl ess%20and%20insecure [Accessed 15 June 2022].

Couldry, N. and Mejias, U. (2019) *The Costs of Connection: How Data is Colonizing Human Life and Appropriating it for Capitalism*, Redwood City, CA: Stanford University Press.

Curry, D. (2022) 'Uber Eats revenue and usage statistics', Business of Apps, [online] 29 June, Available from: https://www.businessofapps.com/data/uber-eats-statistics/#:~:text=%20Uber%20Eats%20key%20statistics%20%201%20Uber,is%20available%20in%206%2C000%20cities%2C%20with...%20More%20 [Accessed 30 June 2022].

De Villiers, J. (2018) 'Fast food deliveries are exploding in South Africa – here are the winners', Business Insider South Africa, [online] 1 August, Available from: https://www.businessinsider.co.za/fast-food-deliveries-are-exploding-in-south-africa-here-are-the-winners-2018-8 [Accessed 14 June 2022].

Gadgil, M. and Samson, M. (2017) 'Hybrid organisations, complex politics: when unions form cooperatives', in E. Webster, A.O. Britwum and S. Bhowmik (eds) *Crossing the Divide: Precarious Work and the Future of Labour*, Pietermaritzburg: University of KwaZulu-Natal Press, pp 143–64.

Gandini, A. (2018) 'Labour process theory and the gig economy', *Human Relations*, 72(6): 1039–56.

Govindarajan, V. and Srivastava, A. (2018) 'Re-examining dual-class stock', *Business Horizons*, 61(3): 461–4.

Hawkins, A.J. (2018) 'Uber Eats expands to 100 new cities in Europe, Middle East, and Africa', The Verge, [online] 12 March, Available from: https://www.theverge.com/2018/3/12/17110008/uber-eats-food-delivery-expanding [Accessed 14 June 2022].

Huws, U. (2016) 'Logged labour: a new paradigm of work organisation?', *Work Organisation, Labour & Globalisation*, 10(1): 7–26.

International Federation of App-based Transport Workers (IFAT) (2020) *A Study About the Response to the Pandemic by the App-based Companies*, New Delhi: IFAT and ITF.

International Labour Organisation (ILO) (2018) 'Resolution concerning statistics on work relationships', 20th International Conference on Labour Statisticians, Geneva, 10–19 October 2018.

International Labour Organisation (ILO) (2021) *World Employment and Social Outlook: The Role of Digital Labour Platforms in Transforming the World of Work*, Geneva: ILO.

Kute, S., Molife, M. and Tshezi, M. (2021) *Workers or Partners? The Political Economy of Uber in Dar es Salaam, Nairobi, and Johannesburg*, Berlin: Friedrich Ebert Stiftung.

Lozano, A.A. (2018) 'Reframing the public sociology debate: towards collaborative and decolonial praxis', *Current Sociology*, 66(1): 92–109.

Maphukata, S., Verachia, S. and Webster, E. (2021) 'Decoding algorithmic control', *Global Dialogue*, 11(3), [online], Available from: https://globaldialogue.isa-sociology.org/articles/decoding-algorithmic-control [Accessed 27 June 2022].

Mason, S. (2018) 'High score, low pay: why the gig economy loves gamification', The Guardian, 20 November.

Mhlana, S., Forrest, K. and Webster, E. (2022) Representation in the informal economy, Unpublished paper, Southern Centre for Inequality Studies, University of the Witwatersrand, Johannesburg.

Mokhoali, V. (2019). 'SA Uber Eats drivers halt deliveries in protest over low pay, working conditions', Eyewitness News, [online] 19 December, Available from: https://ewn.co.za/2020/12/19/sa-uber-eats-drivers-halt-deliveries-in-protest-over-low-pay-working-conditions [Accessed 27 June 2022].

Nocke, V., Peitz, M. and Stahl, K. (2007) 'Platform ownership', *Journal of the European Economic Association*, 5(6): 1130–60.

Pagdens (2020) 'What is the legal employment status of your Uber driver?', Pagdens, [online] 27 January, Available from: https://www.pagdens.co.za/legal_employment_status_of_uber_drivers/#:~:text=Uber%20SA%20objected%20to%20the,of%20the%20Labour%20Relations%20Act.&text=they%20are%20largely%20controlled%20by%20Uber [Accessed 14 June 2022].

PYMNTS (2020) 'Uber Eats partners with South African restaurants for food delivery', PYMNTS.com, [online] 2 January, Available from: https://www.pymnts.com/news/delivery/2020/uber-eats-partners-with-south-african-restaurants-food-delivery [Accessed 14 June 2022].

Qiu, W. (2019) 'Complete list of Google's subsea cable investments', Submarine Cable Networks, [online] 9 July, Available from: https://www.submarinenetworks.com/en/insights/complete-list-of-google-s-subsea-cable-investments [Accessed 26 June 2022].

Sánchez, D.Y. and Maldonado, O. (2022) *My Boss, the App: Algorithmic Management and Labor Process in Delivery Platforms in Colombia*, Future of Work(ers) SCIS Working Paper 36, Johannesburg: Southern Centre for Inequality Studies, University of the Witwatersrand.

Shapiro, A. (2020) 'The changing fortunes of the world's richest', Forbes Winners and Losers, [online] 10 October, Available from: https://www.forbes.com/sites/arielshapiro/2020/10/10/jeff-bezos-and-ex-wife-mackenzie-scott-gain-12-billion-in-anticipation-of-amazon-prime-day-trump-covid/#122ca6cb1df2 [Accessed 14 June 2022).

Srnicek, N. (2016) *Platform Capitalism*, Cambridge and Malden: Polity Press.

Statista (n.d.-a) *Online Food Delivery*, [online] Available from: https://www.statista.com/outlook/dmo/eservices/online-food-delivery/south-africa?currency=usd [Accessed 14 June 2022].

Statista (n.d.-b) *Restaurant-to-Consumer Delivery*, [online] Available from: https://www.statista.com/outlook/dmo/eservices/online-food-deliv ery/restaurant-to-consumer-delivery/south-africa [Accessed 14 June 2022].

Uber (2016) 'Driver deactivation d [p]olicy: Sub-Saharan Africa only', Uber, [Blog] September, Available from: https://www.uber.com/en-ZA/blog/ driver-deactivation-policy/ [Accessed 9 August 2020].

Uber B.V. and Others (Appellants) *v.* Aslam and others (2021) Judgement at the Supreme Court, given on 19 February, Available from: https://www. supremecourt.uk/cases/docs/uksc-2019-0029-judgment.pdf [Accessed 15 March 2021].

Vandaele, K. (2018) *Will Trade Unions Survive in the Platform Economy? Emerging Patterns of Platform Workers' Collective Voice and Representation in Europe*, Working Paper, Brussels: European Trade Union Institute.

Visser, J. (2012) 'The rise and fall of industrial unionism', *Transfer: European Review of Labour and Research*, 18(2): 129–41.

Webster, E. (2020) 'The uberisation of work: the challenge of regulating platform capitalism. A commentary', *International Review of Applied Economics*, 34(4): 512–21.

Webster, E. and Masikane, F. (2021) *I Just Want to Survive: A Comparative Study of Food Courier Delivery Workers in Three African Cities*, Johannesburg: Friedrich Ebert Stiftung and Southern Centre for Inequality Studies, University of the Witwatersrand.

Webster, E., Ludwig, C., Masikane, F. and Spooner, D. (2021) 'Beyond traditional trade unionism: innovative worker responses in three African cities', *Globalisations*, 18(8): 1363–76.

6

Crossing the Divide: Informal Workers and Trade Unions

With Carmen Ludwig

In the preceding chapters we have identified four trends within the labour movement. First is the ongoing marginalisation through the process of informalisation, where unions face a further loss of members, resources and relevance. Second is dualisation, where unions defend existing strongholds and focus on those workers in stable jobs while neglecting the majority of precarious workers. Third, we showed how precarious workers are at the centre of accumulation strategies in the factories east of Johannesburg, where new collective worker struggles are emerging. However, these workers are being 'remade' as precarious workers and are not being organised by a traditional trade union but rather by an NGO. We call this substitutionism, as it describes a scenario where unions are no longer the only actors and other organisations such as NGOs, social movements and cooperatives fill the vacuum by providing specific services. In Chapter 5 we introduced another example of substitutionism: we identified the emergence of a new type of worker in the platform economy and hybrid forms of organisation being created in that arena. In this chapter we identify a fourth trend, one in which traditional unions successfully revitalise by crossing the divide and organising the new workers emerging in the informal economy.

The chapter grew out of our involvement in the TUiT project, designed to examine how unions change, innovate and pursue new strategies to face twenty-first-century capitalism. It was initiated by the FES in 2018 and was aimed at shifting the narrative on trade unions as 'victims of globalisation', and instead highlighting that they 'do have agency and power' (Herberg, 2018: 6). The project identified successful examples of how 'labour can and already does shape globalization'; this included three examples of crossing the divide between the formal and informal in Africa – Ugandan transport workers, Kenyan security guards and Nigerian textile workers (Herberg, 2018: 6).

We have chosen the Ugandan transport union as the main case study as it demonstrates a successful example of union revitalisation in Africa.[1] The union has been substantially transformed from 5,000 paid-up members 15 years ago to become a hybrid organisation – something between a traditional trade union and an informal association of micro-businesses. It is now one of the largest transport unions in Africa, with nearly 100,000 members.

We will begin in Part I with a historical account of the role of trade unions and the distinctive nature of the African labour market. We turn in Part II to an examination of the move to cross the divide between formal and informal workers. In Part III we focus on ATGWU as an example of the successful integration of informal transport workers into what was a traditional union. We pay particular attention to digital organising through Union Apps.

Part I: The African labour market and trade union organisation

Historically, African trade unions were active in the anti-colonial struggles that led to independence (Freund, 1988). While being important actors, trade unions usually played the role of junior partners to political parties, without developing an autonomous social agenda outside and beyond the struggle for political independence. As discussed in Chapter 1, South Africa is an exception as the size of its industrial workforce and the outlawing of the liberation movement allowed an independent labour movement to emerge during the country's liberation struggle. With independence and the introduction of state-led projects, employment in the public sector expanded rapidly. During this phase formal union rights were often protected in theory, but in practice unions in many countries on the continent were subordinated to dominant parties, losing their autonomous capacity to intervene politically.

The phase of market regulation began in the late 1980s. Faced with widespread state indebtedness during the 1970s and 1980s, governments came under pressure from the international financial institutions – the World Bank and the International Monetary Fund (IMF) – to adjust their budgets in line with the neo-liberal orthodoxy of fiscal austerity. They saw unions as organisations 'that represent only a few workers, that they are irresponsible and unrepresentative, and that they stand in the way of the need to shift resources from the public to the private sector, which is assumed to be more productive' (Barya, 2010: 89). As a result, widespread job losses took place under structural adjustment programmes (SAPs) and most unions sought to disengage from the state–corporatist order which seemed to have lost its capacity to deliver. As trade unions began to resist retrenchments, cuts in wages, privatisation and the deterioration of social services, the labour movement emerged as a significant opponent of the one-party states that had come to characterise post-colonial Africa (Beckman et al, 2010).

At the time of the fall of the Berlin Wall in November 1989, 38 out of 45 sub-Saharan African states were governed by authoritarian civilian or military governments. Eighteen months later, half had been forced to commit themselves to multi-party elections and major limitations on executive powers, and some had actually held elections in which incumbent elites – mostly the old nationalist parties – were expelled from power (Decalo, 1992).

The evidence from country studies is that unions in Africa are rethinking their approach to politics, a shift in which unions rely less on their alliance with the ruling party – what could be called a political alliance – and focus more on building coalitions with other organisations in civil society, such as women's organisations, non-governmental organisations and informal economy organisations (Beckman et al, 2010).

During the phase of liberalisation and SAPs, economies were increasingly integrated into the global economy. The loss of control over prices and economic policy tools led to increased inequality and informality (Standing, 2011). The ILO estimates that 89.2 per cent of employment, including agriculture, in sub-Saharan Africa is informal. As shown in Chapter 1, informalisation is uneven across Africa – highest in western Africa (92.4 per cent) and lowest in southern Africa (40.2 per cent). In addition, the majority of Africa's population is young and better-educated than ever before.

Following Henry Bernstein (2007), Africa's labour market is best understood as divided into 'classes of labour' (discussed in Chapter 2 of this book). It is possible to identify five broad classes of labour, as illustrated in Figure 6.1.

With the exception of South Africa, a minority of workers are in formal wage employment – the SER – usually in the public sector. These jobs involve a degree of security through an employment contract, a regular wage, social protection in the form of benefits, and some form of workplace representation. It is what the ILO has come to call decent work (Webster et al, 2015).

Then there are what are called 'own account' or self-employed workers. The ILO estimates that 45 per cent are own account workers, 36.2 per cent are employees, 16.1 per cent are contributing family workers and 2.7 per cent are employers. Some authors have challenged labour statistics that show self-employment as the dominant employment status in the informal economy, as in their view notions of 'wage employment' and 'self-employment' do not capture the nature and variety of employment relations in developing countries. However, the new category of 'dependent contractors' introduced by the International Conference of Labour Statisticians in 2018 should enable a clearer distinction for these concepts (ILO, 2018a).

Figure 6.1: Fluid classes of labour

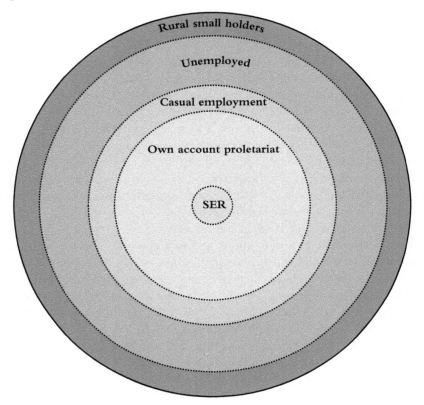

Source: Developed by Carmen Ludwig and Edward Webster.

Own account workers are usually workers involved in informal survival activities such as street traders, reclaimers or small enterprises making clothes or selling goods and services, often employing family members (Berner et al, 2012). These 'self-employed proletarians' engage in complex sets of employment relationships. For example, the workers found at the points where the buses congregate in Dar es Salaam,

> include many occupations – e.g. callers, supervisors, agents, loaders, sweepers, vendors, money-changers (often women, who have bags of small change which they sell for a fee to the conductor who needs change). There is also the *pigga setti* – a seat-warmer (the bus won't leave till it's full) and side-mirror menders. (Spooner, 2018: n.p.)

There are a significant number of workers in the cities involved in casual paid wage work, either temporary or part-time, sometimes paid in kind, and often employed by a third party such as an employment agency or labour broker.

This includes dependent contractors – usually people like Uber workers and other gig economy workers. This is not traditional wage employment but has some characteristics of wage employment because those in this category are dependent on the owners of, say, Uber.

Then there are the unemployed with little or no unemployment benefits as there are no welfare states in Africa, not even South Africa with its extensive system of social grants. The unemployed survive through retreating into their households where they share economic resources (Mosoetsa, 2011) or through various survivalist activities (Sefalafala, 2018). They create what can be called an informal security regime (Webster and Bhowmik, 2014: 14).

Finally, there are the peasants or smallholders based in agriculture, using mostly family labour and often dependent on remittances from household members who may spend their lives oscillating between town and countryside (Scully and Webster, 2019).

This ambiguity over class location raises difficult questions for union organisers. We have raised these questions in Chapter 2: Who is a worker?[2] Is a person who owns one minibus and drives it himself a worker? If she owns two minibuses and hires a person to drive the second one, what is she? If he owns 200 minibuses, what is he? Is a street trader a worker or an entrepreneur? This ambiguity has led to hybrid forms of organisation combining the function of a trade union (collective bargaining) with that of a cooperative (a jointly owned and democratically controlled enterprise) (Webster, 2011).

Part II: Organising in the informal economy

In recent times, in the face of growing informalisation, significant initiatives have been made to organise workers in the informal economy. The pioneer in this field is the formidable Ela Bhatt and the Self-Employed Women's Association of India (SEWA). Formed in 1972 by Bhatt, SEWA grew out of her work with women in the Textile Labour Association (TLA), a union founded by Mohandas Gandhi in the 1920s. Trained as a lawyer and brought up in the Gandhian tradition, Ela Bhatt extended the traditional notion of worker solidarity to a new type of work and worker – the self-employed women in the informal economy.

In the course of her legal work, Bhatt began to realise that the work being done by the wives of the textile workers was not only unpaid domestic work; these women were also performing crucial economic activities such as street vending, embroidering from home, recycling and various labour services. These activities were not only crucial for household income, they were also a major contribution to India's GDP. This became clearer when the TLA asked her to set up a women's department inside the union. She discovered that the women did not need counselling on how to run their households; instead, they needed help in defending their interests as paid workers because they were not protected by any of the labour laws (Bhatt, interview 2010).

Instead of bargaining collectively with an employer, SEWA empowers women economically in the informal economy by bringing together those who own their labour power. To meet the needs of the self-employed, SEWA developed a new type of trade unionism. This combines the trade union notion of collective bargaining with the central idea behind worker cooperatives – that of collective work. To achieve this goal, SEWA has broadened the reach of the union to meet the needs of worker-members as a totality, not simply as producers of goods and services, by creating child-care facilities, credit facilities (including the SEWA Bank) and a range of social security benefits. Their power lies in their collective strength, built through organising ordinary working women at the grassroots level (Webster, 2011).

Initially, SEWA's claim to be a union was rejected, as their members were not seen as workers because they were self-employed.

> When I am asked what the most difficult part of SEWA's journey has been, I can answer without hesitation: removing conceptual blocks. ... The Registrar of Trade Unions would not consider us 'workers'; hence, we could not register as a 'trade union'. ... Without an employer, you cannot be classified as a worker, and since you are not a worker, you cannot form a trade union. Our struggle to be recognised as a national trade union continued until we succeeded in 2007. (Bhatt, in Webster, 2011: 107)

The growing interest in organising informal workers in India has led to two different organisational strategies. On the one hand, there are the attempts by established left unions to extend traditional forms of representation through class politics and political trade unionism. On the other hand, there is the pioneering role played by SEWA in recognising that informal workers are different and require a different form of representation and mobilisation. At one level this involves broadening the role of the union to include a range of new functions such as access to micro-credit and training in entrepreneurship. Established trade unions remain sceptical of this attempt to reconfigure trade unionism and see it as 'depoliticising'. In particular, they are critical of this approach as they feel it is compatible with 'the neo-liberal prescription that the State should hand over many (welfare) functions to NGOs and civil society' (Gillan, 2010: 14).

Types of informal worker associations

Today there are increasing numbers of national and international union organisations that support organising initiatives by informal workers. Bonner and Spooner (2011) discuss an increased interest by the International Trade Union Confederation (ITUC) and other GUFs in organising informal workers, and the growing number of informal workers' associations. They identify three types of such associations: the first type consists of self-organised associations; the second type are traditional unions reaching out and recruiting informal workers; and the third type are conceived and sponsored by external actors like women's organisations, migrant workers' organisations and NGOs (Bonner and Spooner, 2011).

To assess the extent to which informal workers are willing to cooperate with unions, or even to join them as members or affiliates, an extensive survey was conducted in Kenya, Benin, Senegal and Zambia (Traub-Merz, 2020). The study found that although the informal labour force had a low level of awareness of trade unions, those who were aware of unions had a 'fairly positive perception of their role' (Traub-Merz, 2020: 1). Importantly, Traub-Merz found that the informally employed are already organised, but not into trade unions. Instead, around half of the informally employed are 'members of various types of organisations, of which savings clubs, religious associations and cooperatives (including credit unions) are most prominent' (Traub-Merz, 2020: 2). To offset 'overoptimistic' expectations, the article argues for 'strategic recruitment' where 'unions decide beforehand which sectors to focus on, which types of organisation to consider and which form of employment to address' (Traub-Merz, 2020: 3). Such an approach would focus on 'economic sectors in which organising activities by both trade unions and informal sector organisations are ongoing' (Traub-Merz, 2020: 4).

However, organising in the informal economy faces a number of difficulties; this emerged from a study of organising informal workers in South Africa, India and Ghana (Webster et al, 2017). The heterogeneity of circumstances and needs of urban informal workers points to the variations in their organising strategies. It is clear that for some informal workers, collective organising efforts are unlikely to succeed, and for them the only forms of agency possible are individualised resistance, coping strategies or endurance.

Riisgaard (2022) concludes her study of attempts at organising informal workers in Kenya and Tanzania by identifying two competing institutional models. The model favoured by the trade union movement wants to 'extend membership to people in the informal economy so that they can be represented via existing structures and participate in social dialogue, in particular about how to transition into formality' (Riisgaard, 2022: 213). The second model, she suggests, 'seeks to transform the existing tripartite structure to a 3+1 model in order to enable people in the informal economy to represent themselves on an equal but separate footing with formal enterprises and workers' (Riisgaard, 2022: 213). Riisgaard (2022: 213) goes on to suggest that this approach, promoted by WIEGO, 'questions whether the vision of full formalisation is possible and instead emphasises approaches that allow for participation of people working in the informal economy (in their own right) in policy design and implementation'.

Trade unions in transformation

What emerged from the FES's Trade Unions in Transformation project is that major changes in traditional trade unions are necessary if unions are to serve the organisational needs of informal workers. For example, the National Union of Textile, Garment and Tailoring Workers of Nigeria (NUTGTWN) lost 40,000 members between 2000 and 2016 in the face of massive retrenchments in the textile industry as a result of intensified international competition. It turned to the traditional self-employed tailors to try to unite the sector around common interests – the need for cheap electricity and water, and regulation of foreign imports (Andrea and Beckman, 2010). The union also adapted its structures, developed specific training and focused on the problems of self-employed tailors in order to unify the textile workers and regain strength (Bello, 2017). It focused on the professional development of tailors, including seminars on new trends in fashions and financial literacy (Herberg, 2018: 23). Above all, the union gave priority to education and capacity development for female members as a way of promoting women's participation in the union. They amended their constitution to increase women's involvement in leadership structures at all levels of the union, aiming at a target of 40 per cent women representation (Bello, 2017: 15).

The tailors had developed their own associations, in particular the Nigeria Union of Tailors (NUT). However, it lacked political influence, especially for the smaller tailors. Showing a union membership card diminished police harassment significantly (Andrea and Beckman, 2010: 91–3). This allowed the associations and the unions to recruit thousands of self-employed tailors countrywide (Bello, 2017). The renewed membership was based on a series of capacity-training sessions and soft skills development. This was complemented by participation in international platforms with the South African Clothing and Textile Workers Union (SACTWU), the United Nations Industrial Development Organization (UNIDO), IndustriALL and StreetNet International. However, the most successful example of union revitalisation was in the transport sector in Uganda. We turn now to our Ugandan case study.

Part III: Building organisation and challenging tech companies through union apps

The shift to market regulation discussed earlier had a major effect on the labour movement in Uganda (Barya, 2010: 101). The neo-liberal economic policies 'involved SAPs, cuts in public expenditure (except for the coercive arms of the state), dismantling price controls, retrenchment of public servants and privatisation of public enterprises, leading to massive redundancies, wage cuts for existing staff and the widespread casualisation of labour' (Barya, 2010: 101). According to the Ugandan Bureau of Statistics (UBS), by 2003 only 2 per cent of the entire workforce in Uganda had permanent employment in the private sector (UBS, cited in Barya, 2010: 101). The bulk of the population were self-employed (59.2 per cent) or were unpaid family workers (26.1 per cent). By 2006, 117 public enterprises had been privatised, leading to massive redundancies with temporary and casual workers dominating the employer–employee relationship (Barya, 2010: 102). 'In short', Barya (2010: 103) concludes, 'liberalization and privatization have not brought any tangible benefits to workers. Rather, they have resulted in the casualization of labour and the violation of workers' basic rights while at the same time not necessarily increasing employment opportunities.'

The Amalgamated Transport and General Workers' Union: organising informal transport

Founded in 1938 in Kampala, the Uganda's Amalgamated Transport and General Workers' Union faced a near collapse of membership in the 1980s when liberalisation undermined the public transport sector through the introduction of structural adjustment programmes and privatisation. This led to the informalisation of transport and the emergence of mini-taxi drivers and motorcycle taxi riders (known locally as boda boda). In Kampala alone about 250,000 boda boda riders form part of the transport sector. The ATGWU made the strategic decision to organise the growing number of boda boda drivers.

The decision was influenced by the launch in 2013 of an informal transport workers project by the International Transport Workers' Federation (ITF) and their willingness to assist ATGWU to organise informal workers (Spooner and Mwanika, 2018). A crucial feature of these workers was that they were already organised, not into a trade union but through credit and savings cooperatives, informal self-help groups, community-based organisations and, most importantly, associations. ATGWU did not try to recruit individual informal workers but undertook a process of discussions with these associations, eventually affiliating each association as a whole into the union (Spooner and Mwanika, 2018). The union had to find new ways to respond to informal workers whose status and identity ranged between being a worker, self-employed or a small business holder (Webster et al, 2021: 6). A female informal driver explains her work experience in these terms:

'I am a taxi driver, a minibus of 14 car seaters. I drive for the whole day, from Monday to Friday. The boss, who works for an insurance company, owns the minibus. ... On Saturdays, I drive a boda boda to make some extra money. I also own a minibus taxi on a loan. I have a driver for the taxi, a fellow colleague that I am employing.' (ATGWU member, interview 2019)

The unionisation of the boda boda drivers had a dramatic impact – a reduction in police harassment, substantial gains through collective bargaining, reduced internal conflict within the associations, and improvement of visibility and status of informal transport workers (Spooner and Mwanika, 2018).

'When the BRT [Bus Rapid Transit Project][3] came, they were throwing us out of the city centre. And the union stood and said no, we will need time to sensitise our members to be able to operate the buses. Bring the buses, but it is our members to operate the buses. And it was tough; I saw how the union stood for us; this would not have happened if it was us alone. The city authorities are now listening to us.' (ATGWU Member, 2019)

The rapid growth of the ATGWU from 5,000 members to over 100,000 members in just over five years raised new challenges for the union. This new large, fully integrated formal–informal organisation needed to learn how to reform its democratic processes and accountability, and how to maintain solidarity between informal and formal workers (Webster et al, 2021). This demanded considerable structural and procedural change within the union.

With much debate and discussion, both within and between the associations and the union, the structures were adjusted to ensure that the informal workers were included in the governance and management of the union itself. ... As a consequence, the 2018 ATGWU Congress agreed to drop the terminology distinguishing between 'informal' and 'formal' workers, and instead simply refer to 'workers' and 'members' throughout the union's activities, irrespective of employment relationships. It also agreed to move from payments of affiliation fees from the associations towards individual dues payments and [to] ensure that all members have the right to directly stand for election to ATGWU positions. Congress elections resulted in equal informal–formal representation on the union's National Executive Board. (Webster et al, 2021: 7)

A further, unexpected challenge was the entrance of multinational platform companies such as Uber, the Dutch-based company SafeBoda and Taxify in Kampala, threatening the livelihoods of informal public transport operators.

In order to use these apps, riders had to get into significant debt to afford acquiring a rider's permit, phones or a bike through a loan.

'It created a vicious circle of deteriorating working conditions and increased the poverty level of these workers. During the lockdown one or two riders even set themselves ablaze because things were so bad. Once you are captured in the vicious circle you cannot pull yourself out. The pressure, mental problems, accidents are increasing and most have families. The incentive that Uber has promised has not been realised by workers.' (ATGWU Representative, 2021)

Rising to the challenge: developing digital apps

The innovative response of ATGWU to this challenge was the adoption of digital applications as tools to provide service to informal workers, which is an example of unions appropriating digital technology to empower their members (Barrett, 2018). As the ATGWU Representative (2021) explains, it was the boda boda drivers who initially pushed the union towards using digital tools in order to solve the issue of collecting union dues and to build a membership data base through mobile phone applications. In the process, members raised the issue that a digital tool was also needed to connect drivers with passengers as an alternative to exploitation through the multinational platform companies.

One of the associations that joined ATGWU was the Kampala Metropolitan Boda Boda Entrepreneurs (KAMBE), with a membership of 64,000 (Manga et al, 2020: 4). The leadership of the union noticed that some of the association's members had begun to join new market entrants' digital platforms and that there was a growing interest among the boda boda drivers to use such technology (Manga et al, 2020: 6). In 2017, the AGTWU concluded that it needed to support KAMBE in developing its own app, which should serve multiple purposes like the collection of membership dues, developing and maintaining a database, a hailing function and a chat room.

The challenge for the union was to acquire external resources, which it received from the FES. This provided ATGWU with a safe base from which to "venture into the unknown" (ATGWU Representative, 2021). ATGWU also had to find a developer who was interested in developing a software application (app) together with workers, in order to also build the capacity of the association. After a few setbacks, including the temporary poaching of those workers who were involved in the project by SafeBoda and Uber and delays because of the COVID-19 pandemic, the union was finally successful in setting up two applications, which are both in operation.[4]

The first is the KAMBE app, which aims to serve members by facilitating the collection of union dues, managing a members' database and enabling communication among members. Only members of the association and ATGWU have access to the app and to other benefits such as loan facilities and insurance schemes.

The second is the SOT Boda App, which is purely a ride-hailing app. It was developed together with another association in the union, called the SAGULA Online Transporters Association. It can be used by all riders, independently of membership in the union.

The developers are currently in the process of customising the app for a range of prices depending on distance, so that passengers pay a competitive fare compared to the other providers. In contrast to the other providers, riders only pay a small, fixed amount per day to use the SOT Boda App. That way, the main income remains with the drivers. The app was launched in September 2020, and first experiences in its pilot phase are encouraging as the number of riders and passengers using the app are rising. This reflects the initial positive response by riders in a survey conducted in 2019 in Uganda, which showed that respondents overwhelmingly concurred that a riders' own app would be a better option for them than using the other platforms. The survey also revealed the reasons why the majority favoured a union app: improved passenger services, and safety for drivers and passengers (Manga et al, 2020: 4–5).

ATGWU relies on its members to advertise the SOT Boda App because of a lack of money for advertising:

'Drivers are using the current marketing and advertising strategy of the companies Uber and SafeBoda to promote their own app. As the driver is riding this passenger, which he got through Uber or SafeBoda, he tells the passenger: "Next time you want me, please use this application because this is ours." And the riders wear branded reflector jackets and helmets of SOT Boda. That way they are entering and chipping slowly the market share of this established companies without it being overly known.' (ATGWU Representative, 2021)

ATGWU regards both digital tools as an integral part of their organising strategy. Organisers, called 'ambassadors', are trained to inform boda boda riders about the advantages and the functions of the SOT Boda App.

'The idea is that the SOT Boda team is for recruiting riders. Once they get in there, we have organisers to talk to them about the need to be in a collective unit. Those that are willing to join become KAMBE members, where they directly benefit from more services than the ones that are only on SOT Boda.' (ATGWU Representative, 2021)

The hailing app has two functions: one that aims to generate business for riders on fair conditions, and the other a non-for-profit function for KAMBE members. These two functions are separated to ensure the data protection of members, but also to reflect the different roles of the associations and the union. It therefore mirrors the 'hybrid' nature of a union with a large membership of informal workers (Webster et al, 2021).

> 'As associations they have to deal with rider aims and objectives that go beyond the remit of a union. The union is engaging with its affiliates and ensures that the affiliates are able to respond to the needs of their members – without the union changing its posture to being a business entity. ... The associations are independent entities, registered and having their own constitutions with aims and objectives and they are not restricted from doing business. One of the key issues that brings them together is the socioeconomic empowerment of members. If that means undertaking such a business, they can. But as a union we are non-profit, we cannot. This is why we have two different apps.' (ATGWU Representative, 2021)

The different roles of the associations and the union also help to address the different identities of informal taxi and motorcycle drivers – as entrepreneurs, workers and union members.

The challenge remains that not all riders have the technical requirements to use the app. It was discovered, for example, that the app cannot operate on the cheaper smartphone imports from China, which are widely used in Uganda. The rider survey also demonstrated that only 40 per cent of respondents own a smartphone. Other obstacles, according to survey respondents, included not knowing how to use the platform applications, Wi-Fi connectivity and lack of equipment such as high-visibility vests and passenger helmets (Manga et al, 2020: 6).

> 'We have linked up with another local bank to do an affirmative action for workers to access loans to procure helmet, reflector jacket and a smartphone that can handle the app. We have also employed an IT person who is working with the developer to train the ten ambassadors on the functionality of the app.' (ATGWU Representative, 2021)

The ITF response to digitalisation: building union power

The initiative to start organising informal workers and to create their own applications came from ATGWU itself (Spooner and Mwanika, 2018). The ATGWU Representative (2021) explains their main motivation: "If you work in the informal sector, you need to be very flexible and you need to be responsive to workers' demands. If you are not moving with them, they will abandon you".

The ITF has about 700 affiliated trade unions from 150 countries representing about 20 million workers in the transport sector (ITF, n.d.). The support by ITF was primarily aimed at strengthening associational power, not only of its affiliate but within the transport sector as a whole. Associational power refers to the collective strength of workers which is grounded in organisation. It refers to unions' membership and participation, their infrastructural resources, conceptual tools and knowledge, and the capacity to 'optimize their structures so that associational action can be reconciled with the underlying structural conditions and the interests of the members' (Schmalz et al, 2018: 120).

ITF supported its affiliate in Uganda with research, capacity-building workshops and resources at a time when ATGWU was facing decline (Spooner and Mwanika, 2018: 6). The idea of building alliances and working with informal economy associations in the transport sector dates back to the ITF Congress in 2010 (Spooner and Mwanika, 2018: 13). It was the ITFs Education Department that initiated the Informal Workers Project but, as Spooner and Mwanika (2018: 13) argue, it was to some extent 'under the radar' and 'not in the mainstream of priority strategic campaigns' until ATGWU presented their successful model to a 2016 global conference of the Road and Rail Sections of the ITF in Brussels. A resolution was passed at the 2018 ITF Congress, which stated that the Federation would make renewed efforts to bring workers who are in the informal economy into the formal economy, including activities around gig work (ITF Representative 1, 2021).

On the gig economy, ITF's general approach is to develop research, policy frameworks (including model collective agreements) and campaigns. An example for ITF's campaigns is the Rights4Riders network.[5] ITF draws on the experiences of its affiliates but also links up with other global union federations to develop demands in a cross-sectorial perspective.

> 'What ITF can do, given that the global situation varies, is to bring together these contexts, share information, experiences and best practice, provide a platform for affiliates to do this, provide some expert opinion around some of these issues and put all of these ingredients together in order to allow affiliates to develop their own perspectives, which are locally tailored.' (ITF Representative 1, 2021)

When ATGWU started to develop its own applications, the ITF provided advice and support by drawing on its networks such as the FES, by initiating a process of knowledge transfer and sharing in the Federation. The organising app can be adapted to the needs of other unions – a process supported by the ITF (ITF Representative 3, 2021).

'ITF is helping in conducting research because we also discovered that building knowledge is very critical in this area. And then, of course, bringing the different affiliates together for learning and experience is important. Unions in Kenya also want to embark on the journey of developing their applications.' (ATGWU Representative, 2021)

This encouraged experimentation with new ways of building organisation and with digital organising. At the same time, challenging the extensive resources of the tech giants through worker-driven ride-hailing apps remains a major task and entails risks.[6] It is very difficult to achieve competitiveness, and the danger exists that unions might 'spread their resources too thin' in the process (ITF Representative 3, 2021). As an ITF representative explains:

'We have looked at the apps in general with an open-minded and a positive view but also recognising that so much of the way that these companies work is by generating the network effect to find the efficiency and the economies of scale. That is very hard to achieve for a grassroots, alternative, worker-created app that does not have billions of dollars in investment capital behind it to subsidise its operations. It is a very asymmetrical response.' (ITF Representative 2, 2021)

For the ATGWU representative, the need to find innovative ways of responding to the needs of workers in the gig economy is crucial. "As organised labour, we need to stand up and be the voice of these workers if we are to remain as a relevant social change agency" (ATGWU Representative, 2021).

Conclusion: Crossing the divide

In this chapter, we have focused on the strategic choices being exercised by the labour movement in organising informal workers.

The ATGWU made the strategic decision to organise the large numbers of informal taxi and motorcycle drivers by affiliating their already existing informal associations, thus revitalising the union. The union adopted digital tools to provide services to empower their new members and to challenge the exploitation of the multinational platform companies. Together with its associations, the ATGWU managed to develop two apps, which are both in operation and an integral part of the union's organising strategy.

Riisgaard (2022) distinguishes between two competing institutional models in the representation of informal workers. The example of the ATGWU shows that there could be a third way, one in which these two approaches are not necessarily in conflict with each other but could be combined. Central to the ATWGU's strategy has been the direct involvement of informal workers in the process of developing new approaches to organising and representation beyond established routines. In order to represent the interests of informal workers, the union had to be very flexible, also in adopting its structures.

Importantly, where trade unions have taken up the issues of informal workers, unions have also undergone fundamental changes. They often become 'hybrid' organisations, which include different forms of organisations and blur the distinction between traditional unionism, informal workers' associations and cooperatives. An understanding of these new forms of organisation must be at the centre of any attempt to understand an emerging global labour movement.

We turn now in Chapter 7 to examining how to build (global) union power and the possibilities of transnational activism.

Notes

[1] The Ugandan case study is drawn from joint work with Dave Spooner in two separate papers: Webster et al (2021) and Webster and Ludwig (2023).

[2] As Riisgaard (2022: 212) argues, it is 'also a struggle over defining and delimiting who the working class is and, crucially, who should be able to legitimately claim workers' rights'.

[3] BRT is a public transport system designed to improve capacity and reliability while decreasing congestion and pollution. In particular in the Global South, major cities are encouraged by the World Bank and national governments to adopt BRT, raising questions on its political, social and economic design. In Uganda, ATGWU was successful in negotiating conditions in the BRT implementation process (Spooner, 2019).

[4] There is a third application for taxi drivers at the Entebbe Airport, which received approval from the management of the Civil Aviation Authority in January 2020. The app is a response by the Entebbe's Airport Taxi Services Cooperative Society, an association affiliated to ATGWU, to the increasing competition from Uber at the airport (Manga et al, 2020: 6). However, because of the shutdown of the airport during the COVID-19 pandemic, its operation has been delayed.

[5] The campaign was launched in the lead-up to Deliveroo's initial public offering (IPO) in April 2021 around common demands and as a way to amplify organising efforts by members of the network, which includes ITF-affiliated unions and newer grassroots unions (Rights4Riders, n.d.).

[6] Experiences in Colombia demonstrate that the process of creating union apps is challenging given the start-up capital necessary to develop and maintain apps. Small and medium enterprises have struggled to compete with transnational digital platforms (Velez, 2020). Rappi Inc. workers – who work for one of the most valuable digital platform companies in Latin America – joined the National Movement of Digital Platform Workers. As part of the movement, they founded the Unión de Trabajadores de Plataformas (UNIDAPP) to coordinate strike actions with other food delivery organisations across Latin America. It appears that UNIDAPP could not compete, and the workers app has been abandoned.

Interviews

ATGWU Member, Johannesburg, 24 March 2019.
ATGWU Representative, online, 3 May 2021.
Ela Bhatt, Founder of SEWA, Ahmedabad, 5 December 2010.

ITF Representative 1 and 2, focus group, online, 21 June 2021.
ITF Representative 3, online, 1 July 2021.

References

Andrea, A. and Beckman, B. (2010) 'Alliances across the formal–informal divide: South African debates and Nigerian experience', in I. Lindell (ed.) *Africa's Informal Workers*, London: Zed Books, pp 85–98.

Barya, J.-J. (2010) 'Trade unions, liberalisation and politics in Uganda', in B. Beckman, S. Buhlungu and L. Sachikonye (eds) *Trade Unions and Party Politics: Labour Movements in Africa*, Cape Town: HSRC Press, pp 85–107.

Beckman, B., Buhlungu, S. and Sachikonye, L. (eds) (2010) *Trade Unions and Party Politics: Labour Movements in Africa*, Cape Town: HSRC Press.

Bello, J. (2017) *A Case Study of the National Union of Textile, Garment and Tailoring Worker Organisation*, Berlin: Friedrich Ebert Stiftung.

Berner, E., Gomez, G. and Knorringa, P. (2012) 'Helping a large number of people become a little less poor: the logic of survival entrepreneurs', *The European Journal of Development Research*, 24(3): 382–96.

Bernstein, H. (2007) 'Capital and labour from centre to margins'. Paper prepared for the 'Living on the Margins' Conference, 26–28 March, Stellenbosch, South Africa.

Barrett, J. (2018) *Mobile Money for Member Dues: Can Technology Transform Worker Organization?*, Berlin: Friedrich Ebert Stiftung and WIEGO.

Bonner, C. and Spooner, D. (2011) 'Organising in the informal economy: a challenge for trade unions', *Internationale Politik und Gesellschaft*, 2: 87–105.

Decalo, S. (1992) 'The process, prospects and constraints of democratisation in Africa', *African Affairs*, 91(362): 7–35.

Freund, B. (1988) *The African Worker*, Cambridge: Cambridge University Press.

Gadgil, M. and Samson, M. (2017) 'Hybrid organisations, complex politics: when unions form cooperatives', in E. Webster, A.O. Britwum and S. Bhowmik (eds) *Crossing the Divide. Precarious Work and the Future of Labour*, Pietermaritzburg: University of KwaZulu-Natal Press, pp 143–64.

Gillan, M. (2010) 'Trade unions and the political representation of unorganised workers in India', Paper presented to the Labour Movements Research Committee (RC44), International Sociological Association 17th World Congress of Sociology, 11–17 July, Gothenburg, Sweden.

Herberg, M. (ed.) (2018) *Trade Unions in Transformation: Success Stories from All Over the World*, Bonn: Friedrich Ebert Stiftung.

International Labour Organization (ILO) (2018a) 'Resolution Concerning Statistics on Work Relationships', 20th International Conference on Labour Statisticians, Geneva, 10–19 October 2018.

International Labour Organization (ILO) (2018b) *Women and Men in the Informal Economy: A Statistical Picture*, 3rd edn, Geneva: ILO, [online] Available from: https://www.ilo.org/wcmsp5/groups/public/---dgreports/---dcomm/documents/publication/wcms_626831.pdf [Accessed 17 June 2022].

International Transport Workers' Federation (ITF) (n.d.) 'Who we are', [online] Available from: https://www.itfglobal.org/en/about-us/who-we-are [Accessed 15 June 2022).

Manga, E., Hamilton, P. and Kisingu, S. (2020) *Riding on a Union App: Uganda's Public Transport Workers' Digital Response to Platforms*, Berlin: Friedrich Ebert Stiftung.

Mosoetsa S. (2011) *Eating from One Pot: The Dynamics of Survival in Poor South African Households*, Johannesburg: Wits University Press.

Rights4Riders (n.d.) 'Stop Deliveroo's pandemic profiteering', [online] Available from: https://www.rights4riders.org [Accessed 15 June 2022].

Riisgaard, L. (2022) 'What is a worker? framing people in the informal economy as part of the trade union constituency in Kenya and Tanzania', *Global Labour Journal*, 13(2): 209–28.

Schmalz, S., Ludwig, C. and Webster, E. (2018) 'The power resources approach: developments and challenges', *Global Labour Journal*, 9(2): 113–34.

Schmalz, S., Ludwig, C. and Webster, E. (2019) 'Power resources and global capitalism', *Global Labour Journal*, 10(1): 84–90.

Scully, B. and Webster, E. (2019) 'The countryside and capitalism: rethinking the cheap labour thesis in post-apartheid South Africa', in J. Reynolds, B. Fine and R. van Niekerk (eds) *Race, Class and the Post-Apartheid Democratic State*, Pietermaritzburg: University of KwaZulu-Natal Press, pp 20–37.

Sefalafala, T. (2018) Experiences of unemployment, the meaning of wage work: the dilemma of wage work among ex-gold mineworkers in the Free State goldfields, Unpublished doctoral thesis, University of the Witwatersrand, Johannesburg.

Spooner, D. (2018) 'Presentation made to the "Crossing the Divide" Workshop on Innovative Organising in Public Transport', 21–23 November 2018, University of the Witwatersrand, South Africa.

Spooner, D. (2019) *Bus Rapid Transit (BRT) and the Formalisation of Informal Public Transport: A Trade Union Negotiating Guide*, London: ITF.

Spooner, D. and Mwanika, J.M. (2018) 'Transforming transport unions through mass organisation of informal workers: a case study of the ATGWU in Uganda', *Global Labour Journal*, 9(2): 150–66.

Standing, G. (2011) *The Precariat: The New Dangerous Class*, London: Bloomsbury.

Traub-Merz, R. (2020) 'The interest of informal labour', in *Trade Unions: Findings from Representative Country Surveys in Sub-Saharan Africa*, Bonn: Friedrich Ebert Stiftung.

Velez, V.O. (2020) *Not a Fairy Tale: Unicorns and Social Protection of Gig Workers in Colombia*, Southern Centre for Inequality Studies (SCIS) Working Paper 7, Johannesburg: University of Witwatersrand.

Webster, E. (2011) 'Organising in the informal economy: Ela Bhatt and the Self-Employed Women's Association of India', *Labour, Capital and Society*, 44(1): 99–125.

Webster, E. and Bhowmik, S. (2014) 'Work, livelihoods and insecurity in the South: a conceptual introduction', in K. Fakier and E. Emke (eds) *Socio-Economic Insecurity in Emerging Economies: Building New Spaces*, London: Routledge/Earthscan, pp 1–18.

Webster, E. and Ludwig, C. (2023) 'Contesting digital technology through new forms of transnational activism', *Global Labour Journal*, 14(1): 56–71.

Webster, E., Budlender, D. and Orkin, M. (2015) 'Developing a diagnostic tool and policy instrument for the realisation of decent work', *International Labour Review*, 154(2): 3–28.

Webster, E., Britwum, A. and Bhowmik, S. (2017) *Crossing the Divide; Precarious Work and the Future of Labour*, Pietermaritzburg: University of KwaZulu-Natal Press.

Webster, E., Ludwig, C., Spooner, D. and Masikane, F. (2021) 'Beyond traditional trade unionism: innovative worker responses in three African cities', *Globalizations*, 18(8): 1363–76.

7

Global Capital, Global Labour: The Possibilities of Transnational Activism

With Carmen Ludwig

We begin this chapter by focusing on how neo-liberal globalisation has undermined the post-war Keynesian consensus built around the notion of social dialogue and a tripartite social partnership between employers, government and labour. In its place global governance is increasingly privatised, driven by global corporations in pursuit of shareholder value (Bakan, 2020). We go on to examine, in Part I, a private for-profit corporation, BIA, that presents itself as providing a solution for the educational needs of low-income families in Kenya and Uganda through digital technology. Instead local unions found, with the assistance of their GUF Education International (EI), that digital technology was being used to de-professionalise teachers and to cut costs drastically. BIA achieves this goal by substituting qualified teachers with low-paid and under-qualified individuals who transmit scripted instructions to pupils through 'teacher-computers'. By openly advancing this form of low-fee, for-profit provision as an alternative to public schools, BIA represents a direct challenge to public education. Long neglected, we argue that global unions are emerging as players in this contest, helping to build counter power at both the local and global level. Through their intermediary coordinating role at the supranational level, global unions can deepen worker power.

A 'new corporation movement' has emerged, believing that by reimagining capitalism business can simultaneously pursue profit and bring prosperity and well-being to society as a whole (Henderson, 2020). Tech giants such as Uber, Amazon and Google have gained unprecedented levels of power. Their business model is based on a new form of algorithmic control where 'workers' are managed through online platforms, monitored indirectly and expected to produce measurable outputs (Tassinari and Maccarrone, 2020). As argued in Chapter 5, a global process of uberisation of work is taking place. This presents the labour movement with a challenge: on the one hand, it deepens the exploitation of labour on a global scale, while on the other hand, it is leading to opportunities for organisational innovation through new forms of transnational labour activism.

Drawing on the power resources approach, the chapter explores these opportunities through a case study of BIA, where technology has de-professionalised teachers in Kenya and Uganda and undermined education unions. By examining how digital technology changes the workplace and how it is appropriated by workers and their unions, as was the case in the previous chapter, we will demonstrate that the use of digital technology is increasingly contested and that trade unions have found innovative ways to respond to the challenge of new technologies.

The chapter draws on the research on BIA undertaken by EI, the Kenya National Union of Teachers (KNUT) and the Uganda National Teachers' Union (UNATU) (EI and KNUT, 2016; Riep and Machacek, 2016; Riep 2019). In 2021, three interviews with union leaders of EI, KNUT and UNATU were conducted by the authors on the role of the unions and the federation in the campaign.[1]

This chapter evaluates the extent to which global unions constitute, through their intermediary coordinating role at the supranational level, a source of power to challenge the global tech giants. We argue that global unions have played an important role in facilitating local unions' resistance to global corporations. A similar point is made by Fichter et al (2018: 7) when they conclude that '[t]oday's globalised world impacts workers and their unions ever more directly, so that the need for transnational cooperation in defending themselves at home, i.e. linking the local with the global, is growing. In some cases, local associational power is bolstered through the transnational resources provided by global unions.'

This combination of the local and the global has led to the emergence of what Sydney Tarrow (2005) calls 'rooted cosmopolitans'.[2] Rooted cosmopolitans, Tarrow suggests, are activists who think globally, but are linked to very real places. In his words: 'They move physically and cognitively outside their origins, but they continue to be linked to place, to the social networks that inhabit that space, and to the resources, experiences, and opportunities that place provides them with' (Tarrow, 2005: 42).

We take as our point of departure Joel Bakan's (2020) challenge to the 'new corporation movement'. 'CEO activism', writes Bakan (2020: 16), is part of a larger 'corporation movement' of business leaders proclaiming that 'it is time to remake the corporation and redefine its mission and mandate'. Bakan demonstrates how corporations are tapping into new markets while framing this as an engagement for the public good. This phenomenon is most developed in what Chuang and Shih call philanthrocapitalism.

> Philanthrocapitalism incorporates a deep, ideological commitment to market-based solutions to the world's problems. The assumption at its core is that the same techniques, management styles, and value systems that enable corporations to amass tremendous wealth can and should be used to correct the world's social problems. Rather than simply funding third-party initiatives, today's philanthrocapitalists create and manage ventures based on their own ideas of how to fix the world. They invest rather than give, and fully expect to see a return on their investment. (Chuang and Shih, 2021: 4)

Technology is regarded as an integral part of the solution to global problems. Bakan (2020: 91) cites business leaders who argue that 'technologies will substitute for government completely' and 'avoid all the crazy, dyslexic anomalies attached to being human'. According to this understanding, as Sun-ha Hong, an expert in artificial intelligence is quoted as saying, 'we need to get rid of human emotion, we need to get rid of human experience and discretion because they will get things wrong; that we need to rely instead on the more consistent, objective, and rational results of anonymous data and numbers' (cited in Bakan, 2020: 105).

While corporations have significantly increased profits, Bakan argues, the lives of the vast majority of people in the United States and around the world have become increasingly precarious. 'Over the last two decades', writes Bakan (2020: 4), 'workers' wages stagnated, inequality spiraled, public services – including health services – were shredded, good jobs and unions disappeared, and people worked harder for less pay and with less security (if they worked at all)'.

Bakan ends his book on a note of hope on the emergence of a counterforce with grassroots movements working side-by-side with elected officials, such as Bernie Sanders and Alexandria Ocasio-Cortez in the United States: 'Global resistance to corporate power and rule has surged over the last decade, an antidote to both the false hope of the "new" corporation and the growing sense of hopelessness pervasive in society' (Bakan, 2020: 5).

As we will demonstrate, global unions, long regarded as the Cinderella of labour research, have emerged as key players in the trade union movement, building countervailing power to global corporations (Croucher and Cotton, 2009). We draw on the PRA that has emerged as an organisational tool to rebuild labour. We distinguish between four union power resources: associational, structural, societal and institutional power (Chapter 1 of this book; see also Schmalz et al, 2018). The PRA and its relevance for the revitalisation of labour has also been the subject of an ongoing debate in the *Global Labour Journal*.[3] Several case studies demonstrate that innovative forms of organisation are emerging as workers identify and conceptualise new sources of power, but so far little attention has been paid to the global dimension of trade union action and its effect on workers' power (for exceptions see: Birelma, 2018; Fichter, 2018; Schmalz et al, 2021).

Fischer (2021) differentiates between two streams of research on transnational labour activism in global production networks. The first focuses on global structures of the trade union movement and on 'governance struggles' that aim at the transnational regulation of employment relations. The second stream centres on advocacy networks and campaigns with a 'broader political, social and environmental agenda' (Fischer 2021: 372) and on grassroots mobilisation and the recruitment of (non-unionised) workers. Our case studies on the International Transport Workers' Federation (ITF) in the previous chapter and on Education International in this chapter fall into this latter stream by examining two examples of how global unions are challenging the power of global corporations through a combination of local and global union activities.

In Part I we examine the effects of BIA's business model on education. In Part II we demonstrate how global labour, through EI, became a key driver of a campaign against the privatisation of education.

Part I: The McDonaldisation of education

Bridge International Academies is 'a flagship of creative capitalism', Shannon May, Bridge's cofounder, told Bakan (2020: 122). According to BIA, the for-profit company seeks to increase access to education for the poor, to make a contribution to local communities and to the realisation of Sustainable Development Goal 4 on education:

> When free public schools either do not exist or do not offer quality education, ethics of responsibility begs private actors to ensure that children have their right to education enabled through a mixed economy. At Bridge, we cannot stand by while children have either no school they can afford to attend, or only a school where they still cannot read after attending for 4 years. (BIA, 2017)

The BIA business model is designed to meet this demand by selling low-priced products to low-income people. 'We take lessons from global service providers, like McDonald's or Starbucks. We build to scale, we systematize, we standardize. We call this vertically integrated platform, our "Academy in a Box"', BIA co-founder Jay Kimmelman remarked in an interview (cited in Bakan, 2020: 122). The new digital technology is at the centre of this business model. As Kimmelman explained, the technology allows for 'word-for-word, action-by-action scripts delivered in real time to Android-based tablets' (cited in Bakan, 2020: 122).

Concerned about the impact of this 'McDonaldisation' of the learning process, the global union federation EI conducted studies in Kenya (EI and KNUT, 2016) and Uganda (Riep and Machacek, 2016), both countries in which BIA had expanded rapidly. EI's studies found that BIA services were of poor quality, inaccessible for the very poor and disadvantaged, and ultimately unaffordable for most families in the communities in which BIA operates (RESULTS, 2017; Riep, 2019: 7–9). Private companies like BIA represent a direct challenge to public education with this form of low-fee, for-profit provision being openly advanced as an alternative to public schools, often framed in the rhetoric of 'parental choice' (Zuilkowski et al, 2018).

EI's studies demonstrate that the 'teacher-computers' allow BIA to hire low-paid and often under-qualified individuals who transmit scripted instructions to pupils. In Kenya, more than 70 per cent of teachers were found to be insufficiently qualified (EI and KNUT, 2016: 23). 'Teacher-computers represent not only the company's most "innovative" and entrepreneurial effort towards education standardisation, calibration, and economies of scale, but also the most problematic, given that it has fundamentally altered the nature and practice of education itself' (Riep and Machacek, 2016: 25).

BIA teachers are forced to use a scripted curriculum developed in the United States instead of the local curriculum, which raises questions as to whether this approach constitutes a form of re-colonialisation of education in Africa through global capital. As teachers have to follow the lessons on the tablets, they have little or no autonomy to adapt to the learning needs of students or to influence teaching practices and the curriculum. Many teachers questioned the quality of the instructions and materials found on the 'teacher-computers'. At least 46.7 per cent of the teachers argued that following the scripted curriculum did not always work and that it was not effective for helping learners to understand target concepts (EI and KNUT, 2016: 35). Where teachers did not follow the tablet instructions, they usually had to hide this practice from BIA.

As a KNUT representative explained:

'The teachers never went to College, there were just people picked and trained for a few weeks. They were not allowed to teach the Kenyan Curriculum, they were receiving instructions from US early in the morning, through their tablets and that's what they are told to teach. And if you deviate from that teaching they deduct your salary for the day instantly and in most circumstances, teachers were sacked.' (KNUT Representative, 2021)

The representative of the Uganda National Teachers' Union also highlighted the missing interaction between teachers and students:

'A tablet is a tool that one can use in the teaching-learning-process. But this is where you are just being controlled. You are like a robot. Someone is doing the work somewhere and you are here pretending to be the one doing it, which is unfortunate.' (UNATU Representative, 2021)

The crucial point is that new digital technology is being used by BIA to de-professionalise teachers and to cut costs drastically by substituting qualified teachers with unqualified staff. Furthermore, the working conditions of teachers at BIA schools are characterised by low salaries, high workload, long hours, and a lack of job security and benefits. Accordingly, BIA teachers did not perceive their contracts as fair (EI and KNUT, 2016: 22–32).

This commodification of education takes different forms, with private companies being one relevant expression. It is expected that in the wake of the COVID-19 pandemic and the push for online learning, corporations including Google, Facebook and Apple will gain even more influence in the expanding education technology (EdTech) market in the future (Bakan, 2020: 124; Marachi and Carpenter, 2020; Williamson and Hogan, 2020).

In the view of EI, 'it depends a lot on how technologies are used. It's not inherently bad as long as they are used appropriately. But the way it is prescribed by Bridge, it de-professionalises and de-humanises teachers. ... We have also learned from the pandemic that technology cannot replace teachers' (EI Representative, 2021).

Part II: Challenging privatisation: the Global Response campaign

Founded in 1993, Education International is a global union federation that represents 32 million education personnel organised in 383 trade unions from 178 countries. At its 7th World Congress in 2015, the EI decided to initiate a campaign called 'Global Response in Opposition to the Commercialisation and Privatisation of Education'.[4] The aim of the campaign is to 'develop a global response strategy to ensure governments fulfil their obligation to free, quality public education and counter the influence of private actors in education, especially where their activities in education have a negative impact on access and exacerbates inequities within education systems' (EI, 2015).

An important starting point for the campaign is research that sheds light on the extent of privatisation in selected countries and the degree of involvement of private education companies. The aim is to assist the federation and its members to gain knowledge and to raise public awareness about the privatisation and commercialisation of education and its impact on national education systems. Furthermore, the research builds the base for the campaign strategy in each country. The campaigns combine global and local union advocacy activities. An EI representative from the Africa region described the strategy as follows:

'An important goal is to strengthen public education and to prevent the privatisation of education. ... In Africa, the campaign has already contributed a lot to the fight against the privatisation of education. Studies are first conducted in the different countries to better understand the events and contexts regarding the privatisation of education. Then campaigns are developed based on these findings.' (EI Representative, 2021)

The global union federation played an important role in building the capacity of local unions by facilitating the transfer of knowledge and mutual learning. A representative from KNUT told us that the campaign in Kenya first "started through cross-border solidarity" when EI organised meetings with other education unions in Liberia, Nigeria and Uganda to learn from their experiences (KNUT Representative, 2021).

In Kenya, KNUT sought to create awareness among union members and to 'organise from below'. The union used the annual general meetings of its 110 branches across the country to get school representatives and union members involved in the anti-privatisation campaign (see also Bascia and Stevenson, 2017: 18–23). The involvement of members also helped to locate Bridge schools. Parents and communities were informed that BIA is "not serving the needs of the poor" (KNUT Representative, 2021).[5] The union relied on parents from government schools who felt that the existence of BIA threatened the existence of these schools.

Both unions located the campaign in the broader picture of defending public education and to advocate for an increase in funding. As the representative from UNATU (2021) explains: "It was not only focusing on the fight against Bridge, but it was about looking at education as a whole and as a right, where children of school-going age should attain quality education".

In both countries, the campaign centrally included an engagement with members of parliaments and governments, whom the unions found to be responsive. In Kenya, the Minister of Education at the time started an inspection of the infrastructure of BIA schools, which mainly consists of "only corrugated metal sheets, with no windows and wire mesh" (KNUT Representative, 2021). Concerns about safety issues increased in 2019, when a non-BIA school with a similar infrastructure in Nairobi collapsed and killed at least seven children. In response, the government initiated an audit, which found that three quarters of BIA schools did not meet the safety and infrastructure standards (KNUT Representative, 2021). In Uganda and Kenya, BIA was also deemed an illegal operator by the courts following action by education authorities (Riep, 2019: 14). In Kenya, 26 of 45 BIA schools had to close (KNUT Representative, 2021). In Uganda, BIA has been prohibited from opening other schools in the country. It is not clear how many of the initially existing 63 schools are currently in operation; the UNATU representative regards their continued functioning as a violation of the court ruling and an illegal practice.

Both education unions share the opinion that the EI's campaign has made an important contribution to the fight against privatisation in their countries. It is the strength of global union federations like EI to reinforce the actions of the member organisations and to escalate these from a local to an international context. This reflects the fact that private education companies operate globally and that education financing is also partly steered through multilateral institutions. On the international level, the campaign was successful in creating sustained pressure on education corporations, governments and international financial institutions. As a stakeholder in multilateral institutions such as the Global Partnership for Education (GPE),[6] EI also had some institutional leverage to reinforce its demands.

As a result, in 2020 the World Bank's private sector arm, the International Financial Corporation (IFC), decided to freeze any investments in private for-profit K–12 schools.[7] In March 2022, the IFC exited its investment in NewGlobe Schools, Inc., the parent company of Bridge International Academies (IFC, 2022). The policy shift by the IFC was a major achievement, as the World Bank Group's private sector lending arm had promoted education and private providers as an important area for its investment policy. The IFC had invested more than US$10 million in BIA operations in Africa. EI welcomed the decision by the IFC and called on other investors to follow. The federation's General Secretary, David Edwards, commented: 'The World Bank is the largest funder of education in the developing world. Investing in private for-profit operators, such as Bridge International Academies, clearly contravenes the global commitment to inclusive and equitable quality free education for all consistent with Sustainable Development Goal (SDG) 4' (EI, 2022).

The World Bank has played a highly ambivalent role in its position towards school fees and private education institutions. While it promoted user fees in education through its structural adjustment policies in the 1980s and strengthened the role of private education institutions in the 1990s, it has now declared its commitment to free primary education, albeit in a rather weak form (RESULTS, 2017: 10–17).

The struggle against the privatisation of education is taking place in a contested terrain, where considerable vested interests are at stake.[8] Particularly relevant in the struggle against the commodification of education has been the global union federation's ability to draw on societal power by influencing the public discourse and by building alliances with civil society organisations. First, the federation was able to gain attention through issue-setting. The exposure of the negative effects of privatisation on education, and BIA's operating model in particular, received a high media response – on local and international levels. As with other brands, BIA's business model depends on a good public image – even more so when it comes to providing public goods.

Equally important, the struggle against commercialisation was located within the broader aim of promoting access to quality and free public education worldwide, highlighting it as an issue of equity and democracy. This provided a strong frame, which also resonated with other civil society organisations. The broader involvement of civil society organisations was important to build pressure. In 2018, the human rights organisation, the East African Centre for Human Rights (EACHRights), filed a complaint with the World Bank's Compliance Advisor to document grievances in BIA schools in Kenya, to which the World Bank responded by initiating further investigations (Adick, 2020: 273). Since 2015, civil society organisations have written an annual open letter to investors, donor agencies and the World Bank urging them to stop funding BIA. This included the Global Campaign for Education (GCE), an alliance where EI works together with civil society organisations. The letter to the World Bank and its donors in 2019, signed by 173 organisations, stated that '[w]e call on all donors and the World Bank Group itself to take a clear and principled position in support of free, publicly provided education and against the use of development aid to fund for-profit or commercial education' (Civil Society Organisations, 2019).

These initiatives were further supported through protest actions in front of the World Bank building and the worlds' largest education company and shareholder investor of BIA, Pearson's, which also involved civil society and EI member organisations internationally. As the EI representative explains:

'We have also mobilized other stakeholders, especially civil society partners, like members of the Global Campaign for Education in Africa or members of the regional network African Network Campaign on Education for All (ANCEFA). It is about bringing all these partners together and putting pressure on governments. There is a need to expose what is going wrong at the national and global level. There also needs to be global pressure on the World Bank, as the funder of BIA.' (EI Representative, 2021)

Conclusion: Global unions and power resources

We have shown in this chapter how EI and in the previous chapter how the ITF were able to mobilise power resources on a supranational scale in cases where local power resources were constrained or under threat.

These case studies demonstrate the capacity of global unions to act as intermediaries in broadening connections with different actors and strengthening power resources in support of joint campaigns. Although the power of global capital makes it a deeply unequal contest, the involvement of the global unions facilitated the development of unions' counter power. As Ford and Gillan (2021) argue, the power of global unions lies in their transnational character and their ability to connect different spatial levels of union action. They can therefore 'combine different kinds of power resources simultaneously at different scales' (Ford and Gillan, 2021: 4; see also Brookes, 2013; Schmalz et al, 2021).

By mobilising resources through the global campaign against privatisation of schools in Kenya and in Uganda, EI was able to draw on a global network of public support, what we have called societal power. By assisting in the development of an app in the national union discussed in Chapter 6, the ITF was deepening the union's associational power. In both cases, the global union federations initiated a process of generating and sharing knowledge among affiliates, which has been highlighted as particularly relevant in the view of local unions. Lévesque and Murray (2010) argue that the ability to learn and to diffuse learning throughout the organisation is crucial for union revitalisation and the mobilisation of power resources. In both cases, the involvement of global unions has added another layer to this capacity, that of *transnational learning*.

We suggest that global unions can reinforce, but not replace, activities of the local unions on the ground. It is therefore the specific interplay of local and global activities that is relevant to increasing union power. In both cases, the relevance of local unions to engage directly with their governments in order to fight privatisation and to promote the regulation of standards in both sectors was regarded as important.

However, the two cases discussed in Chapters 6 and 7 differ in three significant ways. First, the support provided by EI was important in resisting the privatisation of education, whereas the support of the ITF involved assistance in strengthening the capacity of the union to revitalise. Although they are both key labour issues, they involve quite different strategies and resources. A second difference lies in the ways in which these cases demonstrate the contradictory nature of the new technology. In the case of the education unions, they were resisting the abuse of the tablet by BIA and its use to undermine the union as part of its broader struggle against the privatisation of education. The Uganda case, on the other hand, demonstrates how the new digital technology is contested but also used to strengthen the union. A third difference lies in the relationship between the global and the local. In the case of BIA, the initiative came from EI as a global campaign against the privatisation of education. In the case of the transport sector in Uganda, the initiative to revitalise the union came from the local, from the national union, as an innovative response to its decline in the context of privatisation. They therefore represent two different relationships between the global and the local.

Above all, these two cases suggest that the emerging labour internationalism we identify in this chapter does not involve a choice between going global or remaining local; it requires that unions navigate between the local and the global.

We turn now to our concluding chapter, where we draw on our case studies to evaluate the future of labour in Africa, and the similarities and differences between South Africa and the rest of Africa.

Notes

[1] Due to the COVID-19 pandemic, the interviews had to be conducted virtually. Despite the limitations involved, this had no negative effects on the research process.

[2] A new type of regional network internationalism is emerging in sub-Saharan Africa (McGregor and Webster, 2021). The GLU and its Engage programme have contributed through training a new type of union organiser, one who understands the global context, but is rooted in the local community.

[3] Stefan Schmalz, Carmen Ludwig and Edward Webster (2018, 2019) contributed to this debate as guest editors of the Journal's special edition on Acquiring and Applying Power Resources (Volume 9, Issue 2, May 2018), which includes several case studies on the development and application of the PRA.

[4] The Global Response Campaign formed part of a larger global campaign run by the EI, the 'Unite for Quality Education Campaign'.

[5] According to BIA, the school model serves poor families who live on US$2 a day or less. Research findings demonstrate that the real costs for parents far exceeds the US$6 per month of school fees as claimed by BIA (Riep, 2019: 7–8).

[6] GPE is a multi-stakeholder platform that aims to strengthen education systems in developing countries by assisting governments, civil society organisations, education unions and the private sector. The World Bank Group is a partner, and supervises some of the GPE-funded projects.

[7] The United States term K–12 schools refers to the education system from early childhood education (kindergarten) until Grade 12.

[8] This is also reflected by the fact that BIA has been quick to respond to international criticism, particularly by civil society organisations, but also by the level of intimidation that researchers and trade unionists reported (Riep and Machacek, 2016; KNUT representative, interview, 2021).

Interviews

Education International (EI) Representative, Africa Region, online interview, 16 March 2021.

Kenya National Union of Teachers (KNUT) Representative, online interview, 20 April 2021.

Uganda National Teachers' Union (UNATU) Representative, online interview, 27 April 2021.

References

Adick, C. (2020) 'Globale bildungsallianzen in der internationalen bildungspolitik', in U. Binder and J. Oelkers (eds) *Das Ende der Politischen Ordnungsvorstellungen Des 20. Jahrhunderts*, Wiesbaden: Springer, pp 265–82.

Bakan, J. (2020) *The New Corporation. How 'Good' Corporations are Bad for Democracy*, New York: Vintage.

Bascia, N. and Stevenson, H. (2017) *Organising Teaching: Developing the Power of the Profession*, Brussels: Educational International.

Birelma, A. (2018) 'When local class unionism meets international solidarity: a case of union revitalisation in Turkey', *Global Labour Journal*, 9(2): 215–30.

Bridge International Academies (BIA) (2017) Letter in Response to the RESULTS Report, [online] Available from: https://www.bridgeinterna tionalacademies.com/wp-content/uploads/2017/08/Bridge-Response-to-RESULTS-Report-March-2017.pdf [Accessed 7 April 2021].

Brookes, M. (2013) 'Varieties of power in transnational labor alliances: an analysis of workers' structural, institutional, and coalitional power in the global economy', *Labor Studies Journal*, 38(3): 181–200.

Chuang, J. and Shih, E. (eds) (2021) *Philanthrocapitalism and Anti-trafficking*, London: Open Democracy.

Civil Society Organisations (2019) An Open Letter to the World Bank and its Donors, [online] October 2019, Available from: https://www-cdn. oxfam.org/s3fs-public/letter_world_bank_october_2019.pdf [Accessed 17 June 2022].

Croucher, R. and Cotton, E. (2009) *Global Unions, Global Business. Global Union Federations and International Business*, London: Middlesex University Press.

Education International (EI) (2015) 'Privatisation and commercialisation in and of education', Resolution, 7th World Congress, 21–26 July 2015, Ottawa, Canada.

Education International (EI) (2022) 'World Bank to exit investment in for-profit school chain Bridge International Academies', [online] Available from: https://www.ei-ie.org/en/item/26362:world-bank-to-exit-investm ent-in-for-profit-school-chain-bridge-international-academies [Accessed 17 June 2022].

Education International (EI) and Kenya National Union of Teachers (KNUT) (2016) 'Bridge vs reality: a study of Bridge International Academies' for-profit schooling in Kenya', [online] Available from: https://www.ei-ie.org/ en/item/25702:bridge-vs-reality-a-study-of-bridge-international-academ ies-for-profit-schooling-in-kenya [Accessed 17 June 2022].

Fichter, M. (2018) 'Building union power across borders: the transnational partnership initiative of IG Metall and the UAW', *Global Labour Journal*, 9(2): 182–98.

Fichter, M., Ludwig, C., Schmalz, S. and Steinfeldt, H. (2018) *The Transformation of Organised Labour: Mobilising Power Resources to Confront 21st Century Capitalism*, Berlin: Friedrich Ebert Stiftung.

Fischer, K. (2021) 'Global labour and labour studies', in A. Komlosy and G. Musić (eds) *Global Commodity Chains and Labour Relations*, Leiden: Brill, pp 361–78.

Ford, M. and Gillan, M. (2021) 'Power resources and supranational mechanisms: the global unions and the OECD guidelines', *European Journal of Industrial Relations*, 25: 1–19.

Henderson, R. (2020) *Reimagining Capitalism: How Business Can Save the World*, London: Penguin Business.

International Financial Corporation (IFC) (2022) IFC Project Information and Data Portal: Bridge International Academies, [online] Available from: https://disclosures.ifc.org/project-detail/SII/32171/bridge-intern ational-academies [Accessed 17 June 2022].

Lévesque, C. and Murray, G. (2010) 'Understanding union power: resources and capabilities for renewing union capacity', *Transfer: European Review of Labour and Research*, 16(3): 333–50.

Marachi, R. and Carpenter, R. (2020) 'Silicon Valley, philantrocapitalism, and policy shifts from teachers to tech', in R.K. Givan and A. Schrager Lang (eds) *Strike for the Common Good. Fighting for the Future of Public Education*, Ann Arbor, MI: University of Michigan Press, pp 183–8.

McGregor, W. and Webster, E. (2021) *Building a Regional Solidarity Network of Transnational Activists: An African Case Study*, Sao Paulo, Brazil: Tempo.

RESULTS Educational Fund (2017) 'From free to fee. Are for-profit, fee-charging private schools the solution for the world's poor?' [online] Available from: https://www.results.org/wp-content/uploads/From_Free _to_Fee.pdf [Accessed 7 April 2021].

Riep, C. (2019) *What Do We Really Know about Bridge International Academies? A Summary of Research Findings*, Brussels: EI.

Riep, C. and Machacek, M. (2016) 'Schooling the poor profitably. The innovations and deprivations of Bridge International Academies in Uganda', [online] Available from: https://www.right-to-education.org/resource/ schooling-poor-profitably-innovations-and-deprivations-bridge-intern ational-academies [Accessed 7 April 2021].

Schmalz, S., Ludwig, C. and Webster, E. (2018) 'The power resources approach: developments and challenges', *Global Labour Journal*, 9(2): 113–34.

Schmalz, S., Ludwig, C. and Webster, E. (2019) 'Power resources and global capitalism', *Global Labour Journal*, 10(1): 84–90.

Schmalz, S., Conrow, T., Feller, D. and Rombaldi, M. (2021) 'Two forms of transnational organizing: mapping the strategies of global union federations', *Tempo Social*, 33(2): 163–82.

Tassinari, A. and Maccarrone, V. (2020) 'Riders on the storm: workplace solidarity among gig economy couriers in Italy and the UK', *Work, Employment and Society*, 34(1): 35–54.

Tarrow, S. (2005) *The New Transnational Activism*, Cambridge: Cambridge University Press.

Williamson, B. and Hogan, A. (2020) *Commercialisation and Privatisation in/ of Education in the Context of Covid-19*, Brussels: EI.

Zuilkowski, S., Piper, B., Ong'ele, S. and Kiminza, O. (2018) 'Parents, quality, and school choice: why parents in Nairobi choose low-cost private schools over public schools in Kenya's free primary education era', *Oxford Review of Education*, 44(2): 258–74.

8

Changing Sources of Power and the Future of Southern Labour

In the early 1970s the apartheid state seemed to be all-powerful. Indeed, the coercive capacity of the state appeared so powerful to eminent sociologist Heribert Adam (1971) that he argued that it was not possible for Black workers to go out on strike. He was not alone: it was a time globally of deep pessimism about the future of labour. Neo-Marxists, such as Herbert Marcuse, had abandoned the industrial working class altogether and were focusing their theories on groups outside the traditional working class, such as students. Others kept their classical Marxism intact, insisting that labour struggles are essentially economistic and can only be transcended by a vanguard political party. Some offered a version of 'dependency theory' which focused on the claim that imperialism blocked national economic development. At best, this conception of change relegated labour in the Global South to a secondary position. At worst, workers were identified, with little in the way of evidence or argument, as a privileged 'labour aristocracy' aligned to metropolitan capital.

In the coastal city of Durban, South Africa, in the early months of 1973, construction workers stopped work, followed by workers in the large textile mills surrounding Durban. Many of them were women workers, but mostly they were men. They stood beside their machines, stopped working, and those mills fell silent – large mills that employed thousands of workers. They moved outside of the factories and danced down the streets (IIE, 1974: 15–25). As they danced, other workers joined in. And before they knew it, the factories in Pinetown and Durban had come to a standstill. And the power of workers became visible and audible, as they cried Amandla![1]

At the same time, the study of labour in Africa was changing. 'By the mid-1970s', Bill Freund (1988: 22) wrote, 'a new generation of scholars had discovered the working class and, armed with more flexible means of considering the application of class, they began to change the way labour in Africa was being written about'. Two key books published in the mid-1970s reflect this new class paradigm by academics: Sandbrook and Cohen's (1975) *The Development of the African Working Class* and Gutkind et al's (1979) *African Labour History*. Importantly, Freund added, this new paradigm did not assume that the working class would form a particular kind of political party; indeed, it was critical of African nationalism and de-emphasised colonialism while increasing attention to capitalism and focusing on 'hidden forms' of worker consciousness (Freund, 1988: 23). 'The reality', Freund (1988: 24) commented, 'requires us to make sense of how labour is organised in agriculture as well as industry, of what actually goes on in the many facets of what political economists call the informal sector of the economy'.

To capture the changes taking place in the study of labour, we have divided this concluding chapter into four parts. In Part I we draw lessons from South Africa's past. Then, in Part II we draw together our six case studies on the unmaking, remaking and making of working-class formations: this somewhat counter-intuitive phrasing will become clear in the course of that part of the chapter. In Part III we summarise our findings on the changing power resources of workers, and in Part IV we return to our central theme on the future of labour. We conclude by arguing that we need to move away from the standard narrative of the end of labour. Labour has a future, but not in its current form. Our research highlights that precarious workers do have agency and power. New and hybrid forms of organisation are forming on the margins of the labour movement in Africa and elsewhere. These embryonic organisations point in the direction of labour's future, but point is all they do.

Part I: Lessons from the past

There were no trade unions for Black workers at the time of the 1973 Durban strikes, but there were people who realised that if their power was going to be sustained, they had to turn that power into some form of permanent worker organisation. In the wake of the strikes, initiatives to organise workers across the country began (Maree, 2019). Quite quickly one started to see the emergence of national industrial unions – a textile union, a clothing union, a transport union, a chemical union and a metal union. In order to build these organisations, it was necessary to learn lessons from the past (Maree, 1984). One key lesson was the need for worker education: How can we learn from the past attempts to organise Black workers? How do we build a common position, a consensus? How do we avoid conflict between ourselves?

Another lesson was that the history of labour is replete with predictions of the end of labour. It is worth noting the pessimism that faced the labour movement in the 1930s in the United States. As labour historian David Brody has argued:

Perhaps one of the more famous stories illustrating the labor movement's unpredictable course is the one historians often tell of multitude and solemn pronouncements made by august labor scholars in 1932 heralding the certain death of the American labor movement. These dire predictions, of course, were issued literally on the eve of the dramatic and widespread upsurge of labor organizing that began in 1932. (Brody, 1980, cited in Cobble, 1992: 82)

The changing nature of unions in the twentieth century

Faced by the de-skilling of craft work through the Fordist assembly line in the United States, the bargaining power of the traditional craft union had been undermined in the 1930s. Instead of adapting their organising strategy to recruit the new semi-skilled assembly-line workers, the craft unions stuck to their skill-based organising strategy. But side-by-side with the decline of the craft union, labour in the United States was about to experience its most dramatic upsurge. The emergence of the assembly-line technologically linking together the factory workforce – so that when the line stopped every worker necessarily joined the stoppage – gave these semi-skilled workers a new source of power. A different kind of trade union – the industrial union based on the shop floor – was emerging. A new generation of union organisers had begun to build workplace bargaining through shop stewards at plant level.

Something similar was happening in South Africa as the old white-controlled craft unions resisted the rise of the Black semi-skilled worker and their shop-floor-based industrial unions (Webster, 1985: 156–76, 216–30). Gradually the industrial unions grew, but it was not easy. Some of the activists were banned under the so-called Suppression of Communism Act, confining them to their homes where they could only meet people on a one-to-one basis. A few were even assassinated. But importantly, these emerging industrial unions were such a force that the LRA was amended in 1979, and unions of Black workers were recognised as part of the official collective bargaining system. Before then, Black workers had not been classified as employees. It was an historic moment when the LRA came into effect on 1 May 1979, recognising Black workers as employees.

But there was a problem for these emerging unions – they seemed to be narrowly focused on collective bargaining. Of course, tactically, that may have been necessary in those early days, because if you were seen to be 'political' you were arrested under the Suppression of Communism Act. The pressures built up, and soon the trade unions had more power than any other organisation in civil society. The popular movements of the national struggle, such as the ANC and the Pan Africanist Congress (PAC), were banned, and many of their leaders and members were in exile.

As the crisis deepened, many people felt that these trade unions should be part of the broader national liberation struggle. So they started to form alliances (Lambert and Webster, 1988). Stay-aways – essentially, general strikes – became commonplace. Students demanded a decent education. People in the townships demanded public services. All of these forces came together in a general strike in November 1984 – an alliance between workers, students, their parents and the churches in a struggle for liberation (Webster, 1988).

Drawing on the analytical framework introduced in Chapter 1 we can now see how different sources of power – structural, associational, societal, institutional – were realised in order to build the modern labour movement (see Figure 8.1).

The 1973 strike – clearly illustrating structural power, with its capacity to disrupt in the heart of the economy – was a fundamental source of power. Then we have associational power (the establishment of collective worker organisation) and societal power (the need to form alliances with other groups). Institutional power – the power of the law, the Labour Relations Act, a bargaining council, labour market institutions such as the CCMA – consolidates worker power by giving workers certain rights.[2]

As a result of its steadily growing strength, the labour movement went on to play a key role in the transition to democracy. Through the disciplined and strategic use of power, it effectively challenged inequality in the workplace and more broadly in the labour market. Through combining mass action with negotiations, it was able to build a powerful movement that entrenched workers' rights in the law and created new labour market institutions that gave labour a direct voice in policy making.

Ironically the racialised nature of the apartheid state facilitated the organisation of Black workers. In the 1980s, large numbers of migrant metalworkers on the East Rand (now Ekurhuleni municipality), were housed in single-sex hostels with a common set of grievances; this contiguity made organisation into the new industrial unions much easier. As the union organiser of the metal union at the time explained:

> It is easy to get hold of everyone in a hostel. It is an advantage when you organise. They are close to each other, living in the same conditions. It brings together a lot of different factories, sometimes ten representatives in one room. And they preach unions to each other all the time. (Quoted in Webster, 1985: 209)

But the world of work and politics has changed dramatically over the past four decades, especially in the nature of the labour process and the employment relationship. New hybrid forms of organisation have begun to emerge.

Figure 8.1: Interactions between various sources of power

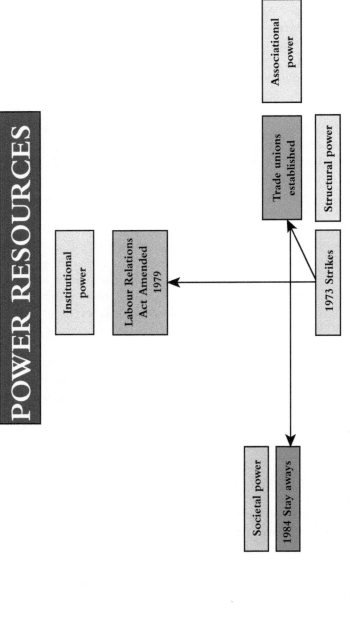

Source: Developed by Edward Webster.

New hybrid forms of organisation emerge in the twenty-first century

Faced by dramatic changes in the world of work through automation and the so-called Fourth Industrial Revolution (4IR) as well as a growing representational gap as traditional unions fail to represent the growing numbers of precarious workers, could the role of labour be revived in post-colonial Africa? Could organised labour 'cross the divide' and broaden its constituencies to include the growing numbers of precarious workers trading on our streets, working from home, or employed on short-term contracts by labour brokers?

The answer is that in spite of exploring ways of organising precarious workers as we showed in Chapters 2, 3, 4 and 5, South African trade unions, unlike in Uganda as we saw in Chapter 6, have so far made little progress in crossing the divide. Instead we have begun to see the self-organisation of precarious workers such as street traders and labour broker workers, assisted by amendments to the labour law and the re-emergence of labour-supportive NGOs.

There is an important difference between the struggles on the East Rand in the 1980s and the struggles today in Ekurhuleni: workers and unions of the 1980s were driven by their opposition not only to exploitation, but also to the oppression that accompanied a racial state (Webster and Englert, 2020). The racial state was itself a double-edged sword: it facilitated control over Black people but it also provided the perfect conditions for collective solidarity. Although the rise of a democratic state has created new opportunities for strengthening union rights, the changing employment relationship, as we showed in Chapters 2, 3 and 4, has re-divided workers on the shop floor and weakened their workplace bargaining power.

More importantly, the incorporation of trade unions into existing labour market institutions has led these unions to defend the system, to the benefit of permanent employees rather than the growing numbers of precarious workers. However, a 2014 amendment of the LRA to allow for precarious workers to become permanent has opened new opportunities for workers' struggle to take advantage of amendments to the law.

The crucial difference between the past and the present, however, is in the attitude of workers towards trade unions. In the 1980s, the majority of the emerging unions had no doubt that their trajectory was the construction of worker-controlled trade unions, and they were willing to register them under the amended LRA and to participate in bargaining councils. Today in Ekurhuleni there is a real distrust of existing trade unions among many precarious workers and the institutional settlement of which they are a crucial part. Instead of establishing a trade union, the precarious workers we studied are forming worker committees or councils on a plant-by-plant basis. To understand these dramatic changes we need to return to the Marx–Polanyi dialectic introduced in Chapter 1.

Part II: The unmaking, remaking and making of working-class formations

As discussed in Chapter 1, Silver (2003: 170) identifies how capital overcomes impediments to accumulation through various fixes (spatial, production, financial and technological). And accompanying such fixes, especially where new iterations of capital formation are concerned, are processes of new class formation.[3] While Silver emphasises the process of working-class formation in new sites of industrialisation, such as India and China, and processes of remaking in the growth of service workers in the industrialised core, we have been concerned with processes of unmaking, remaking and making in sub-Saharan Africa. Here labour market indicators demonstrate the persistent dominance of agriculture in Kenya and Uganda, and show how employment in industry has tailed off in South Africa, along with the general economic decline of many of its subsectors.

Drawing on the findings from our six different case studies, we summarise in Table 8.1 the ways in which the African working class is being restructured. As we see in Table 8.1, two distinct 'types' of struggles are generated in response to capital's efforts to overcome impediments to accumulation. The old sections of the working class – the municipal workers, factory workers, bus drivers and school teachers – are unmade and remade. They resist the 're-commodification' or 'ex-commodification' of their labour power through the attack on their wages, employment relationships and the social wage. These conflicts are framed as 'Polanyi-type' struggles, as workers resist 'the spread of a global self-regulated market' (Silver, 2003: 20). They are drawn from workers who gained significant rights and improved material conditions during the heyday of the post-colonial era – essentially to de-commodify their labour power by regulating its sale and ultimately taking it out of the free market. Often the attack on this section of the working class results in the 'unmaking' of its traditional location within the relations of production. 'Marx-type' struggles, on the other hand, emerge from new sections of the working class that are made or re-made through the various capital fixes and new capital formations (Silver, 2003: 20). This is clearest in our factory case studies where previously unionised workers are remade as casualised and externalised workers and a new class of precarious workers emerges from the young and previously unemployed workers. It can also be seen in the making of a new class of street traders and waste pickers in the growing informal economy. The impact of the new digital technology creates a new class of platform-based food couriers, boda boda riders in Kampala and 'teacher-computers' in Kenya and Uganda. As our studies show, when capital restructures, different sections of workers are compelled to organise using various organisational forms and to mobilise different sources of power.

Table 8.1: The unmaking, remaking and making of working-class formations

	Unmaking (of the SER)	Remaking (as precarious work)	Making (into a new class)
Street traders (Chapter 2)			Street traders in South Africa are new workers. Street trading was illegal under apartheid
Municipal workers (Chapter 3)	Unionised workforce under SERs are unmade	Workers are outsourced and the municipal structures corporatised	A new class of informal workers, such as waste pickers, is made
Manufacturing in South Africa (Chapter 4)	Unionised SER workforce eroded	Casualising and externalising previously unionised SER workers	Young workers and previously unemployed brought into manufacturing workplaces as precarious workers
Platform service economy (Chapter 5)			Making of a new but precarious class of platform workers delivering food
Transport industry in Uganda (Chapter 6)	Unionised bus drivers under SER retrenched		A new transport worker emerges on motorcycles, the so-called boda boda drivers
Teachers in Kenya and Uganda (Chapter 7)	Attempt to de-professionalise teachers	Attempts to re-make a class of unqualified computer teachers	A new class of unqualified teachers begins to emerge

In assessing the conclusions and implications of these case studies, our focus is on the question posed by Silver, whether we should 'expect this general crisis of contemporary labour movements also to be temporary', as was the case with earlier crises, or whether the mobility and restructuring of capital globally has condemned the labour movement to permanent decline' (Silver, 2003: 167). From the global perspective adopted by Silver, 'we should expect to see new working class formations and emerging labour movements in the leading industry/industries of the twenty-first century … the late twentieth century crisis of labour movements is temporary and will likely be overcome with the consolidation of new working classes in formation' (Silver, 2003: 171).

Silver goes on to argue:

> The twentieth-century trend toward increased workplace bargaining power ... is at least partially being reversed in the twenty-first century. The bargaining power of many of today's low wage workers in producer and personal services is closer to that of workers in the nineteenth century textile industry than that of workers in the twentieth-century automobile industry. (Silver, 2003: 172)

Lacking strong structural power, 'textile workers successes were far more dependent on a strong (compensatory) associational bargaining power (trade unions, political parties, and cross-class alliances with nationalist movements)' (Silver, 2003: 172). She concludes that 'we might expect the weight of associational power in the overall power strategies of labour movements to be on the increase' (Silver, 2003: 172).

To what extent are Silver's observations confirmed in our case studies? We turn now to our findings on the changing use of power by precarious workers.

Part III: Changing sources of power

As is clearly demonstrated in our six case studies, summarised in Table 8.2, we see the very limited use of structural power and the difficulties of mobilising associational power. Both constraints are due to class fragmentation which impacts workers' bargaining power and the ability to disrupt production processes. Trade unions have not managed to systematically organise precarious workers, and the new emerging forms remain embryonic. However, what is distinctive in our studies is the increasing orientation of workers towards societal power and institutional power.

Let us begin with the street traders discussed in Chapter 2. Although informal traders are distinctive from traditional workers in that they do not have a direct counterpart to negotiate with, they have adopted similar organising tactics. However, instead of making their demands to an employer, their demands are made to local and national state authorities. The difference from traditional union organising lies in the weight that informal traders give to the different power resources. The informal traders study demonstrates that experimentation in organising vulnerable workers is underway outside of the traditional unions through associations, platforms, umbrella organisations, international NGOs such as WIEGO and new types of global unions such as StreetNet International. In other words, rather than drawing on support from traditional trade unions they are establishing coalitions or alliances – what we call societal power.

While the legal organising tool is used widely by traditional trade unions, our study of street traders suggests that informal traders rely on the courts to

Table 8.2: Experimenting with different sources of power and the impact on labour

	Structural	Associational	Societal	Institutional
Street traders in South Africa		XX	XX	XX
Municipal workers in South Africa	XX	X	X	XX
Manufacturing workplaces in South Africa	X	X	XX	XXX
Food couriers	X	X	XX	X
Transport drivers and riders in Uganda	X	XXX	X	XXX
Teachers in Ugandan and Kenya		X	XXX	XX
Total	5	9	11	13

Key: blank = no observable experimentation or impact; X = experimentation and low impact; XX = experimentation and medium impact; XXX = high experimentation and high impact

a greater extent. For example, attempts by municipalities to clear pavements of traders' stalls and to confiscate traders' goods has twice been successfully challenged in the South African Constitutional Court (the country's highest court). Institutionalised labour rights and institutionalised dialogue procedures such as NEDLAC – what we call institutional power – is a source of power that informal traders have drawn on because their structural power is weak.

Our second case study is drawn from Chapter 3, which discusses the failure of municipal workers to prevent the casualisation of their work. It demonstrates the limited impact of the strike weapon – that is, structural power. In spite of a two-week strike in April 2011 and the imaginative campaign against management corruption, SAMWU failed to sustain the organisation of precarious workers and to broaden their support in the community or to form alliances with their organisations. This failure to draw on societal power and challenge the new 'rules of the game' contributed to the decline and fragmentation of the traditional union. It also led to the rise of tenderpreneurs[4] and the financialisation of the union. Significantly we see the making of a new class of informal waste pickers organised into the South African Waste Pickers Association (SAWPA).

Our third study, examined in Chapter 4, covers four factories in Ekurhuleni – Reckitt Benckiser, PFG Building Glass, Simba Chips and Pioneer Foods. Historically, factory workers have relied on their craft skills to bargain for better wages and working conditions but with mechanisation and the rise of shop floor based industrial unions they switched to workplace bargaining. In only one of the four workplaces was a strike attempted, and it failed. Instead these workers are struggling to build associational power at workplace level and three of the workplaces are working closely with a labour-based NGO, the CWAO. Significantly they have relied quite strongly on the labour market dispute institution, the CCMA, and the 2015 amendments to section 198 of the LRA which gave important new rights to workers, enabling them to access permanent jobs directly within the company at which they work. The possibilities of 'permanent jobs' through legislative change and their popularisation by organisations like the CWAO convinced some workers to begin to organise at factory level. Factory committees were formed at some workplaces and, with the help of the CWAO, institutional power was drawn on and cases were taken up with the CCMA.

Our fourth case study, described in Chapter 5, is of digital workers who, despite their highly individualised labour processes, have created worker-driven messaging apps and chat groups where they share information, develop a shared identity and announce local direct action. Although their classification as self-employed weakens their associational power, the potential for associational power is dramatically increased when workers meet face-to-face at work zones and begin to form a collective identity. Although they have engaged in collective action, this has had a limited impact. Instead they have formed a relationship with a supportive international NGO, the FES, and are putting forward demands to regulate their work and thus strengthen their institutional power.

In the fifth and sixth cases, the transport drivers and riders in Uganda (Chapter 6) and the teachers in Uganda and Kenya (Chapter 7), the shift away from the use of structural power is quite sharp. Instead of strike action both case studies focus on building associational power. Transport workers' structural power has been weakened through privatisation and informalisation processes. They built associational power, with the help of the global transport union federation, by crossing the divide between traditionally organised workers and the new informal boda boda riders. This dramatically increased the membership of the union. In the case of the teacher unions and their campaign against for-profit education providers, they successfully broadened their scope by drawing on support from civil society organisations. In both cases, local associational power is bolstered through the transnational resources provided by global unions.

In sum, our analysis of workers' power implies that workers can build their strategy by choosing which power resources to develop and mobilise. As our six case studies demonstrate, due to low structural power precarious workers are giving priority to associational, societal and institutional power. In reality, organised labour does not develop its power in isolation from other important wielders of power, namely capital and the state. Therefore, the concept of power resources cannot be understood as a universal and static formula but needs to be located within the strategic environment in which workers find themselves (Gallas, 2018).

As the historical, political and social context differs, the use of power also takes different forms, as it is both dependent on specific institutional arrangements and historical developments and continuously restructured by the logic of global capitalism. For instance, in Africa unions have been profoundly shaped by the politics of national liberation. The political nature of African trade unions is made clear by Buhlungu.

> The emergence of trade unions was more than merely a response to conditions of economic exploitation. It was simultaneously a response to the conditions of political oppression created by colonialism, particularly the denial of political rights and the violation of the dignity of workers and the general population of the colonized. (Buhlungu, 2010:198)

Part IV: The future of labour

What implications do the findings from Table 8.1 – the unmaking, remaking and making of working class formations – and Table 8.2 – experimenting with different sources of power and its impact on labour – have for the future of labour? As discussed in Chapter 1, Visser (2019) identifies four trends: marginalisation, dualisation, substitution and revitalisation. We find this framework useful but the boundaries between the trends are not sufficiently fluid and do not seem to capture all the trends in the Global South. We reconstruct Visser in two main ways: first, we see marginalisation and dualisation as linked; and second, we identify a fifth trend.

First, through externalisation and casualisation there is on-going marginalisation of traditional trade unions in Africa. It is clear that the picture of unions in Africa is bleak. They are weak, fragmented and largely in the formal economy. Only about 5 per cent of formal workers are unionised in sub-Saharan Africa, with 24 per cent in South Africa (Schulz and Greven, 2020). As Schulz and Greven write in their useful report on the state of unions in sub-Saharan Africa:

> Trade unions suffer from a decline in membership. ... Trade union leaderships are often disconnected from their members and the link to the world of work – represented mainly by shop stewards in the workplace – is gradually being lost. ... This crisis of internal representation also means that fewer and fewer workers are joining the trade unions because they no longer trust them. (Schulz and Greven, 2020: 3)

They go on to identify the specificity of organising workers in the Global South – that is, the high proportion of informal workers:

> Trade unions are unable to represent the great majority of workers, because a considerable part of the working population earns its living in the informal economy, far away from defined employer–employee relations. … Due to the internal and external representation crisis, it cannot be said that trade unions represent the interests of the majority of the working population. (Schulz and Greven, 2020: 3)

Where unions exist, they are mainly in the public sector, although there have been some innovative responses in various other sectors in recent times. Often these responses are the result of support from global unions such as UNI Global Union, the International Transport Workers Federation (ITF), and the Building Workers International (Schulz and Greven, 2020).

As can be seen in Table 8.2, the case studies reveal very little impact of labours' traditional source of power – that is, structural power. In four cases, structural power has had little or no impact. In the three cases where the strike weapon was used it had a low impact; it either failed as in the case of Reckitt, or had limited impact. There was a similar result in the cases of the municipal workers and food couriers in Johannesburg.

As we show in Chapter 4, the rise of externalisation and casualisation in the manufacturing sector is having the effect of unmaking an older industrial workforce that was well unionised and generally employed in a standard employment relationship. Instead of organising the new layer of precarious workers, established unions such as FAWU are being marginalised by defending existing strongholds. In focusing on those workers in stable jobs, they are reproducing the dualities in labour markets. The effect of this is unfortunately to buttress capital's dualised workplace regimes which, we have seen, also eventually leads to the marginalisation of these unions. This is what Jelle Visser calls *dualisation*, although it is clear from this example that marginalisation and dualisation are linked.

SAMWU, in the Johannesburg Municipality, is another example of dualisation, where unions defend existing strongholds and focus on those workers in stable jobs. This opens up a growing representational gap as growing numbers of precarious workers are left without a voice. Another example is the manufacturing sector, where we see the entrenching of dualised workplace regimes based on hegemonic control over unionised, permanent workers and despotic forms of control over workers under precarious forms of employment. While capital's fracturing of the labour process in recent decades has allowed it to overcome past impediments to accumulation, it simultaneously deepens the age-old wage-labour contradiction which lays the basis for the re-emergence of struggles from below, although under new and increasingly more precarious and difficult conditions.

These challenges from below lead to a third response, what Visser (2019) calls substitution. This describes a scenario where unions are no longer the only actors and other organisations such as NGOs, social movements and cooperatives fill the vacuum of workers not having adequate representation by providing specific services and alternative organisational strategies. A distinction can be drawn between two forms of substitution. One approach is the development of legal firms, such as LegalWise and Scorpion, that have been set up as alternatives to unions (Sefalafala, 2011). Another approach is exemplified by the establishment of a Labour Desk by the Economic Freedom Fighters (EFF) to intervene in all labour-related issues to protect the lives and dignity of workers. An example of this second type of approach includes those NGOs set up to give advice to vulnerable working people (Wilderman, 2013). Some human rights activists see a real dilemma with this form of 'substitutionism' (for example, Heywood, 2018: 9). While Heywood (2018: 7) makes clear the 'unquestionable contribution to many struggles for democracy and social justice' of the NGOs and philanthropic organisations, he suggests that they also play 'a hugely controlling and limiting role over those struggles, which are supported and which not'. The support of these organisations in funding movements for social justice is, he believes, a double-edged sword; it provides the key resources for their success, but the funding relationship 'creates a loss of independence and unsustainability' (Heywood, 2018: 10).

Finally, unions successfully revitalise. But to revitalise, Visser (2019: 19) argues, unions need 'the courage to innovate and experiment with new forms of association, use digital tools, and broaden unions' reach through coalition-building with other civil society groups'. The clearest case we have of successful union revitalisation is the ATGWU in Kampala. By reframing informal boda boda riders as workers and therefore potential union members, they were able to foreground associational power and dramatically expand the union from a declining 5,000 members to over 100,000 members. By forming an alliance with the established union, and gaining concrete support from the ITF, the boda boda riders were able to draw on associational and institutional power, which led to a decline in police harassment.

An example of the use of societal power was the campaign by EI to resist the de-professionalisation of teachers in Uganda and Kenya. They did this by successfully influencing the public discourse (through research and protest actions) and by building alliances with civil society organisations.

However, in both the cases just discussed, union innovation led to the revitalisation of a traditional union, either by broadening their membership base in the case of the boda boda riders, or by successfully campaigning against the attempt to 'unmake' their teacher members. Our research points in the direction of a fifth response, one in which traditional unions are not revitalised but instead new workers are experimenting with new forms of power and hybrid forms of organisation among the growing swathe of precarious and informal labour in the Global South. We will call it an experimental trend that is emerging in parts of the Global South.[5] This trend shares the following three characteristics.

First, the subordinate position of the South under this phase of neo-liberal and financialised capitalism ensures that Africa retains its role as a source of resource extraction and cheap labour. As argued in Chapter 1, surplus value is increasingly created through low-paid, labour-intensive work in the Global South and appropriated by multinational corporations (and their financial backers) that are headquartered in the Global North.

Second, the scale of the informal economy and the resulting reserve of labour makes it difficult to build sustainable worker organisation. Where work is precarious and workers easily replaceable, it is difficult to build a workforce that is able and willing to pay regular membership fees to a union. The result is collective action without sustainable collective organisation.

Third, these new forms of organisation are largely self-organised but often rely on NGOs for support. In our studies, one example is the food couriers discussed in Chapter 5. Here, through participatory action research and the support of an international NGO, the Friedrich Ebert Stiftung, these platform workers have begun to develop union-like hybrid collectives offering mutual aid. The CWAO is another example where an NGO has facilitated the organisation of casual workers in the factories east of Johannesburg into workplace-based informal committees (Chapter 5). The support given to the organisation of street traders by WIEGO is another example (Chapter 2).

Conclusion

By re-entering the 'hidden abode of production', we are able to uncover the logic behind capital's restructuring initiatives and establish a clearer picture of union and worker responses. What emerges from our case studies is that we need to move away from the standard narrative of the end of labour. Our research highlights that precarious workers do have agency and power. New and hybrid forms of organisation are forming on the margins of the global economy.

The question raised by these findings is whether these embryonic forms of worker organisation – what we are calling the Southern trend – are sustainable and could become the foundations for a new cycle of worker solidarity and union growth. Working from home – often with no physical workplace and limited face-to-face interaction with fellow workers and no regular working hours – has rendered the establishment and maintenance of worker solidarity increasingly difficult. In earlier stages of capitalism, the growth of factories brought large numbers of workers together with common grievances and the capacity to come together collectively and withdraw their labour. In spite of the changes brought about by globalisation and digitalisation we have shown how informal solidaristic groups among workers (often along ethnic or clan lines, as demonstrated in the case study of food couriers) continue.

These embryonic organisations point in the direction of Southern labour's future. If a revitalisation of labour is to take place, there will need to be tolerance and support on the part of traditional trade unions toward the innovative strategies and experimental forms of organisation that are emerging. There is a need to reconceive the traditional workplace, to include the street, workers' homes, the shopping mall, the airport and the smartphone. Clearly there is a need to broaden unions' reach through coalition building but unless this is accompanied by the repurposing of corporations and the state for the public good to service people, communities and nations, these emerging associations will be unsustainable (Mayer, 2013). Cross-national agreements that shift away from labour-saving to labour-using technical change will be required. This will necessitate addressing the weaknesses of the institutions of global governance in regulating the power of the global corporation (Kanbur, 2017). This points to the importance of bolstering global institutions such as the ILO, and global unions which are supporting the organisation of gig, farm and other workers. The ILO is the only tripartite UN agency that incorporates worker, trade union and employer representatives, crucially allowing for nation states to adopt empowering legislation, such as R204, permitting informal economy workers to transition into the formal economy.

The strategic challenges facing labour will require innovative organisational forms in order to build independent worker organisations that draw on the old and the new sources of power emerging in the digital age. For labour to move out of the shadows of the digital age is not only a massive organisational challenge; it is also an intellectual challenge. It requires confronting the global knowledge system now under the influence of global capital. As our examples demonstrate, global unions can play an important role in this regard. Encouraging first steps in this direction have also begun, with the establishment of such institutions as WIEGO and the Global Labour University (GLU)[6] but the challenge is enormous (Williams and Webster, 2021).

We end on a note of caution. The history of labour is replete with examples of august experts who have predicted the end of labour. Indeed, we began this chapter with Heribert Adam's prediction in 1971 that strike action was not possible in apartheid South Africa. Arguably more than ever in the history of capitalism, society's direction is uncertain and the future of labour hangs in the balance.

Unions are important because they have historically performed the role of converting 'their organisational space into a political space and contributing to the development of democratic institutions' (Jose, 2002: 12). By performing this role, 'unions came to occupy a unique position as the purveyors of social cohesion in society' (Jose, 2002: 17). This broader role of labour lies at the centre of the 'experimental' Southern trend we have identified. Workers and their organisations are drawing on a neglected source of power, what we have called societal power, which involves coalitions including those with NGOs. In parallel with the use of traditional notions of associational and institutional power, they are rebuilding worker organisation, as we have shown in our case studies. To effectively use this source of power, worker organisations have to engage more directly in the public arena, form coalitions with other civil society actors and become part of a broader counter-movement.

While it is important to support civil society organisations, there is a danger of downplaying the role of the state. Based on a study of three campaigns promoting codes of conduct – the Sullivan Codes in apartheid South Africa, child labour involved in rug-making in India, and repression in the apparel industry in Guatemala – veteran labour scholar Gay Seidman (2007: 139) suggests that labour 'activists should focus their efforts on shoring up weak states, reinforcing national institutions rather than trying to replace them with even weaker NGOs'. She concludes:

> in the long run, states offer more effective instruments for intervening at work than even well-intentioned NGOs. ... State inspectors can legally insist on access to the workplace and enforce compliance with standards defined by national law; they stand in a very different relation to workplaces and to employers, with legal sanctions backing their enforcement efforts. (Seidman, 2007: 143)

This points to the importance of pressurising particularly weak nation states to adopt worker rights in a variety of areas including in laws governing migrant, social protection, labour, local government, small business and other arenas impacting workers' lives. Global interventions take on an added importance as the traditional factory, where workers were brought together in large numbers and could be easily organised, has declined. Workers are often atomised and isolated.

Worker activists also need to target state and other national institutions which have the power to deliver services such as pensions, unemployment benefits and other forms of social protection. Crucially nation states need to strengthen inspectorates to monitor state institutions in their delivery of worker benefits and services. Laws and regulations are ineffective without successful delivery, an area which worker organisations must crucially oversee.

While building a capable and democratic state is a long-term goal, it would be wrong to see voluntary initiatives as in opposition to the state. Local organisation needs to be supported to ensure that global and national rights and regulations are implemented and that bargaining with local state institutions can take place. Importantly, this includes the role of traditional trade unions, as well as other players in cooperatives and associations. This level takes on a new importance as work becomes more precarious and the informal economy grows at local level. This will involve new and experimental ways of organising and implementing worker rights.

Notes

[1] Amandla is a South African political slogan calling for power to Black working people.

[2] Institutional power can be a double-edged sword: it gives rights but it can also co-opt leaders into management (Englert and Runciman, 2019).

[3] Or as Munck (2013) argues, these fixes result in cyclical processes of capital formation that 'make, unmake and remake' the working class. In this chapter, we turn Munck's chronology on its head. We begin with unmaking, as the first stage of restructuring under neo-liberalism is the erosion – that is, the unmaking – of the SER.

[4] A South African term for persons who use their political connections to secure government contracts for personal advantage.

[5] This is not to suggest that experimentation is not taking place in the Global North where a range of grassroots organisations are emerging, such as Intercategory Syndicate (SI Cobas) in Italy. Our argument is that these experiments in the Global South are shaped by certain features of its labour market.

[6] In response to the impact of unregulated market-led globalisation, the ILO initiated in 2003 the GLU to strengthen the intellectual and strategic capacity of unions. The assumption behind the GLU is that the shift to neo-liberal globalisation requires analytical skills that are best acquired in advanced courses in a university, rather than within traditional trade union courses.

References

Adam, H. (1971) *Modernising Racial Domination: The Dynamics of South African Politics*, Berkeley, CA: University of California Press.

Buhlungu, S. (2010) *A Paradox of Victory. COSATU and the Democratic Transformation in South Africa*, Pietermaritzburg: University of KwaZulu-Natal Press.

Cobble, D. (1992) *Dishing It Out: Waitresses and their Unions in the Twentieth Century*, Urbana, IL: University of Illinois Press.

Englert, T. and Runciman, C. (2019) 'Challenging workplace inequality: precarious workers' institutional and associational power in Gauteng, South Africa', *Transformation: Critical Perspectives on Southern Africa*, 101: 84–104.

Freund, B. (1988) *The African Worker*, Cambridge: Cambridge University Press.

Gallas, A. (2018) 'Class power and union capacities: a research note on the power resources approach', *Global Labour Journal*, 9(3): 348–52.

Gutkind, P., Cohen, R. and Copan, J. (eds) (1979) *African Labour History*, London: Sage.

Heywood, M. (2018) 'The transformative power of civil society in South Africa? Innovative forms of organizing and rights-based practices – an activist's perspective', Paper presented to conference 'Overcoming Inequality – A Transitional Compass', 4 September 2018, Southern Centre for Inequality Studies, Johannesburg.

Institute for Industrial Education (IIE) (1974) *The Durban Strikes 1973*, Johannesburg: Ravan Press.

Jose, A.A. (ed.) (2002) *Organised Labour in the 21st Century*, Geneva: International Institute of Labour Studies.

Kanbur, R. (2017) 'Tony Atkinson and what can be done about inequality', *Journal of Economic Inequality*, 15: 115–19.

Lambert, R. and Webster, E. (1988) 'The re-emergence of political unionism in contemporary South Africa', in W. Cobbet and R. Cohen (eds) *Popular Struggles in South Africa*, Trenton, NJ: Africa World Press, pp 20–41.

Maree, J. (1984) 'The Institute of Industrial Education and worker education', *South African Labour Bulletin*, 9(8): 71–99.

Maree, J. (2019) 'The Durban Moment: turning temporary worker action into a permanent democratic trade union movement … and then…?', *Transformation*, 100: 53–77.

Mayer, C. (2013) *Firm Commitment: Why the Corporation is Failing Us and How to Restore Trust in It*, Oxford: Oxford University Press.

Munck, R. (2013) 'The precariat: a view from the South', *Third World Quarterly*, 34(5): 747–62.

Sandbrook, R. and Cohen, R. (1975) *The Development of the African Working Class: Studies in Class Formation and Action*, Toronto: University of Toronto Press.

Schulz, B. and Greven, T. (2020) *Trade Union Developments in Sub-Saharan Africa*, Bonn: Friedrich Ebert Stiftung.

Sefalafala, T. (2011) 'Mineworkers opt for private legal scheme', *South African Labour Bulletin*, 36(4): 24–6.

Seidman, G. (2007) *Beyond the Boycott: Labor Rights, Human Rights and Transnational Activism*, New York: Russell.

Silver, B. (2003) *Forces of Labor: Workers' Movements and Globalisation since 1870*, Cambridge: Cambridge University Press.

Visser, J. (2019) 'Can unions revitalise themselves?', *International Journal of Labour Research*, 9(1–2): 17–48.

Webster, E. (1985) *Cast in a Racial Mould: Labour Process and Trade Unionism in the Foundries*, Johannesburg: Ravan Press.

Webster, E. (1988) 'The rise of social movement unionism: the two faces of the black trade union movement in South Africa', in P. Frankel, N. Pines and M. Swilling (eds) *State, Resistance and Change in South Africa*, London: Croom Helm, pp 174–96.

Webster, E. and Englert, T. (2020) 'New dawn or end of labour? from South Africa's East Rand to Ekurhuleni', *Globalizations*, 17(2): 279–93.

Wilderman, J. (2013) *Worker Advice Offices in South Africa: Exploring Approaches to Organising and Empowering Vulnerable Workers*, Johannesburg: Chris Hani Institute.

Williams, M. and Webster, E. (2021) 'Public sociology and worker education: the story of the Global Labour University in South Africa', in L. Hossfield, C. Hossfield and B. Kelly (eds) *Routledge International Handbook on Public Sociology*, London: Routledge, pp 315–26.

Index

References to figures appear in *italic* type; those in **bold** type refer to tables.
References to endnotes show both the page number and the note number (175n2). Index
entries for persons interviewed are only given when both first name and surname are supplied.